Aix Marks The Spot

Also by the Author

THE STARSTRUCK SAGA

Starstruck

Alienation

Traveler

Celestial

Starbound

Earthstuck

NOVELLAS

Miss Planet Earth
(Pew! Pew! - The Quest for More Pew!)

The Horrible Habits of Humans
(Pew! Pew! - Bite My Shiny Metal Pew!)

Miss Planet Earth and the Amulet of Beb Sha Na

Head over Heels (Starstruck Halloween Short)

Aix Marks the Spot

Copyright © 2020 by Sarah E. Anderson

All rights reserved. No part of this publication may be reproduced, distributed, or transmitted in any form or by any means, including photocopying, recording, or other electronic or mechanical methods, without the prior written permission of the publisher, except in the case of brief quotations embodied in critical reviews and certain other noncommercial uses permitted by copyright law.

For permission requests, write to the author, address: saraheanderson@protonmail.com

First Printing, 2020
Sea Breeze Books

ISBN:
978-1-7344495-0-1 (Ebook – EPUB)
978-1-7344495-1-8 (Paperback)

Editing by Cora Corrigall
Cover Design by Sarah Anderson
Book Design by We Got You Covered Book Design

WWW.SEANDERSONAUTHOR.COM

same with the other cheek. My eyes went wide.

"Jean-Pascal," he took a drag from his cig, grinning wide. *"Enchanté, ma belle. T'as besoin d'un coup de main?"*

"Eh..."

"Ah, no French?" the grin faded, but only for an instant. I could understand the confusion: every email he had ever sent me I had fed through a translator and written my reply right there in the same box. Every email he or Mamie received had been in French: just not *my* French.

"Help... you?" He made a gesture, as if to reach for my bag. I nodded, pressing the handle of my suitcase into his hand. He rolled it to the back of his tiny car, stuffing it into the surprisingly large trunk. He then took a long look at my carry on, shrugged, and threw it on the back seat.

"You 'ave ez-ry-ting?" he asked earnestly, and again I nodded. He indicated the passenger side of the car with a sweeping gesture of his hand, tossing the now used up cigarette into a nearby ashtray, because of course those were everywhere. *"En route, alors."*

He pulled out of the flashy new carpark of the Marseille airport and around the multiple roundabouts that stood between us and the highway. Surprisingly, the tiny little car was doing quite well, and roared to life on the freeway.

"Iz not far," he said, still keeping that jovial smile on his face. "Did you 'ave good trip?"

I nodded again, before realizing he couldn't see me. A little, muffled *"Oui"* was all that I could muster.

"Ah! Ze girl speaks!" he let out a light laugh. "Iz zis your first time in France?"

"Oui, Désolé, mon Français c'est... très mal..." I blurted out, my hands digging awkwardly into the foam of the seat cushion. I didn't want to have to talk to the stranger. After Mamie had agreed to let me stay, she still passed me on to this friend of hers for airport pickup. She was much too busy with who knows what to actually pick me up herself.

"My English, your French..." he didn't have to finish for me to understand where he was going. We were doing the best we could: we may have needed to translate each other's emails, but we had still managed to find each other at the airport, so all in all, we probably were not doing as badly as we thought.

Conversation didn't matter anyway: within a few minutes of smooth driving on the highway, even with the wrinkled stranger in his ratty hat, I had still drifted off to sleep, rocked by the slow rhythm of the old car.

I hadn't been one of those girls dreaming of going to France all my life, and if I had, I would have picked Paris as my destination of choice: all those art

For my Mom and Dad
Who chose Provence

one

YOU ALWAYS TOLD ME THAT THE FIRST TIME I CAME to Provence, it would feel like coming home; instead, it felt like an exile.

It was never supposed to be like this. You were going to be the one to show me the places you fell in love with when you first came here, all those years ago, and dad would take me to the spots he discovered as he grew up beneath the pines. But neither of you were with me now. Instead, I spent eight hours crammed into the tiny economy seat on the back of a full flight, on my way to meet a woman neither of you had spoken to for the entirety of my existence, trying not to think about Jazz as she now lived out our summer of fun on her own.

Having hours alone to reflect in the flight from Philadelphia – not to mention remembering every vivid detail of the accident that put me on this plane in the first place - did wonders to one's mood. Having to wait another five in a crowded airport, all to willingly cram myself back into another metal sky canister, now that was just masochistic. To make my day even worse, I would be spending the next hour or more in a tiny car with a complete stranger who didn't speak a lick of English.

He said I would recognize him by the old straw hat he wore, but that had been an understatement: it was easily the rattiest panama I had ever laid eyes on. In thick jeans and a light blue shirt, it was almost as if I had never left the states. He looked exactly like a farmer from any commercial I had ever seen for fresh juice.

He stood before an absolutely tiny red car, which I wouldn't be exaggerating if I said it hadn't been driven since WW2. It was even more ancient than a Volkswagen bug. The cherry on top of this ever-growing cake was that it was a bright, ladybug red.

"Jamie?" he asked, the name rolling off his tongue like a bad stereotype. He sounded like he was asking how I liked my PB&J's - Jammy.

"Jamie," I said, insisting on the long 'a' sound, holding out my free hand to shake his, but instead he plucked the cigarette from his mouth and pressed his cheek to mine, smacking his lips, and repeated the museums waiting to be discovered, the beating heart that connected all the things that I loved. I hadn't wanted to see the south, and certainly not in the dead of summer. From what I heard, no one had introduced this country to air conditioning yet.

But I deserved it. I deserved every kind of punishment you could throw at me: I almost killed you, so it made perfect sense you didn't want to see me again. I would respect that, stay out of your way as you learned to walk again. Even if it meant living with the stranger dad once called his mother.

I was woken up by a smell, rather than a sound. My eyes slowly fluttered open to see a completely empty road, lined with fields on either sides, grasses tall and jagged in mismatched colors. Beautiful sycamore trees shaded our drive, keeping the sun from my face. Jean-Pascal was slowing the car to a stop, which didn't bother me at first, until I realized what the white things starting to drift into my vision actually were.

Sheep. Or goats, I suppose, I never could tell the difference. The one thing I could tell you about them is that they smell so much worse than their picture book counterparts. The stench seeped through the windows and deep into the fibers of my skin.

The car finally stopped, the herd of goat things now crossing the road in full force. With the air suddenly stagnant, I could feel the heat of the day cloying at my skin, beads of sweat beginning to trickle from my brow, even down my back.

"*Tu peux bouger tes fesses?*" my driver threw open his car door and yelled to the herd. "*M'enfin!*"

At first, I was convinced he was speaking to the sheep, until a woman appeared out of nowhere, her blonde dreadlocks stuffed into a floppy sun hat, which she tipped to Jean-Pascal as she strode up to him.

"*Salut, vieux,*" she said cheerfully, before going off on some tirade in French, the two of them playing off each other like old friends. She was incredibly young to be a shepherd, looking for all intents and purposes like a backpacking college student. But I hadn't heard any stories of college students travelling Europe with herds of sheep.

Or goats. I still wasn't sure about what they were just yet.

The herd was still crossing the road as she spoke, three large dogs keeping them steady as they moved from one pasture to the next. Across from us, two cars were also waiting for them to pass, though one of them had the driver leaning out, rapidly snapping pictures with his phone.

"*Bon, à plus!*" she said, waving lazily at Jean-Pascal as she turned back to her herd. The last of them had made it across the asphalt, and the other stream of cars was slowly beginning to move again. *"Ciao, Poulet!"*

Jean-Pascal laughed at this, closing the car door and shaking his head. He turned to me and let out a single, proud "Woof!" before hitting the gas once again.

"Woof?"

"Woof!" He contorted his face, obviously concentrating hard. "Farming. Woof! Do you see?"

I did not see, but I also did not care. All I wanted right now was a hot bath, a hot meal, and a warm bed. But as I was starting to get warmer the longer I sat in this car, I was starting to question whether those priorities were lying.

The car was making an odd noise as it drove, an overwhelming *chirp chirp chirp*, and I wondered if it was all that safe. I clutched the seat and held on tighter. I was exhausted, but there was no way I could go back to sleep now.

We drove around a small little lake, one so tiny it could have been called a pond, then across a river, this one wide enough to deserve that distinction. The fields here were lush and green, the road still shaded by large sycamores, even this far from civilization. When we finally drove through towns, they too were barely large enough to be called that. It seemed everything was done smaller in France.

"Almost there," said Jean-Pascal, "*Bientôt.*"

He waited for a response, his eyebrows raising playfully, urging me on.

"*Be-n-toe,*" I repeated, and that smile of his grew tenfold. "Soon?"

"*Bravo!*" he cheered, "*Je te jure, tu seras bilingue quand j'aurais fini avec toi.*"

Not knowing a word of what he just said, I just smiled and said "*oui.*" He seemed to like this a lot.

I knew the fundamental basics of French from you and dad: when both your parents are French lit professors, it would be embarrassing for their daughter not to. But the second it was actually up to me to open my mouth and speak, the words dried right up. All I could say to strangers were yes, no, please and thank you, and that was it. Not a great start to a conversation.

The farmland fell away as buildings appeared on either side of the road. Somehow, with no transition at all, we had reached a village. The houses that lined the street were ancient, their stones crumbling beneath wooden shutters and clinging ivy that made entire walls burst green with life. These alternated with modern homes, though I wasn't quite sure if they were all that modern, just not as old looking as the others. Ancient or modern, laundry hung out the windows, cars were parked in driveways, and they gave the distinct homey feel.

And then, as we swung around a large road, my jaw dropped. Because there, right there, just a few feet away from me, was a castle.

It didn't have towers or turrets as I had been imagining since I was a child. In fact, it was more like a large house, simply ancient and made entirely out of stone, and still, somehow, undeniably a castle. Trees grew around the foot of the fortress, tall and majestic, cypress reaching for the sky as the pines spread out like parasols. A flag waved at the top, striped yellow and red, which I'm pretty sure wasn't French at all.

Jean-Pascal slowed the car for me, all so I could gawk at the castle through the windshield. He was grinning again, and I could almost feel the excitement pulsing through him.

"Welcome to Lourmarin," he said, proudly, "welcome home."

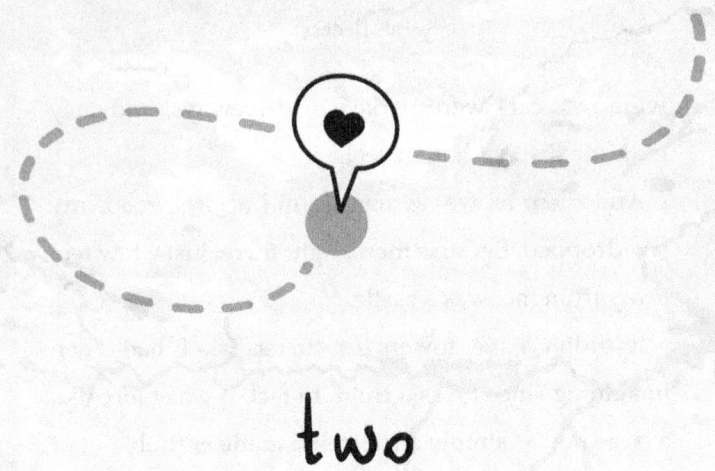

two

SADLY, THE CASTLE WASN'T GOING TO BE HOME FOR the rest of the trip. Jean-Pascal got the old car moving again as people caught up behind us on the road, and he drove away from the beautiful castle, buggy chirping as we went. He looped back around, and I realized he had only driven us by the castle for my benefit. It hadn't actually been on our way, but even in my tired state, I was glad to know it existed.

I had only seen my grandmother in a single picture before. In it, she was in her very early twenties, her long brown hair down past her waist, a bouncing baby boy in her arms: my father. Her husband stood beside her, beaming, built like a lumberjack but dressed like a fisherman. It was the only image I had of the woman, or my grandfather for that matter, who passed away a few years after it was taken. My father didn't have any other pictures of them in the house.

We were now outside of the village, coming up on a gate – imposing wrought iron with rock walls on either side - and Jean-Pascal was slowing, not to mention casting more furtive glances my way, indicating without words that this was the big moment.

The gate groaned as it slid open, and Jean-Pascal turned up the gravel path, driving along a tall rock wall as the road slowly sloped upwards. At the top of our climb was a single old stone fountain, about the size of the car itself, dry, dark under the shade of a circle of trees. Jean-Pascal rounded the fountain, parking the car facing down the hill.

As the car shut off, the sound of chirping stayed in my ears. For a second, I wondered if my tinnitus was back: after the accident, I had heard ringing for days. Jean-Pascal opened his car door and stepped out.

"*Tu connais…* do you know the *chant des cigales*?" He asked, waving his hands at the trees. I shook my head. "Chirp chirp chirp!"

I hadn't been imagining the sound, though it hadn't been coming from the car, but from all around us, a restless, endless wail of chirping. Like the crickets on a hot summer's night, when I visited my other grandmother in her house in the suburbs. Only this was during the day, and so loud I could barely hear myself think.

"A *cigale*? What is that? Is it an alarm?"

"Is bug," he replied, "Ci-cah-dah, I tink!"

Jean-Pascal grabbed my suitcase from the trunk, gesturing that I should get my bag from the back seat. We stepped out of the trees, and there it was: my grandmother's house, the one I had heard so much about from my father as he regaled me with stories of growing up in Provence. It was much larger than I imagined: three floors - none of them straight - built back into a cliff face, surrounded by trees almost as large as it was. The outside was the same old stone as the village houses, with bright green plants clinging to the sides. The shutters were painted a faded sky blue, casting a sharp contrast against the bright pink buds that blossomed from bushes on either side. The walls looked stained in places where the stones had been replaced, like someone had spilled coffee before the paint had dried.

A woman came flying out of the house, door slamming behind her. I didn't even have time to see her before she scooped me up into a tight hug, her tears falling into my hair as she held me close. I dropped my bag, and, without thinking, hugged her back.

The woman who threw my father out of his home,

his entire country. The woman who had never spoken to me until two weeks ago. The woman who hadn't so much as written a letter in the seventeen years I was alive. My Mamie.

A Mamie who was certainly not crying like a woman who wanted nothing to do with me.

"Ma chérie, mais comme tu es belle!" She said between tears, holding my face in her soft hands and taking a step back to look at me. For a split second, I thought someone was making a joke, that someone had thrown wrinkles and a wig on my father. The resemblance was uncanny: I could see right where he had gotten his nose, those familiar smile lines under his eyes. But then that second flickered away, and I was back to looking at my grandmother. Her own eyes were a vibrant shade of blue to match the deep sky above us, unlike his wooden brown. Her once chocolate hair was now silver white, and unlike my gran, she hadn't taken to dying it.

She smoothed my hair away from my face. So that's where I had gotten it from. It was strange to see my own straight hair on a complete stranger. Your hair had always been wavy and beautiful in way I could never replicate. She touched it delicately with her long fingers, realizing this at the same time I was.

She stepped back, holding me out now at arm's

length, moving her hands to my shoulders but refusing to let me go. This time she took me in a little more questioningly, sweeping her eyes over my entire face, picking out my baggy grey shirt from U-Penn, and my favorite blue Levi's which I had found in a goodwill years ago and was certain were imbued with comfort magic.

She herself was wearing loose fitting white trousers and a black tank top, which showed off her trim figure. Another difference between me and her: I had inherited your curves while she seemed to have been plucked straight out of a patch of string beans.

I met her gaze, and we held it for a few seconds. Maybe even minutes. Neither of us knew what to say: a grandmother meeting her granddaughter was supposed to be one of the first things in a baby's life, but I was no longer a baby. Far from it. Right now, we were two strangers who happened to be related by blood, who happened to share hair and a nose, who were excited and terrified by the prospect of living together for the next few months.

Finally, she dropped her hands from my shoulders, cracked a smile not unlike Jean-Pascal's, and slowly, very carefully, enunciated in English.

"It is so very nize to meet you," she said, the 's' sounds scooped up by the chirping around us, leaning in to kiss me on both cheeks. I would have to get used to this. Her skin was cool against mine. "My darling Jamie, I am so 'appy you are 'ere."

"*Enchanté, Mamie,*" I said. "*Merci* for having me."

"*Bon, je vous laisse,*" said Jean-Pascal, returning from the house suitcase-less. The sweetheart had taken it inside for us without even asking, leaving us to our moment. He leaned down to kiss Mamie on both cheeks, though she had to wipe away her tears first.

"*Merci, J-P,*" she replied, and added a string of words I couldn't pick up. He reached down and held her hand in both of his, exchanging a sweet smile with her before walking over to me.

"*A bientôt,*" he said, leaning forward. I did the cheek kiss thing, proud of myself for understanding without too much prompting.

"*A bientôt, Jean-Pascal,*" I repeated in my broken-up accent, which made him beam. One word learned today: ten thousand more to go.

And then, it was just the two of us. My grandmother and me.

And we had no idea what to say.

The initial excitement of our first meeting was already wearing off, replaced by an urge to get to know each other. I wanted to burst out with questions, to ask why I had never met her until today, or why she

Aix Marks the Spot

was so different from all the things I had heard about her. And it was obvious she had questions too: she kept starting to say something, then closed her mouth, only to open it again, all without making a sound.

"Je te sers de l'eau?" she finally asked, so awkwardly it looked like she was cringing.

"Um, what?"

"Tu parles Fraçais?"

I shook my head. No, I did not speak French. I barely understood it, for that matter. My parents had tried, but languages had never clicked for me. I was a much more visual learner: colors were my language, paints my words.

Mamie's entire face fell at this, and she emitted a soft, almost heartbroken, "Oh." Shamed cascaded over me like a wave.

"I'm sorry," I said, and I meant it

"T'apprendras," she shrugged, but whatever enthusiasm she had had just minutes ago had already faded. *"De l'eau?* Water?"

"Yes please," I replied, adding the new words to my mental list, but they would be gone within a few hours for sure. *"Oui, Merci, S'il te plait, beaucoup."*

She laughed, though the smile never reached her eyes. I must not have been saying any of this right. But if I had been making mistakes, she didn't try to correct me.

She reached for my bag, but I grabbed it first, worried that she wouldn't be able to lift it. Her arms didn't look like they had any muscle on them. Empty handed, she waved me along to follow her, taking me into the house through a small door on the side.

It wasn't the front door, though I'm not sure which door was supposed to be. This one led to what seemed to be a cave. The second I stepped inside, the heat of the day was suddenly gone, and in its place, I felt the cool and refreshing cold of darkness.

It was like being underground. The light came through the doorway and a single small window above an old sink, where Mamie went to fill a glass with cold water. I took it eagerly, chugging it down. The water tasted cool and crisp, though a little salty.

"How waz your airplane?" she asked, not that she sounded all that enthusiastic for a reply. She had probably expected me to speak a little French, and for this to have been something, I don't know, cute between grandmother and granddaughter. Instead, now, it was coming off a little patronizing.

"*Très bien*," I replied. Very good, the same words my French teacher Madame Lemaitre used when I occasionally replied correctly back in her class. Not that anything I learned there seemed to be helping. I could

Aix Marks the Spot

tell Mamie my name, age, and ask many questions about monkeys, but couldn't tell her anything about myself.

"Do you want to see your room?" she continued, struggling over the vowels. I nodded, handing her back the now empty glass.

The house was surprisingly dark, and difficult to navigate. Most of the shutters were closed to keep out the heat of the day, though propped slightly open so that some light could filter in, but it wasn't much. The hallways were tight, my bag scraping along the wall as we walked.

Mamie led me to the top floor, taking so many turns I wondered how I would ever remember the way back down. There, at the very top, at the end of the hallway, a door was ajar, light flowing in through the open window. It filled the hallway with a warm, caramel glow, the world basked in sepia. Mamie turned around as if making sure I was still following.

"Your fazer's room," she said, indicating the door, "I 'ave not touched."

She took a step back, indicating I should go in. It didn't look like she would be following me. But I didn't care: I was instantly in awe.

The room was small, square, furnished simply with a matching wooden desk, bed, and wardrobe that looked like they were out of an antiques catalogue. The bed was massive, dressed in white linens, a lavender wand sitting on the end and filling the room with the gentle, calming scent. The desk and bookcase were stuffed full of books, some ancient hardcovers, others old paperbacks: my father's books, from when he was still a student.

"Bathroom," said Mamie, opening a door next to the wardrobe, revealing a small room with yellow and green tiles. I realized it shared a wall with the cliff face, keeping the room cool.

"And ze toilet," she added, almost an afterthought, pointing to a door directly outside my room. "*Séparé*. Az you say, separate."

I dropped my bag next to my suitcase, which sat on the chest at the end of the bed, waiting for me to unpack it. Jean-Pascal had been immensely kind to bring it up for me. I wondered idly how well he and my grandmother knew each other, before getting distracted by the window and rushing to it, practically flinging myself outside as I took in the view.

The entire valley spread out before me. Green exploded on the rolling hills, dotted here and there with small traces of civilization. In the distance, I could even see the Lourmarin castle peeking through the trees. Right below the room, I could see my Mamie's patio, and, of all things, a bright blue swimming pool.

"Thank you," I said, so overwhelmed with emotion I couldn't figure out what to say next, "thank you, Mamie."

"I am so 'appy to see you," she said.

She placed her hand on my cheek, running her thumb over my ear. She looked once again like she had something important to say, licking her lips to make difficult words slide out more easily, but instead she returned her hand, and smiled.

She left without another word.

three

ONE THING PEOPLE NEVER TELL YOU - OR THEY DO, I just chose to ignore them - is that travelling makes you tired. Even though I had tried to sleep on the plane and even managed to catch a short nap in the car ride over, the second I hit the bed I felt so overwhelmingly exhausted that I fell backwards and was out like a light.

When I woke up the next morning, the room hadn't changed at all. The only thing to tell me an entire day had gone by was the way the shadows seemed to have moved in a single blink. It was hot, my skin was sticky, and my face itched like you wouldn't believe.

I sat up, groggy. I hadn't even bothered to take my shoes off, so I did now, blinking the film of haze out of my eyes as I freed my toes from their rubber prison cell. I let out a breath of relief as they expanded in the heat.

Aix Marks the Spot

The room seemed smaller today. Maybe it was a trick of the light, but after a good night's sleep it was almost claustrophobic. So, this was going to be my cell for the next three months. My punishment for my near deadly mistake. Like Napoleon at St-Helens, only reversed: trapped inside France instead of kept out of it.

I took a deep breath and pushed myself onto my feet. My back creaked, echoed by the floor as I put my entire weight on it. I shuffled to the bathroom, where I practically fell on the toilet. It was lower than back home, and uncomfortable to sit on without a seat. I stood up to flush, before realizing there wasn't one. Oh. Crap.

I had just gone in the bidet.

Who the hell puts a bidet in a bathroom but doesn't put the stinking toilet? I vaguely remembered Mamie mentioning the separate room last night, but... why?

Grabbing the showerhead, I threw the water on full blast and aimed it at the tiny porcelain bowl. Water flew up the ugly yellow tiles of the wall. I held back tears of frustration as I drenched the bathroom. I couldn't even use the toilet properly in this country.

I threw my sticky clothes into the corner and stepped into the shower stall, putting the head back where it was supposed to be, which was far, far too low to be convenient. Mamie had left soaps and shampoos for me - *shampooing* was both self-explanatory and hilarious, *Après shampooing* I could guess was conditioner, and *gel-douche* must have been the soap, because I sure as heck hoped my grandmother wasn't buying me a douche. There was a lot of guessing - and I melted into the warm embrace of flowing water.

I did have to duck to get the hair. I wondered how on earth any woman in this country could shave in a cubicle so small. I could hardly bend over. Maybe that's where the stereotype of hairy European women came from: small, insufferably tight showers.

Clean and starting to feel more awake, I shuffled to the sink, inspecting my face. I almost screamed: in just a single night, I had either developed acne from the plane, or become a banquet for mosquitos. By the itch, I guessed the latter. As the steam began to dry, the red in my face remained, and with the burning, the urge to scratch.

Not even one day into this country, and already I was having a bad reaction. Was it possible to be allergic to France?

I left my clothes in the corner and grabbed new ones from my suitcase, slipping on gym shorts and a baggy old tee. Finally, clean, dressed, and sufficiently awake, I grabbed my phone.

6:34 am.

Impressive, I had slept through the night and emerged from my exhausted nest as a morning bird. Equally impressive was how high the sun was in the sky, how loud the cicadas were chirping, and how many missed calls waited for me on my phone now that I actually opened it.

Realization hit me like a punch to the face. I hadn't set the correct time zone. It was already noon, and I had slept through half the day.

I flew down the stairs, realizing halfway down that I had no idea which direction anything was in this crazy house. I stopped at a landing that could well have been a living room, with an old purple couch in the corner and a wooden coffee table covered in magazines that couldn't actually say *Philosophie*, could they?

A door leading outside stood ajar, and I walked through, emerging into the summer heat and right in the middle of cicada song. I didn't know how I would ever get used to the sound, how anyone could get used to it. It was like living inside an electrical socket.

We were on the second floor, the door leading to stairs that brought me right down to the pool, and, thank god, to the kitchen. Inside, Mamie was sitting on a stool, round glasses that hadn't been replaced since the seventies perched on the tip of her nose as she read a worn white paperback.

"*Coucou, ma puce!*" She exclaimed, catching me staring at her through the kitchen window in a totally non-stalkery way. "*Bien dormi?*"

Not sure what any of that meant and catching a whiff of something meaty and magical wafting out her window, I gave her a smile.

"*Bonjour, Mamie,*" I replied, stepping into the kitchen. It was so much cooler down here, no wonder she was reading in the dark. "Did my parents call?"

"*Tes Parents?*" she looked a little taken aback, though I wasn't sure what by. "*Ils ont appelés hier soir. Rapelle les après qu'on déjeune?*"

"Um…" I wet my suddenly dry lips, "*Je comprends pas?*"

At least I knew how to say I didn't understand. But the look on Mamie's face was heartbreaking, as if she had expected me to emerge from the room having fully assimilated the French language in my sleep, and now her only granddaughter was stabbing her deep in the back.

"Late-her," she said, making the phone symbol with her hand, "*telephone* later."

"Thank you," I replied, then added "*Merci,*" for good measure.

"*Tu m'aides a mettre la table?*" she asked, making no attempt to sprinkle in any English. She pointed to a cabinet, and from context I understood she wanted the table set. She pointed out the door, towards the shaded spot near the pool, where a wooden table waited, alone.

I took the plates and utensils, walking them out to the table in silence, my mind racing to make sense of the situation. She was obviously frustrated I didn't speak any French, but she wasn't trying to speak English, either. What was it dad was always saying? Conversation goes both ways. And this sure wasn't a conversation.

I don't know what she had expected: the perfect bilingual granddaughter to waltz into her life, now that she was finally ready for her. For us to act like we had known each other since I was born, that she had watched me grow from a baby to the person I was now. But she had waited too long for any of that.

Mamie came out to the table with a heavy cast iron casserole in her hands. I reached to help her, but she had already made it all this way without any trouble - she was strong, and younger than she looked.

She dished out a massive slice of pork roast and potatoes, covered in a sweet-smelling mustard sauce with chunks of garlic sitting on top, handing me the serving spoon while she returned to the kitchen for a bottle of water and a bottle of pink wine. She poured us glasses of water first, pointing to the wine while saying, in her drawn out, rolling French accent, "*later.*"

The roast was excellent, so moist that it melted on my tongue, and the mustard had just enough kick to balance out the gentle creaminess of the sauce and juices. I dove right in, not realizing how hungry I was. I hadn't eaten since we had lunch on the plane.

"Iz too… *lourd* for summer," she said, struggling to shape the words, "but I make for you."

"I'm so happy to be here, *Mamie*," I said. Well, lied.

"Um-hum," she replied, utterly unconvinced.

The tension was so thick I had an easier time slicing the pork. I wanted to say something, anything, but the words stuck in my throat, unable to pass the language barrier.

"Say Tray Bon," I said, and Mamie smiled gently. But it was not enough to win her over.

I ate a meal with this familiar stranger, trying to sort through all I knew about her. I knew she was a writer here, which is part of what inspired dad to study literature at university, where he met you when you shared graduate classes. You had wanted to study abroad, left in search of a degree, and came back with a husband and, later, a daughter.

But there was an entire chapter I was missing between "(French) boy meets (American) girl" and "man leaves his homeland, vowing never to come back again, his own mother refusing to see him." What could he have done that was so horrible his mother disowned him so completely?

I finished my water and she poured me a little wine. We clinked glassed. Drank. I wasn't a fan: it was too sour, too sharp, like licking a cold fork. I didn't finish my glass.

After lunch, Mamie and I cleared the table, washed the dishes together (me drying), and she went upstairs, with no intension of coming back down again. I didn't particularly mind. I had had my awkward fill of her for the day, and didn't want to draw out all the tense, one-way conversations.

I finally spotted her up on a terrace, like she was on top of her own little tower, typing away madly on an old mechanical typewriter.

Huh. So that was how it was going to be.

four

"YEAH, IT'S SUNNY HERE," I SAID TO YOU. Understatement of the century: the heat was so astoundingly strong that I could barely move. My own sweat kept me stuck to every surface I had the misfortune of touching for too long.

I had thrown myself back onto the bed, keeping the phone a little distance from my ear, as that too was, astoundingly, sweating as well. I stared up at the ceiling, at the cracking white plaster and sturdy brown beams that held the roof above my head.

The windows were closed against the cicada sound, but it made the room so stuffy I couldn't think. I experimented with closing the curtains while the windows remained open, but it wasn't much better.

"And what are you doing so far?" You asked.

"I had lunch with Mamie, but she's working now," I said, extrapolating, "it's hard to talk to her. I don't think she likes me."

"Nonsense, of course she likes you!" dad interjected, "you're her granddaughter. What's not to like?"

The fact that I put my mother in a wheelchair, for starters, maybe? How much had dad told her about the accident? About why he was sending me away?

"Have the two of you made any plans yet?" you asked, your eagerness seeping through the phoneline. "Is she going to take you to Aix? Oh, how about the St Victoire?"

"We haven't really talked at all," I said, too tired to filter my words. "I don't think she wants anything to do with me."

"Don't stay cooped up in the house," you said. "Go out. See things! Do stuff! Practice your French!"

"You mean, my non-existent French?"

"There's nowhere to go but up, darling."

There was a silence, and for a second I thought the phone had gone dead. But the longing in your voice remained like a string knotting us together, you wanting to be here, me wanting to be home with you. If I could drag you through the Atlantic network cables, and somehow download workable legs along the way, you know I would.

"Just try to have a good time," you said, finally taking a deep breath. " Thanks for being so understanding about living with your Mamie while I recover. It's good to know that I don't have to worry about you still having a great summer. It's just easier this way."

"Sure, sure." Just because you and dad both had said it, didn't make it true. I knew you resented me for what I did for you. I knew you needed time away from your life-crushing daughter. You needed space: space to walk again, and space from me.

I gave you that space. I ruined everything, and I would do anything to make it right again.

"I love you, baby bear," you said. And for a moment, I believed you. Using almost forgotten nicknames as terms of endearment was a low blow.

"I love you too, mama bear."

"And I love you!" Dad piped in. "Sorry, I'm trying to work things out with billing. But I love you!"

"I love you too, Dad," I said, feeling a pang to my heart. He didn't really have to do that right now. It was just another stab to remind me what I had done.

I hung up, staring up at the rafters again. If I stared long enough, I could imagine lines of ants walking up and down them, living the world of Mamie's upside-down house. I wondered if I could live upside down. It was better than living pushed to the edge of things, unwanted by my parents or my grandmother.

At least there was one person who wanted me, and that was Jazz. The two of us had spent weeks planning our summer: me, with my brand-spanking-new driver's license, and her, with her mother's old Toyota. We were going to get out of the city and explore as much of the state as we could. Well, within reason: we had to be home by curfew, but that wasn't hard. All we wanted to do was sketch.

When we both got into the Barnes's Foundation's summer program, we knew that the universe really did want us to be artists. Together, because that's what best friends do. But my parents didn't care how prestigious it was, after the accident: the only thing that mattered was getting me far, far away from them.

So now she was learning the secrets to the finest of fine art, while I was trapped in this house, with not even my own language to comfort me.

I needed the internet. I pulled out my computer, feeling relief flow through me as I heard the familiar boot-up jingle. Now I would just have to ask Mamie about the Wi-Fi password, if she had one.

What I didn't count on was her not having Wi-Fi at all.

I had 3G on my phone, though, which made a small difference. It was enough data for my parents to call me (pre-approved oversea numbers and all) and have a trickle of internet. I looked up Jazz on Messenger, realizing she was probably at Barnes right about now.

Jazz,

Message me when you get out? I need to talk to someone. I'm going crazy over here.

Don't call tho. I don't have much data and I don't think my parents got your number approved. I have a lot I need to say, and I honestly can't handle another phone call right now. If I hear your voice, I'll probably have a(nother) break down.

I didn't get a message back until the middle of the night, but I was already awake: you're a jerk, jetlag. Not to mention the entire French countryside trying to start a concert. At one point I thought a woman was screaming, but it turned out to be a bird. A flipping bird.

Jazz was just getting off from the second day of studio art training, and it was obvious she loved it, despite how much she played it down for my sake. She told me how the teachers hated her work and made her redraw the same apple over and over again to get the shading right.

She might have said it to make me feel better, but it turned my insides to knots. I needed that kind of criticism. I would never improve my portfolio if people kept lying to me about my work. I was mediocre at best, but passionate. I would have killed to be in her place right now, apples and all.

I told her it was late, and I was going to sleep. There's nothing like seeing your best friend live *your* life without you to make you feel the brunt of this punishment.

It was my fault. I deserved this. I rolled over in bed, pushing the pillow over my ears, and tried to cut out the noise of the frogs.

five

EVERY NIGHT HAD A PERFECT MOMENT. THE CICADAS signed off, one by one, and quiet fell over the rolling hills of Provence. This moment was pure bliss. The sun set fast here, so there were only a few minutes of twilight, where the world looked odd, all filtered in blue, while some of the cliffs still shimmered in pink.

And then. *Then.* Taking up the relay from his cicada friends, you would hear a lone and tearful *ribbit*.

It sounded like a rubber band being stretched, about to snap. Another responded, lower than the first. Then a third. And then the entire world sounded like it was the seat of a frog concert. Birds would join, hooting or screaming. It sounded like a drunken rave that just wouldn't end.

That's also when the mosquitos came out to play.

With all the frogs chatting back and forth, I would only hear the whine when it was too late. The high-pitched hum shot past my ear, but I missed it because I was already too busy scratching the new bite on my arm.

So, I closed the windows. For a minute, I had perfection: no mosquitos. No frogs. My ears would ring as they noticed the absence of sound.

And then the air itself would try to suffocate me.

It was so hot in the room I could feel myself sweating through my pajamas. So, I was faced with the dilemma: do I open the windows and breathe, but leave all this exposed skin at the mercy of the mosquitos, or did I close said windows and suffocate in my sleep?

I switched every night. When I would wake up from a mosquito free sleep, I was so covered in sticky sweat I swore - never again. But the next night, after waking to new mountains on my legs, I couldn't remember the pain of those sweats. And the next morning I... and so on. That was all considering I fell asleep at all.

I still managed to get into the semblance of a routine. Slowly, I was waking up earlier and earlier, falling asleep more or less when my head hit the pillow. Even so, there was nothing interesting to report at all.

I wasn't quite sure what I was allowed to do: I swam in the pool and read the books I brought along. Mamie didn't have a car, so I couldn't go anywhere. She didn't have internet, so I couldn't do anything. All of her books were in French, so I couldn't read. How dad managed to grow up here at all completely baffled me. I could completely understand why he left.

But the worst was that it had gotten to the point where I just couldn't draw anything. I was in Provence, the land of artistic inspiration, but every time I picked up a pencil, I got the shakes. Nothing in my head made it onto the paper.

Mamie had made a roast on the first day, but since then most of our meals had been salads, meatballs, and fruit. She seemed really into Swedish meatballs, though I'd never seen her leave the house once to buy them.

During the day, she had this terrace outside her room where she would sit and hammer at a typewriter for hours on end. Sometimes, she would call me things like *choupette* which I think were supposed to be affectionate, but then she would turn cold and lock herself in her room again for hours on end. I asked her about the Wi-Fi, but she said that whiffy is distracting, and I couldn't get over that.

Friday morning, despite managing to wake up at the very reasonable hour of 9 am, I came downstairs to find the entire house abandoned. Mamie must have locked herself away in her study already, which was not exactly new, but she usually greeted me in the morning and shared her coffee. I took some, though I hated the taste, just to try to impress her, to spend a few more minutes trying to bond, but she would always leave before I was anywhere near finishing my mug. I would dunk it down the sink.

This morning, instead of Mamie and the coffee, there was a note waiting for me. A short list of groceries she needed, and a crisp blue 20-euro bill folded in half sitting on top of it, pinned down by a key ring with a large beeper on it.

Hungry, and finding the fridge sorely in need of a refill, I was caught in a tight place. Usually, if you told me to pick up groceries, it was an easy chore to do, especially now that I could drive on my own. But it dawned on me that I had no real way of getting into town even if I wanted to.

My stomach grumbled; my cue to leave. I strode up the stairs to Mamie's room two at a time, finding her room locked. Lovely. I knocked. No answer.

I stuffed the note into my pocket with the bill and ran downstairs and outside, taking a step away from the house to see if she was on her *terrasse*. My hunch was right: she was sitting on her little overlook, hunched over a typewriter, cigarette hanging limply from her lips.

"Hey!" I called. No answer. "Mamie!"

"*Quoi?*" she yelled back, neither pausing not looking up, "*Je travaille! Ne me dérange pas quand j'écris, tu comprends?*"

I certainly did not *comprend* any of that. Except maybe the word comprend.

"*Comment...* How do I get to the *village?*" I shouted again, cupping my hands around my mouth to make sure she understood every word I said.

"*En velo!*" she said, "*en bas!*"

Velo, velo... velociraptor was the only equivalent I could think of.

"Velo?" I asked up again.

"*Bicyclette!*"

She wanted me to bike into the village? With groceries? I could have laughed, but there was nothing funny about this. I felt sick to my stomach, which wasn't great considering how hungry I was.

"*Passe à la boulangerie en premier,*" she said, of which I only picked up the word *boulangerie*: bakery. She must have heard my stomach rumbling all the way from her perch. Suddenly, the idea didn't seem all that unappealing anymore. The thought of a real French croissant melting in my mouth was enough of an encouragement to leave the house as any.

I found Mamie's bike leaning against the wall beneath the kitchen window and pushed it down her steep driveway. There was a basket in the front, properly convenient. I clutched the gate beeper tight in my hand: this was my first freedom in five days, and no matter how small, I would embrace it.

The cicadas were singing with a vengeance this morning, so loud that they drowned out the sound of me tapping the kickstand and pushing myself onto the road. I remembered the way to the village easily enough, as there was only one real road here, after all. One road, but no bike lane, and a ditch on either side of the asphalt. Worst design ever. If you're thinking of biking across Provence… don't.

The bike was old, but once it got going, it handled rather well. I kept to the side of the road, cringing every time a car even came close to me. The cicadas were covering up the sound of motors, leaving me terrified I would get run over at any moment.

The village of Lourmarin started right across the street from the castle. I hadn't paid any attention to it as we had driven by it the first time: I mean, there was a freaking castle there, for goodness sakes. Now that I had time to focus on it, I could see the clocktower reaching up from the center, and the tightly wound homes and houses that spun up to it.

Was I allowed to bike through? There weren't any signs telling me not to. I picked up the pace and rolled into town.

The place was gorgeous, like I had fallen into a postcard. Clinging plants covered the street corners, flowers bursting from pots and terraces. Fountains trickled, replacing the sound of the diligent cicada's chirp.

The streets were narrow, homes on either side close enough together to give me small relief from the sun. They were a mishmash of ancient and crumbling, along with recently renovated, smooth stucco next to peeling old plaster. A woman sat in a metal folding chair outside her home, smoking a cigarette as her little poodle slept under her feet. I rode past her, feeling her eyes on me, though I supposed there was nothing else to look at anyways.

Everything seemed to be sloping upwards. I kept pedaling, though the streets were getting steep, until I reached the top. There was a church, bell tower and all, and no bakery to be found. People were already out and about even this early, but when I started to ask for directions, I found the words dried up in my mouth.

I truly had no idea what to say.

I turned the bike around and picked another road at random, riding down the slope and keeping my feet on the pavement in case I needed to brake. There, finally, I saw something promising: bread in the window, so I parked the bike and went on in.

Fresh loaves rested in wicker baskets along the wall, while the counter was full of pastries and tarts. The smell was heavenly, like melted butter and hot sugar. My mouth watered in an instant, and my stomach responded with its now familiar rumble.

"*Bonjour,*" a woman walked in from the back, wiping flowery hands on an apron. "*Puis-je vous aider?*"

"I… um… English?" I sputtered, and she smiled.

"What would you like?" she asked again, the words heavily accented, but clear. I felt relief wash over me.

I checked Mamie's list, recognized the word baguette, but nothing else. I handed it to the baker.

She pulled down two seed covered baguettes, an olive filled loaf from under the counter, and a flat, golden bread with leaf shapes cut out. Each she slipped into a separate paper bag, placing them on the counter beside her.

"*Ce sera tout?*" she asked, handing me back the shopping list, "Is zat all?"

I just couldn't help myself. The massive pile of beautiful flaky pastries was just winking at me from under the glass, arranged from left to right from the classic to the elaborate: mounds of croissants and pain-au-chocolats, moving into rows of sweetened buns, until reaching the lines of glazed eclairs and carefully balanced cakes. Small tarts full of fruit or just plain chocolate preceded the larger versions of themselves, works of art every single one.

My eyes fell on the bun in the middle, a beautiful, golden thing with white icing on top so smooth it looked like princess Elsa's doing.

But as I tried to find the name, I froze up. I couldn't get the words out of my mouth. Instead, I found myself falling into the familiar.

"Un croissant?"

I hated the way my voice sounded as I said the word. I would never get the slick French accent like Mamie who spoke like silk. The baker didn't seem to mind, or maybe she didn't notice my embarrassment. I fed the bill Mamie had given me through the change machine, thanking her for the food as I took the bags - the only French I could manage, but it seemed to make her smile grow.

"A bientôt!" she said, as I left.

"Merci! A bientôt!" I replied, beaming as I went back to the bike and placed all the bread in the basket. There, I had done it: a successful, semi-French interaction. The conversation had me bursting with confidence.

Well, semi confidence. I would have to figure out what that gorgeous silver bun was in order to get one next time. The croissant looked so usual and familiar beside it.

It didn't taste familiar, or even usual for that matter. The second the flaky pastry touched my lips, the butter seemed to melt on my tongue, filling my mouth with sweetness, magically still warm from the oven. I practically tumbled backwards, falling onto the stoop of someone's door. I couldn't blemish this experience by biking at the same time, no: this was something I would have to take the time to enjoy. I tried not to scarf it down, I really did. But there was something simply magical about warm butter pastry flakes in the morning.

France: where even your cheap breakfast is a delicacy.

Riding my bike through the small streets of the village, baguettes poking out from my basket, I felt like I was living the French ideal. All I needed now was my beret and my striped shirt. Instead I was in a t-shirt from a charity fun run, my running shorts riding a little too high up for comfort. Even though it was the middle of summer, many people around me were wearing full length dresses and even slim fitted jeans. I couldn't understand them.

I turned a corner and practically crashed into a market stall. I slammed on my breaks just in time, as my wheel delicately bumped the table.

"Oh mais, fais attention!" An older woman - not even

the stall owner, mind you - swiped an arm at me, batting the air instead of my face.

"Sorry!" I exclaimed, and she rolled her eyes.

"Touriste…"

I got off the bike and decided to push it instead. It was still early enough that the marketplace wasn't too busy. The stalls were bright and clean, close together in this cramped space. There were tables set out with massive wheels of cheese, others with baskets full of dried hams and meats. Touristy looking stalls had bundles of lavender, and berets on display, though I had yet to see an actual French person wear one yet. A farmer had all of his fruits and veg in wooden crates, calling out prices to people as they walked by, who then usually stopped to exchange banter.

I went there first, sure that most of the things Mamie wanted me to get were veggie based. Luckily, the man had signs up, so I could match the words on her list to the names of the food. I rehearsed what I was going to say in my head, how I would pronounce the words, how much of each I wanted… should be easy.

"Vous avez choisi?" he asked, leaning out over his stall and beaming at me, his moustache bristling.

In an instant, all the confidence I had gained from the bakery was gone. The words dissolved off my tongue. I found myself staring at the farmer, mouth suddenly dry, at a complete loss of what to actually say.

"*Vous voulez un peu plus de temps?*" He asked, and it was obvious he was trying to keep the patronizing tone from his voice. Or maybe I was just imagining it out of sheer embarrassment.

How could I go from knowing what to say one second, to a completely bumbling idiot in the next? Faced with a real Frenchman, who looked so much like a stereotype that it hurt, I couldn't utter a word.

"*Je voudrais... je veut... s'il vous plait...*" I managed to blurt out, but none of those were actual orders. I shoved the shopping list forward in shame.

The list looked tiny in the man's massive hand. He read it, nodding to himself, then grabbed a paper bag from behind the counter.

"*Cinq pamplemouses,*" he said, encouragingly, taking grapefruits from the display. He paused, meeting my gaze, eyes wide and encouraging, an expectant look on his face.

I reached for the money, but he shook his head quickly, "*Pamplemouse?*"

"*Pamplemouse...*" I repeated after him, and he put them in the bag.

"*Un kilo de tomates,*" he said, taking the tomatoes. I got it this time, repeating after him as he put them in the bag. With each new word, he smiled wider.

"Une barquette de fraises," he said, holding out the strawberries, smacking his lips, *"Et elles sont tres bonnes!"*

"Un kilo d'oranges!"

"Un kilo d'orages!" I replied. Instead of his usual smile, he burst out into laughter, practically dropping the oranges on his counter.

"Mais, Mademoiselle, il n'a ya pas un nuage dans le ciel!" he said, guffawing, his laugh deep enough to shake his entire stall.

"What?" I stammered, feeling a burst of fear run through me. What had I said?

"He says there's not a cloud in the sky," came a voice, "so it'll be very hard to give you a whole kilo of storms."

I turned, expecting maybe to see Jean-Pascal, but instead there was just a boy. He looked about my age, wearing a light blue shirt and a pair of peach shorts. His hair, a dark shade of brown, was cropped up on the sides, though what was left was wavy and carefree, a little curl resting on his forehead like a modern, French, Clark Kent. He was kinda cute, if you were into the 'I just got out of bed or spent hours trying to look like I did' look.

"Laisse la tranquille, Valentin," said the farmer, packing up the last of the storms I ordered.

"Je ne l'embête pas, je viens l'aider," he said, throwing up his hands defensively. *Aider*, I got that word - he was here to help.

"You speak English?" I asked, simultaneously confused and relieved.

"I game," he shrugged, like that answered all my questions, "need a hand?"

"Yes, yes, please!"

I paid the farmer, taking my bags full of food and putting them in the basket with the bread, careful not to crush anything.

"La semaine prochaine, tu les connais tous, avant de me revoir!" he said, winking, before letting go of my small list.

"What did he say?" I asked my impromptu translator.

"He said next week you know zem all," he replied, "looks like you've got homework!"

I liked the way he said 'them', the *th* not even attempted, just completely replaced by a Z. Zem, like a new pronoun or something waiting to be discovered.

I pushed my bike along as he read the list, checking my basket for the foods I had already purchased. At this point, I only had coins left, and they jingled in my pocket as we strolled along.

"It looks like you have ezeryting but your *saucisson*

and cheese," he said, handing me back the list. "You shop for you?"

"My Mamie," I took it and slipped it in the pocket along with the money. The way he rolled his r's... No, Jamie, stay focused here. Don't let a cute accent distract from the job at hand. "She speaks French, I don't."

"You here for the summer, then?" he asked, "visiting?"

I nodded. He didn't need the details. "And you?"

"Local. I live with my mozer in the *village*," he gestured down the road. "I'm Valentin, by the way. And you are…?"

"Valentine?"

"Valentin," he exaggerated. It was as if the entire last syllable was scooped from his mouth before he could finish saying it.

"Jamie," I replied, not willing to embarrass myself further by trying again.

"Jammy?"

"Jay- Mee."

"Not hard at all to say," he replied, chuckling. "Ok. *Saucisson?*"

We stopped at one of the stalls with the dried hams, and he stepped up to the owner to chat. He seemed to know everyone in the market: perks of being local, I supposed.

"Who's your Mamie again?" he asked me, "She didn't say what kind of *saucisson* she wanted, but Marc might know."

"It's Colette," I replied, butchering her name, "Colette Martin."

The butcher's eyes went wider than dinner plates.

"C'est elle la petite-fille de Colette?" he stammered, and Valentin nodded, the curl on his forehead sliding up and down.

The two of them chatted as I waited in my corner, the man shooting glances in my direction every few seconds, as if to check I was still here. I wasn't sure if he expected me to run away or if he thought I would go up in a puff of smoke. The way he was talking made it sound like my grandmother was some kind of witch.

Valentin finally wrapped it up, and I got my log of dried meat. Was it some kind of salami?

"What was he saying?" I asked, "About my grandma?"

"Oh, nothing," Valentin shrugged, "just small village drama. You know how it goes."

"I don't," I replied, "I'm from Philadelphia. That's not exactly small-town living."

"Philadelphia? Rocky, yeah?" he put his fists in the air.

"Yeah, Rocky," I laughed, but my heart wasn't in

it. I wanted to know what people were saying about Mamie.

"The last thing on the list is the cheese," said Valentin, "and the note said it was for you to choose. How much coin do you have left?"

I counted my cash, but it wasn't even ten euro. Valentin didn't seem to think that was an issue.

"What kind of cheeses do you like?" he asked, before shaking his head. "Wait, don't answer. You don't know real cheese."

I scoffed. "Don't know real cheese? Please. I shop the good stuff."

"Yeah? What color? And how flat?" He rolled his eyes, leading us to the table I had seen earlier with the big wheels of cheese. If I had looked closer earlier I would have seen the rows of small round ones in crates, each a different shade of white, and some covered in spices.

"Our cheese is good," I muttered.

"If you left it outside, would bacteria completely avoid it?" he laughed. "Trust me. You've never had real cheese before. I don't trust anything called cheese by a country that puts it in a can."

"We do not…" my mind flashed back to when I was eight, spraying cheese whiz on crackers.

"Exactly. Let me make you a selection."

"Are you... you sure it's not too much trouble?"

"Oh, this is pure torture, talking to you," he said, "I'm going to call the firemen, have you taken away for endangering a Frenchman!"

"The firemen?"

"That's what you pick up on?" he asked, lifting an eyebrow, which just made his Clark Kent curl rise up. "What's wrong with the firemen?"

"I'm so confused right now."

"Me, too."

He didn't look confused, though. He looked... cute. And I couldn't believe I was suddenly hyperaware of how well-proportioned he was. While his shirt wasn't tight, it still showed the slight definition of his pecs through the light fabric. And his eyes... his eyes were the same shade as the blue sky above, and twice as deep. If he stopped talking, I could swim in them all day.

"Um, anyway," he said turning to grab the attention of the cheesemaker. I felt my face flush red as I realized he must have seen the way I was looking at him. I stuffed my hands in my pockets and tried to get that piercing blue gaze out of my head.

"To make a proper cheese assortment, you need something hard, something aged, something creamy, and something strong," he explained. "So, I'm making sure you get some comté, some camembert, some fresh *chevre*, and some aged *chevre*. Goat's cheese, is that alright with you?"

Any goat cheese I ever had was in log or pre-crumbled. The little round patties the cheesemaker was wrapping in wax paper were practically melting in his hand. I had no idea what I had just gotten into.

I paid the man, and Valentin had done his math perfectly: I ended up with just two euros left. I handed it to my guide.

"For your troubles," I said, and he laughed.

"Wow, two euros!" he clasped it in his hands like a prayer. "*Merci*, My lady! I will be able to buy a new goat with these riches! My lady is fair and kind!"

I couldn't help but snort at the ridiculous act.

"Seriously, though, thank you," I said, placing the cheese delicately on top of my now very full bike basket. "I don't know where I would be without your help."

"Probably still asking strangers to sell you storms," he replied, "but if you still want one, I'll try to track one down for you."

I pushed my bike forward, not wanting to go home just yet. It was amazing to finally speak English like this: it made me realize just how much I missed being home. How much I missed you. And dad too, of course: but I would always be worried about you.

"Hey, if you ever need me to translate for you again, come and find me, ok?" he said, pointing up at an open window. "That's me right there. Valentin Faure. Ring me, and I'll come down. I'd give you my number, but I don't want to sound like a stalker."

"Oh, please do," I said. I practically shoved my phone into his hands. "Your number, I mean. I don't want you to sound like a stalker either. But… It would be nice to have someone to talk to, you know, who actually speaks my language."

"Or, maybe, you've been speaking French this whole time!" He took my phone and added himself to my contacts as *Valentin (Fresh out of Storms)*. It made me giggle an unnaturally girlish giggle when he handed the phone back.

"If that's too cheesy," he said, "then you haven't had any *fromage* yet."

It was easy to laugh with this guy. Maybe it was just the fact that I hadn't had anyone tell me a good joke in days - or even try to - or that I missed being able to be heard, understood, but I wanted to be around him as long as I possibly could.

"Better get your groceries to the fridge," he said, "before the heat gets to them first."

"Yes, yes, true," I said, climbing on my bike, "See you around, Valentine!"

"Valentin," he corrected, rolling his eyes, "See you around, Jammy!"

As I biked back to Mamie's home, basket brimming with fresh food and hope, I wondered why my name sounded so delicate on his tongue, even though he had butchered the pronunciation. I didn't mind being Jammy when he said it like that.

six

MY MOOD PRETTY MUCH INSTANTLY SOURED WHEN I rode home to the quiet house.

Mamie didn't seem to have moved the entire time I was in the village. That wasn't a big deal, but she didn't move after I told her I was back, either. I found myself unpacking the basket of groceries alone, stuffing things into the fridge almost haphazardly since I didn't know where she liked things to go. Dried salami: was it even a fridge thing, or a cupboard thing?

They say the opposite of love is hate, but it really isn't. It's indifference. Had she always been this way? If so, I could understand why dad left. I had no idea what she was like when he was growing up: none of the stories he told me involved her. Stories of running around the hills, swimming in the Durance river, escaping close calls with boars: Mamie was either never present, edited out, or he just flat out refused to tell me stories where she actually played an active role.

At least now I had a new activity I could add to the list of things I could do all day, and that was texting the cute French boy I met at the market, who, let me say it again for the people in the back, *actually spoke English*. Maybe the universe did care about me after all.

I had only just left him at the market, though. Was it too soon to send him anything?

Before I could even attempt to make first contact, Mamie appeared in the doorway, ashtray in hand. She dumped the contents in the trash before finally turning to me, scanning the food I had yet to put away.

"*Tu as faim?*" She asked, "*tu veux déjeuner?*"

Faim and *déjeuner* I had gotten down: hungry and lunch. Important words for survival, after all.

"*Oui, Mamie,*" I replied.

The woman opened the fridge, grabbing some tomatoes, which she promptly sliced and threw into a bowl. I did my best to be helpful, setting the table (inside, today: it was too hot out now, even under the shady pines), and taking the cheese from the fridge to arrange them on a small plate. Mamie seemed to approve.

She ladled out a spoonful of her tomato creation on my plate: just sliced tomatoes swimming in olive oil, with chopped basil on top. She dug in without saying a word.

I followed suit. Meals with Mamie were a mixed bag: on the one hand, I love food. On the other, well, I didn't quite love Mamie.

"*Lourmarin, c'est...*" I struggled to find the words from my tiny vocabulary list, "*très belle.*"

"*Beau,*" she corrected curtly.

"But a town is feminine, right? *Une Ville?*" The French were very hung up on the masculine and feminine of words, which seemed completely randomly assigned. A town was feminine, but a village was masculine. A fork was feminine, and a knife was masculine. No idea about the spoon, we hadn't covered it in class.

"*La ville est belle, mais Lourmarin est très beau,*" she said.

"*Je ne comprends pas.*" I did not understand, I really didn't.

"*C'est comme ca.* Iz the way it iz."

I finished my tomatoes in silence, following Mamie's lead by sopping the juices up with a slice of bread, which I then gobbled up. It was such a simple thing, but it tasted like heaven.

Valentin was right about the cheeses. The chèvres, even the old stinky one, was creamy and melted in my mouth. The comté was like a manchego, but with a good salty bite to it. And the Camembert was the stinkiest of the lot: but it was gooey and strong, once you made it past the smell.

Mamie threw some cling film over the plate of cheeses and put it back in the fridge before I could go back for seconds. Her way of saying that the meal was over. We cleaned the dishes in silence and she was off again.

I went swimming, alone. I wandered around the garden, alone. From outside I could see Mamie typing away on her terrace, outside but somehow still locked in her room. I had no idea how she even managed to write out in this heat with those stupid cicadas chirping all day long. I couldn't understand her. How she thought, how she spoke, how she and dad couldn't have talked in the past seventeen years. Why she claimed to have wanted me here, but now denied me any of her time.

I was a ghost haunting her house. I had to get out.

"What do people actually do around here?" I finally texted Valentin, while sitting in the cool of the kitchen, my phone my only connection to the outside world. I just couldn't wait in solitude any more.

"Who is this?"

"How many of your friends text you in English?"

"Ah! American Girl!"

"The one and only," I replied, though that was an

Aix Marks the Spot

overstatement if I had ever seen one. Way to play it cool, Jamie.

"To answer your question: It's summer," he texted back, "so we rest."

"But it's so dull." The words left my fingertips before I realized how rude I was sounding. "I mean, it's hot out, what do we do for fun?"

"I play video games. We swim, we hang out." He texted back quickly. Too quickly. Probably because he was just as bored as I was.

"But I don't know anyone to hang out with."

"You know me. Come over? My mother wants to say hi."

His mom? He had talked about me to his mom? Unsure of if this was cultural or just a little creepy, I threw caution to the wind and texted him back. I mean, anything was better than lurking in the dark rooms of Mamie's fortress.

"*Je prends le velo*," I said, words carefully rehearsed. I'm taking the bike. Mamie looked down from her terrace, pulled a drag off her cigarette, and called back a single, emotionless -

"*On mange a 19 heures.*" We eat at 19 hours. Seven. By her tone, it wasn't hard to tell that she would be eating then, with or without me.

I biked back into the village. The market was gone

now, leaving the square empty in its wake. Restaurants and bars had filled the space with small round tables and plastic chairs, locals and tourists alike sitting for their late lunches, finishing coffees and wines. It was weird to see both at the same time.

I found my way to Valentin's house, though it was hard to tell if I had the right one. When he had pointed it out to me earlier, I had taken a sudden interest in the curve of his jaw. A split-second fascination, but enough for my brain to memorize the perfect angular chin and not the location of his house.

Curse these raging teenage hormones.

I stopped by the stoop and dismounted the bike, leaning it against the wall and pulling out my phone.

"I'm at your door," I texted, reveling in the whoop of the message soaring off.

I waited outside for what felt like hours, keeping my head down and eyes on my screen to avoid the passing glances. I must have stood out like a sore thumb, and the longer I waited, the worse it became. Not a single passerby was wearing sport shorts; the only other person with paint on their shirt was the literal painter who came by, carrying a ladder and casting me a questioning glance. I half expected him to stop and ask if I was his new intern.

When Valentin finally came down, he took off his

sunglasses, leaning forward.

"*Salut*," he said, extending his cheek. It was awkward, fake kissing a complete stranger, but he didn't seem bothered by it at all.

"Hey," I said, playing it cool. No, I am not blushing from kissing the cute French boy, not at all. "What's up?"

"You can put your bike in back," he suggested, opening his door wide.

I was surprised he even had a garden in a place this small. The house was narrow but tall, and he led me straight through a tiny hallway, into a square garden about the size of my bedroom. We propped the bike up against the fence that split us from the house next door.

Even though the garden was small, it was surprisingly lush. Potted bamboo hid most of the surrounding fence, making a cozy spot for old lawn chairs under a parasol. A tabby cat lounged on one of them, sunning himself.

"That's Leo," he said, pronouncing it Lay-o, which seemed rather fitting for a lazy cat. An ear twitched, signaling he knew we were here, but couldn't be bothered to move. "Come on. Let's eat *gouter*. You hungry?"

Gouter, it turned out, was the official name of the afternoon snack. At 4:30 every day, Valentin informed me, everyone - though mostly kids, really - had their biscuits, or chocolate milk, or fruits. Whatever made them happy.

"Dinners are late," he said, "kids get hungry. Schools usually finish around this time so it's a good excuse to eat."

His kitchen looked almost like my parents' back home, only a quarter of the size. Their fridge was smaller than the one we kept in the garage for sodas. As I leaned against it, Valentin cleared through the kitchen cupboards, trying to find something appropriate for us.

"Oh god, you have Oreos?" I hadn't had anything familiar in almost a week, and the mere sight of the blue packaging had my mouth watering. Surprisingly Pavlovian response.

"Like home?" he asked, proud of himself.

They tasted even better after almost a week without them. I never thought, of all things, I would miss Oreos so much. Though having an afternoon snack gave me all kinds of home cravings: cookies and juice. Peanut butter and jelly sandwiches. Chocolate milk.

"Zis is Jammy?"

I turned to see a woman about my mother's age, twisting her long brown hair into a bun. She smiled as she stepped into the kitchen, cheek first.

"I'm Jamie, Hi," I said. I knew the drill: Cheek, kiss, cheek, kiss.

"*Mathilde*," she replied, "*enchanté*. You are the American?"

I nodded eagerly. I could see Valentin's face in hers: in the way her lip curled slightly, so that she was constantly smiling, or in the fierceness of the brows, bushy and untamable.

"The girl of Henri Martin?" she asked. My face flushed: once again, it hadn't occurred to me that people would actually know my family here. But I should have known better, seeing as dad spent the first twenty-odd years of his life here.

"Yes, that's my dad," I said, and her smile grew.

"I went to school with 'im," she laughed. Her accent was strong, but her English was incredibly good. Miles ahead of my French. "My little brozer was in his class. Zey were, as you say, *inséparable*. What is he?"

"She means to ask what he does now," Valentin interjected.

"Iz what I said." Mathilde ruffled her son's hair, which was quite a feat, seeing as how he was a whole foot taller than her.

"My dad teaches French Literature at the University of Philadelphia," I replied. "His focus is on the Lumières period."

"Oh, *Chaud!*" she said.

"Show?"

"*Chaud,* hot," said Valentin. What the hell, was she calling my father hot? "we say it to mean 'impressive'."

"*Bon, je vous laisse,*" she said, while grabbing an Oreo from Valentin's pack. "*Ciao!*"

She left through the front door, munching on the cookie as she went. I turned to Valentin, confused.

"*Ciao?* Isn't that Italian?"

"Is it?" he shrugged, already moving on to something else. "We walk from here."

"Walk? Walk where?"

"I just thought you might want to see a real castle," he replied, "many tourists do. And the one at Lourmarin is really nice: did you know it was the first of its kind in the entire region?"

"Of what kind?" I asked, before I realized what was going on. "Wait, you realize you don't have to give me a tour or anything, right? I don't need to be treated like a tourist."

"You are one though, are you not?" He asked, cocking his head to the side as he stuffed his phone down into the pockets of his shorts. "*Allez.* What's the point of being in Lourmarin if you don't see the castle?"

I couldn't argue with that. There was something deep inside me which was yearning to see a real castle:

to see the places I had read about in fairy tales, better than any movie. And this stranger was just going to show them to me like that?

I couldn't tell if the town was quieting down, or if the sugar had made me drowsy. You could feel the end of the day in the air, a general winding down of time itself. A small café we passed was filling up with patrons, sipping cream colored drinks with ice full to the top, glasses sweating. While the sun still looked high in the sky, the shadows were getting longer, the world more drawn out. The cicadas were still going strong, but they now seemed to add ambiance.

It took us all of five minutes to reach the castle. It was surreal that something so massive and imposing was just... there. Doors unlocked, ready for us to explore.

Well, after we dished out some cash, sure.

"You owe me 3 euros," said Valentin, as he handed me my ticket.

"Um, I don't actually have any money on me right now," I said. He shrugged, but not like a little shoulder shrug: he shrugged with his *entire body*. It was the most exaggerated thing I had ever seen, but apparently it constituted language here, because that was his full response.

The castle was refreshing after the heat of the sun. It was a relief to be behind stone walls. The rooms were confusingly furnished: it looked old, but it was the kind of things Grandma loved to find while antiquing. It didn't exactly match the whole castle vibe. One of the rooms, with an oddly flamboyant blue and red ceiling, was filled with little tables of all shapes and sizes. Too dainty for the heavy walls that surrounded them. The whole interior gave off a light and airy feel, nothing like the Hogwarts I was expecting. The only thing that was even half medieval looking were the gigantic fireplaces.

Valentin explained about the first foundations of the castle placed in the 12th century, how more was built upon it in the 15th, how the guys who came after in the 16th made it the first renaissance castle in Provence, and so on. It seemed like everyone who came through wanted to leave their mark on the place.

"It was almost demolished in 1920," he continued, "But some rich man bought it, and with a group of friends and workmen from the village he restored and furnished it. He was killed in a car crash right after they finished."

"Oh, wow," I said, "that sucks."

"But he was a good man. He left the château, his art and furniture collections, and his libraries to the French Academy for Art and Science in Aix, so long as they open the place up to the arts, at least during summers. That's why there's a photography exhibit. And concerts."

"Wait, seriously? They have concerts here?"

"Yes. There's even an amazing music festival, but you just missed it."

"What the heck?"

He grinned and left it at that. He led me to a twisty stone staircase: now that's more like it.

"Look, it's a double twist stair," he said, "very renaissance."

He knew the castle like the back of his hand, showing me details I would never have seen on my own. He was like my own personal tour guide, translating the French signs and adding in his own twist.

Wait. Wait. Was this a date? The last time I had gone out with anyone, it had ended badly. Really, really badly. If I hadn't dated Charlie, I probably wouldn't have been at that party that night, and I wouldn't have been in the car when the accident occurred. There wouldn't even have been an accident. It was a good enough sign as any that I shouldn't be dating. It would only end poorly.

Not that I would have minded a date with Valentin… I mean, talk about cute. Everything about him was perfectly… interesting. The way he rolled his r's and z'ed his th's. Or how that curl swung back and forth on his forehead. Or, how much he seemed to know about the renaissance.

"Are you, like, into History or something?" I asked, and realized I sounded so, so basic. Was that even a thing in Europe, basicness?

"I love it," he said, beaming, "I love letters. History, literature, poetry. Iz my life."

And he was a nerd on top of it all. A cute, nerdy French boy wanted to show me around a castle and knew exactly what cheeses I was going to like. Talk about a fairy tale.

We left out the back, exiting onto a terrace with a beautiful little square pond and flowers everywhere. The outside of the castle looked smaller now that I had seen the inside, but no less beautiful.

"So, uh…" I started, trying to make conversation. He turned his eyes on me and my heart skipped a beat. Why was I feeling anything right now? The days of isolation were doing wonders to my heart.

"Valentin! Salut!"

Out of nowhere, what I could only call a bombshell appeared. She must have been a model or something, her long chestnut hair so straight it could have been spun of silk. Even though there was no breeze, it seemed to waft in the wind. She bent over to kiss Valentin on both cheeks, as he cheerfully greeted her back, a firm hand on her shoulder.

Oh.

"Jamie, this is Chloë," he said, turning to face me, "Chloë, Jamie."

"*Enchanté*, do you do ze *bise?*" said the model, leaning down for me to kiss both cheeks.

"Chloë and I are in the same class at *lycée*," he said, "though she lives in Cadenet. *Qu'es ce tu fais la?*"

She answered something I didn't catch, and they laughed. In an instant they were in deep conversation, hands flying as they spoke. And in that same moment, all hope I had drained out of me.

If I didn't have a bike to pick up in his garden, I would have slipped away right then and there. But instead, I was forced to endure a conversation in a language I didn't understand, between two people who were more than friendly, one of whom I had started to feel the semblance of a crush for.

Well. I could have had a crush on both of them at this point. Chloë was so gorgeous my heart melted for her also, though everything melted in this heat.

"*Bon, j'y vais, le bus va passer,*" she said, after what must have been an hour, "*A toute!*"

"*A toute!*" Valentin replied. It was only after she was out of sight that his attention returned to me. "Chloë is trying to sign up for driving. She is a waitress to pay it."

"Oh," I said, "I just got my license back home. But I don't think I'm allowed to drive here."

He nodded. "I need to learn, but iz too expensive. I do not have a thousand euro at the moment. Maybe after my *Bac*."

I didn't know what to pick up on first in that sentence, the ridiculously expensive cost or whatever the heck was wrong with his back. I was realizing now just how burned out I was, exhausted from trying to keep up with all the details all day.

That was the first night that I didn't have jet lag keeping me up. The first night I didn't give a crap about the cicadas and frogs. For once, I was happy and full: confused about things, sure, but I had spent time with an actual human being that I could actually communicate with, and that changed everything.

Though I still woke up the next morning with a face full of mosquito bites.

seven

JEAN-PASCAL ARRIVED AROUND NOON, DRIVING not a ridiculous old car like the one he had picked me up in, but a brand-new silver thing that looked like it could power through swamps.

"*Donne-lui un coup de main*," said Mamie, as I put down the plate I was drying.

"What?"

She jerked her head in his direction. I could see him out the door, carrying a grocery bag. Ah. So that's where she got her groceries from, when she wasn't sending her estranged granddaughter to market for her.

I dashed outside, taking the bag from his hands, and he thanked me, returning to grab what was left. Together, the two of us unloaded the bags and bags of food.

"*Alors?*" he asked me, as he closed the now empty trunk of his car. "How is it?"

"How is what?"

"France!"

How was I supposed to answer that, exactly? The country is hot, the countryside is noisy, the language is hard, my grandma won't speak to me, there's a cute boy, but the girls my age are gorgeous, and…

"*Salut, JP,*" said Mamie, interrupting my train of thought by kissing the man on both cheeks. And then they were off, chatting again, old friends who didn't need the awkward girl standing around in a corner.

Frustrated, I climbed the stairs back to my room. My bed was becoming the one place in the house I didn't feel unwelcome. When boredom and heat collided, I would lay on it, staring at the ceiling, trying to think my way out of here: I would imagine I was with Jazz, sketching: they had moved on to structures, and were now strolling around Philly, trying to capture the most striking details of the city. I hadn't even seen a building from this century since I had gotten here.

I grabbed for my backpack. The only book I had brought for the trip I had read three times already. My computer was useless without the internet. My sketchpad lay empty on the desk, all my inspiration and skill dried up, shriveled in this heat.

Aix Marks the Spot

Last resort? Dad's books.

There was no denying he had a great collection, though I could only understand half the titles. It's not everyone who decided to do a masters in French lit, and from what dad told me, his studies were grueling. When I complained about my essays for English, he would always tell me how at my age, he was already writing philosophy dissertations. He was probably exaggerating.

The books on dad's old shelf looked just like those at home: I wondered how many he had had to buy copies of when he moved, abandoning these ones when he left behind France. Most all the spines were cracked.

The bottom shelf was far more interesting. Where above he had all the great philosophers and poets, below were the red and yellow spines of hardcover comic books. I pulled them out one by one. Asterix and Obelix. Tintin. Gaston Lagaffe.

Just as I was pulling out a water damaged copy of *Lucky Luke*, a note dropped out.

I paused, frozen, unsure of how to react. On the one hand, this note was probably something dad had forgotten, or maybe hidden. On the other, he had abandoned when he fled his mother. Was I supposed to read it, was I even allowed to?

I put the Lucky Luke on the growing stack of comic

books, on top of *Asterix et Cleopatre*. The letter was yellowing with age but wasn't brittle: it must have been written around the time that dad had left. I turned it over, shocked to see it was a few pages long, typed up on a typewriter like the one Mamie had. Maybe the same one.

What the hell, I thought, sitting down on my bed, dad didn't have to know I was reading this. Who was going to tell him?

Mon Amour,

Tadaa! You see, I told you I was going to do something for our six months together! And you thought I would be too busy with my thesis. Well, it just goes to show you never to underestimate me and my will to create elaborate schemes.

(Being broke probably doesn't help. Student life is the best life).

Happy six months, mon chou! Six months of late nights in the library writing all those horrible dissertations, of memorizing Baudelaire after Baudelaire, of catching trains to anywhere just to get out of it all. Six months of picnics on the beach and old men

Aix Marks the Spot

yelling at us to speak French to each other.

Seeing as how our year is almost over, and our relationship had just hit this monumental milestone, I'm sending you on a mission. A treasure hunt. And it's not going to be easy, mind you. I'm not going to cut you any slack just because you're defending your thesis in a few days. I am too, and yet I still had the time to put this together for you!

At the end of the hunt, I promise you, there will be a surprise you won't want to miss. Well, unless this hunt has completely put you off me. I'd say I completely understand, but it wouldn't make any sense after I went to all this trouble to put together this crazy thing I knew you would adore.

Now, it won't be a long trip. Not if you're smart about it. And I'm not giving you any hints unless you're completely and irrevocably stuck. In which case, I guess you'll just have to owe me. We'll work out my price later.

Five stops, that's all I'm giving you. Only places that mean something to us, that we've been to together. They won't be easy but they're definitely not impossible.

Your first clue is to go to the spot where

we first kissed. Here's your hint: blackcurrant beach. Remember how we used to joke about the name?

You're probably also remembering that we didn't kiss on that beach. And you'd be right. We were out with Seb and his friends, only a month into the year, already decimated by the course load. Seb had suggested a beach day, and pretty much the entire masters was on board. I came by train, you took your scooter. It was only early October, but it was still as hot as summer. The entire beach was filled with tourists.

Seb suggested we move the picnic into the calanques. Getting to Port Miou was a hassle, and it must have taken us an hour to all get there and even start the actual hike. We carried bags of food and towels and so many bottles of water. We knew each other vaguely from class, but that day we shared the straps of a massive beach tote, and we talked the entire way over the cliff and back down again. We just clicked on every level, making jokes about Victor Hugo's crazy love life and how Pagnol might have over-romanticized country living.

By the time we reached the beach, the sun was high, we were starving, and I had a crush on you.

Aix Marks the Spot

I remember how your stomach kept grumbling, as if trying to join the conversation. But Seb wasn't convinced by the crowd. He claimed the next beach over would be even better. That he knew a path that would get us all there so much faster than the usual route.

There was grumbling, but we got back on the trail again. This way was steeper, and for a few minutes we joked that Seb was taking us to the middle of the forest to kill us off and spare himself the competition for grant money at the end of the year. But then we reached the top of the cliff, and the world fell away beneath us, and I felt in that instant that I was soaring with you.

Those calanques. I can see them a million times, but it will always take my breath away. It's as if nature fell asleep while adjusting the colors and made everything brighter and more vibrant than anywhere else. It's enough to show you that the impressionists were not as far off as anyone thinks.

Of course, Seb's shortcut was as ridiculous as Seb himself. How someone so wild could make it this far in a freaking literature degree, I will never know. The guy starts climbing down a sheer cliff face in his flipflops. No one wanted to follow until he pointed to the trail marker painted on the side of the stone, and you laughed and said that someone had to go first.

So of course, I did. I wanted to impress you so badly it hurt. I didn't know at what point in that hike you went from being my tote buddy to someone I wanted to know on the deepest level of my soul. Maybe it was when you responded to your stomach with velociraptor noises. I don't know. But I climbed down that cliff, letting Seb guide my feet to the footholds.

And then, of all things, this three-legged dog trots down the cliff. Three legs! I had never seen anything like it. The entire crew was laughing and clapping. If a three-legged dog could climb Seb's stupid cliff, we'd be ridiculous for failing.

After the cliff, things got far easier. We followed the trails left by wildlife, finally reaching that uncomfortable pebble beach, but the sun hit the water so perfectly that it might as well have been heaven. As if god himself was smiling upon us, there was not a tourist, or even a local, anywhere in sight.

Aix Marks the Spot

Just us.

We swam, ate the bounty we had so carefully carried over the cliffs, broke out the rosé in our plastic cups, cheered our good fortune and booed our strictest professors. There were some caves you wanted to explore on the way down, and I offered to come with you, desperate to show you I was as brave and cool as I thought I was.

I don't know who kissed who up in that cave. We only had a minute before Seb and some others arrived to explore too, and the moment was over. But in that kiss, I fell totally and irrevocably in love with you.

There. That should give you everything you need to find the place.

Love,

Your (not so) secret admirer.

I put the letter down, shaking.

Dad. Dad had written the letter to you, planning an adorable anniversary present you never got to find. If any of my boyfriends had given me this, I would have married him on the spot.

Well, if any of my relationships had made it past the

Sarah Anderson

two-month mark. Current record was 47 days.

My hands were trembling so much, I stuffed them under my legs to hold them still. I felt as if I had just intruded on an intimate moment. The letter was not meant for me, and it was like I had stolen the joy from someone else. These feelings were not for me. My stomach knotted with the guilt.

The letter sat on the bed, continuing to exist, defying my imagination. I could not have conjured up something so beautiful even in my wildest dreams. My heart was so full, I felt as if I could soar.

And then, it hit me. If this letter could make me, a random girl, feel as if she could fly, then maybe, just maybe, it could make you, the person who was meant to read it, pull through this.

I had to call you. I had to show you this magnificent letter, to prove just how much dad loved you, even all the way back then. Especially then. In my mind, after you read it, you would push yourself off the couch and wrap your arms around dad, completely cured.

All my mistakes wiped clean.

The phone was in my hand before I could even think. I opened up contacts. Recent calls. I was ready to hit that green button, and then…

A new thought pushed through. This was the start of a treasure hunt, which meant there were more letters like this one out there. Out beyond the confines of this room, there were five clues and a treasure intended for you to find.

Seventeen years ago, though.

I fell back onto the bed, the gears in my head spinning in a wild intense whirr. What were the odds they were still out there? What were the chances I could find them, solving all of dad's clues along the way, get all the letters, and send them to you? That would quintuple your chances of recovering completely. And finding the treasure... not only would you be fully healed, everything else would be fixed, too.

I would be forgiven for hurting you in the first place. For destroying all of our lives.

But there was one major hurdle in the way of finding the clues: one, I had no idea what anything meant. Blackcurrant beach? I didn't even know there were beaches here until a few minutes ago. Well, I knew there was Nice and Monaco and so on, but those were far away, right?

Which brought me to problem number two: distance. If I had my car, there wouldn't be an issue, but I was in France, too young to be on the road by their standards, and of course no idea where I was going.

I sunk deeper into my pillows. So much for that plan.

But I had no other choice. The universe had given

me this one chance to fix my mistake, and I had to take it. This would be my only shot. And if I failed, I would never make things right.

   I had to call in reinforcements.

eight

"COME ON, PLEASE, YOU'RE THE ONLY PERSON I know here," I begged. I'd let you guess who I called, but then again, he was the only guy I knew here.

"What exactly you want from me?" Asked Valentin.

"I need to get out of Lourmarin," I stammered, "I need to find a place called Blackcurrant Beach. I'll bike over."

"No, it's fine, I'll come to yours."

"You know where I live?"

"Everyone here knows where Colette Martin lives," he said, as if that cleared anything up. "I'll text you when I reach the gate, so you can let me in."

"You sure it's no bother?"

"Mom has been complaining about how much time I spend in the house. This will get her to stop bothering me."

"Awesome." I found myself grinning. "I'll wait for your text."

I hung up and rushed to put things away. Not that it was my house, and not that I was bringing a strange boy into my room - wait, why I was I bothering? If Mamie was anything like my mom, she would definitely not approve.

Maybe I should text him and tell him not to come at all. I hadn't even asked her if it was alright to invite a stranger into her home. I hadn't asked her if she knew about the letter, either.

But you had never received the letter. Something between Dad writing it and actually giving it to you had gone drastically wrong. Something between him and Mamie, which broke their relationship forever.

She couldn't know about the letter. There was no way I could ask her without tipping my hand. Then again, she probably would judge me for not having asked in French.

I got Valentin's text a few minutes later, way faster than I had expected. When I reached the gate, he was leaning against an old white scooter, helmet propped up on his head, shading his eyes from the sun so he could read his phone screen. I let him in.

"Hey," he said, looking worried. "You ok?"

"Yeah, yeah, I am," I said, though my heart was

racing a mile a minute, beating so hard in my chest I thought it was going to burst out and just keep on beating, like in an old horror movie. "Why?"

"You look… ignore me."

He pushed the helmet back down and hoped back on his bike, which puttered to life with a little less enthusiasm than a toy version of one.

"Need a ride up?" he asked.

"Me? Ride on that?" I snorted. "Yeah, no."

"What? You think I'm going to get in an accident? On twenty meters of gravel?"

"I just… no thanks," I repeated. I would have to touch him for that, and though I quite liked the idea, I liked it too much for this to be a good plan. "I'll close the gate. Meet you at the top."

He rode up, the bike sputtering as the tires spun on the gravel. When I reached him at the old fountain, he was pulling off his helmet, his brown hair slicked down with sweat.

"This is so cool," he said, "being in Colette Martin's garden. This is insane!"

"I thought you said everyone in town knew her?" I asked, "you haven't been here before?"

"Maybe I made a mistake. I meant that we all know *of* her. You know how famous she is." I shook my head, and his eyes bulged. "You don't know how famous she is! She's Colette Martin! Author of *Sens et superstitions?* Or *Se Fondre Dans Le Sud?*"

Again, I shook my head. Grandma, a famous author? I knew she wrote, and I had seen her books lying around, but I never thought she was actually famous. I had never heard her name used outside of the family anyways.

"Ques'ce que tu fais la?"

The woman in question came storming out of her house, hands on her hips. Valentin put his helmet down on the seat of his scooter, smile wiped from his face. He looked terrified, and for good reason: Mamie's hair was flying out away from her, an *orage* if I ever saw one.

"C'est Jamie qui m'a invité," he said, nervously, *"Pour, eu…"*

"Cours de Français," I interjected, shooting him a nervous look. It would have been a poor French class back home if I hadn't learned how to say the words 'French Class'. My pronunciation was crap, but instantly it turned Mamie's frown into a gasp of surprise.

"Un cours?" she asked, *"Jamie, c'est toi qui a organisé ca?"*

"Je apprends Français," I said, slowly enunciating every syllable. Maybe she had asked me about food or the weather, I don't know, but I had to answer

something. *"Il apprends Anglais.* Conversation?"

He learns English. I learn French. The perfect cover, since, technically, it wasn't a lie. And apparently, exactly what Mamie had wanted to hear. She marched up to us, proudly putting her hands on my shoulders, leaning down to kiss my forehead. I could feel her gently shaking as she took her hand back.

"Je suis fière de toi, ma puce," she said. And I didn't need a phrasebook to tell me she was proud of me: I could feel it in my very bones. This was the Mamie I wanted to know, the one who actually seemed to like me.

"Venez, je vous prepare le gouter," she said, waving for us to follow, *"Tu t'appelles comment?"*

They chatted in French, Valentin blushing and babbling nervously. I guess he must have liked her books. Mamie sliced us the baguette Jean-Pascal had bought that morning, putting it in a basket on our tray, along with a massive jar of Nutella. It hadn't been opened yet.

"Je l'ai prise pour toi," she explained. I nodded, trying to split the words in my head. *Toi* meant me, so I guessed she had bought the jar just for my visit. Or had asked Jean-Pascal to bring it.

Mamie was an odd woman. She could spoil me with sugary treats one second, then admonish me for not speaking French the next. Luckily, she seemed to appreciate the effort I was making - even if it was a total lie.

In the end, Mamie didn't care at all that there was a boy in my room: so long as he was teaching me French, I suppose everything was permissible. I blushed thinking of some other French words I knew, lyrics to a certain Moulin Rouge song, which involved some *voulez vous*.

"*Alors*," said Valentin, peeling back the golden film and spreading the Nutella on thick, "is that what you called me over for? A French class? For your information, my English is perfect, thank you."

"Perfect?" I raised an eyebrow.

"Better than your non-existing French."

"Fair enough," I replied, spreading myself my own Nutella slice. Was it just me, or did it taste better than American Nutella? Smoother, sweeter. Maybe it was the fresh bread that it was smeared on. I didn't care what had happened to it, it was simply magical.

"So, why am I here?" he asked, already done with his entire slice.

"Because you told me not to come to yours."

"If you're not going to tell me, I'm going home." He took another slice of Nutella nonetheless, showing me he had no intention of living up to that threat.

"It's because of this," I said, getting up to retrieve the

letter from where I had stashed it in the desk drawer. "My father wrote my mother a letter seventeen years ago, before he left France and never came back. It's a treasure hunt."

"Oh! A *chasse au trésor*."

"A hunt is called a chase?"

"A *chasse*, yes," he explained, going for Nutella slice number three, "which, ironically, is also the name for the toilet flush. You see? I'm a good French teacher."

"Chase 'o treasure," I said, "it sounds like an Irish pastime."

"But you won't forget it this way," he said, chewing his bread. I was starting to lose any belief I ever had in the sexy Frenchman stereotype. Maybe it just didn't apply to teens.

But then he smiled again, and I felt my heart race inside my chest all over again.

"Anyway," I continued, "I want to find these letters dad left my mom. To make her feel better."

"Better about what?"

"About her spine being damaged," I said, cringing at the harshness of my words. Valentin stopped chewing.

"Is she alright?" He seemed genuinely worried about her, despite never having met the woman before. There was an earnestness in his eyes I had never seen before.

"She will be," I said. You will be, once I finish this hunt, I'm so sure of it my heart aches. "She was in a car accident, but she's recovering. She's learning to walk again. It's slow, and it hurts. I'm only here because there's no room for me at home while she's in therapy."

"*Merde,* I'm so sorry," he said, standing. He reached as if to hug me, but dropped his hands, realizing as I did that we didn't know each other well enough for that. Just telling him this made me feel closer to him, but it was still weirdly too soon.

"Anyway. I *need* to find this next clue. Finishing the treasure hunt dad made for her will cheer her up. The treasure will change everything."

"Are you sure?" he said, forcing a smile. I didn't like how pitying his gaze had just become. "It has been, how long, sixteen years?"

"Seventeen, I think," I said, "but I have a good feeling about this. We won't know they're there until we try."

"We?" he asked, sitting again, "wait. I did not say anything about going on a treasure hunt."

"Oh come on, please?" I begged, "I don't know anything about anywhere, here. I don't have a car, I don't speak French…"

Aix Marks the Spot

"I don't have a car either."

"But you don't even know where we're going!"

"And you do?"

I let out a breath of frustration. I don't know why I expected this perfect stranger to just drop everything and join me on this quest, but he was my only hope.

"I need to find a place called Blackcurrant beach," I said, pointing at the letter. Not that he could read it from over here. "It's where the first clue tells me to go."

"Blackcurrant beach," he repeated incredulously, "it's in English? Or has it been translated?"

"The whole letter's in English."

"Then it had to be a play on words. But I don't know what a Blackcurrant is in French."

"Oh," I said, my heart sinking. I had thought the Frenchman would be a wealth of knowledge. But it sounded like I was back to square one without even beginning. And I had already shared my Nutella with him.

"I can google it?"

He looked up at me, his phone already in his hand, and for a split second I thought he was going to apologize. But why would he? He hadn't done anything wrong, I just... if I had told any of my friends back home about a secret treasure hunt, they would have come running. Valentin's go-to response seemed to be 'not possible.'

"No Wi-Fi," I said, "and I don't think my mother would have had a smartphone 17 years ago, anyways."

"You don't have whiffy?" he asked, incredulously, "*Merde.*"

He held out his hand. It took me a minute to realize he wanted the letter, but when I did, my heart went from slowly sinking to plunging into my gut. This was my letter. Well, it was your letter, and I was already trespassing by reading it myself. It felt like showing him might jinx the entire operation. But at least he seemed like he wanted to help, just a little bit.

"There might be other clues in there," he suggested, "have you seen how long it is?"

"It's just…" I paused. There weren't any actual words for this. Not words that I knew of. "It's personal."

"If you want my help, you have to help me help you," he said.

I gingerly handed him the paper and leaned back against the desk, watching him read. Had dad invited you up here for Nutella, when you were first invited over? Did he lean on his desk the way I did now, talking about books and raving about confusing languages?

"*Oh! Si tu pouvais lire dans mon coeur, tu verrais la place où je t'ai mise!*"

"What now?"

"If you could read my heart, you would see the place I have given you there. Flaubert. I just... I can see why you want your parents to have this back. It's beautiful."

I watched him read again, the words fluttering through my mind.

"Port Miou," he said suddenly, poking the letter so hard the paged ruffled. I cringed, feeling as if he had poked me right in the chest. "I got it! They went to Cassis!"

Miou was a real place? I thought it was another pun of dad's. Something weird to do with cats, maybe.

"What does that have to do with blackcurrants?"

"I think cassis is the French word for that kind of berry. You know, like a blueberry, but black?"

"And that's a beach?"

"Well, Cassis is a town, which has a beach," he explained. "If you pronounce the 's' at the end, it's the fruit. If you don't, it's the town. But tourists and Parisians all pronounce it Cassisss. Which is so annoying: I mean, you don't pronounce it Parissss, do you?"

"I mean, we pronounce the s..."

"In English, maybe, but not in French. It would sound stupid."

I thought about it, running all the instances of Paris through my head. It didn't make much of a difference either way.

"So Dad wanted mom to go to Cassis beach?" I asked, careful not to pronounce it poorly, dare I insult my translator. He nodded.

"But not the main beach, and he's right. Especially at this time of year, the tourists take over. They went to the calanques, which, by his description, sounds like they went to En-Vau."

"I'm going to be honest here, I only understood about half of those words."

He looked up from the letter, grinning. It was funny how his smile changed all of his features: one second, he almost fell into the 'dark-and-mysterious' category, and the next, he was as goofy as a five-year-old. I tried not to laugh. He seemed almost excited at the prospect of telling me any of this, more excited even than being invited to follow a super-secret treasure hunt.

"So the calanques are like…" he search for the word, struggling a little. Holding out his hand, he ran a finger along the negative space. "Fjords?"

I couldn't help it, it caught me so much by surprise I practically chocked.

"Fjords? What, in France?"

"You'll understand it when you see them," he explained. He placed his right index between his left thumb and forefinger. "This is Cassis." He moved his index between the middle and index fingers. "This is

Port-Pin." Then he moved his finger two slots over, so it was between his pinky and ring. "And this is En Vau. It's a bit of a walk, but it's beautiful."

"Great," I said. "How do I get there? Can we leave right now?"

"It's pretty far away," he said, "Like, a two-hour drive from here? And you said *we* again. I am not sure I can go."

"Why not?" Every time a window opened, someone slammed a door in my face. Two hours. Damn. "Come on, beach trip! What else could be better?"

"I don't know. Sleeping?"

"You must be joking."

"No, I'm Valentin."

If there wasn't an open pot of Nutella on the bed right now, I would have tossed a book or a pillow at him, anything. But I didn't want to waste it.

"Seriously, though. I have no idea where I would be going. You know the place, right?"

He nodded. "Every summer I would go with my grandparents. It's my favorite place."

"Then why not come with me?" I said. "I'll give you half of the treasure!"

"No thank you!" he laughed, "the treasure is probably chocolates, or a pen, or... I don't know, something that had to do with your parents. Not an actual treasure."

"I can… I can get you an autograph from Mamie?"

He paused for a moment, contemplating the offer. And I found myself staring at his bright blue eyes, trying to understand what was going on in that head of his. He had to help. He just had to, or the hunt would be over before it even started.

"You really want this, don't you?"

I nodded, faster than I ever had in my life. Felt like a headbanger at a metal concert.

"Fine. But I'm not paying for your transport!"

"Can you drive us?"

"On my scooter? No way! It barely makes it to Pertuis and back. We'd have to take the highway and… no thanks."

"I have my license," I said. He might be able to speak French, but I could drive a friggin' car. Take that, fairness. "Maybe I could ask Jean-Pascal to lend me his car."

"Ah, but can you drive…" he struggled over the word, making a zig-zag motion with his right hand. The guy did so much of his speaking with his hands. "The not-automatic?"

There must have been a breeze, because those doors just kept slamming in my face. It seemed as though every option was being shut down, one after the other.

"How does anyone even get around here?" I wanted to rip my hair out from the roots. This was maddening.

"Trains and buses," he shrugged, "we can take one tomorrow."

"We?"

It hit me suddenly just how much he was helping me with this. Just how wide that goofy grin was getting. Just how little Nutella he had eaten since reading the letter - as in, no Nutella at all.

"Well, I did say you were paying," he said.

"You're really going to come along?" I could have kissed him right then and there. I didn't, though, I had some restraint at least. "You are so getting an autograph!"

"I still don't think we'll find anything," he shrugged. "but I feel sorry for a girl with no *whiffy*."

I smiled. I guess I really did have a friend here.

nine

"*JE PARS,*" I SHOUTED UPSTAIRS TO MAMIE AS I stepped outside into the garden. It was only 7 am, but the sun was already up high, making it feel like noon. Stepping outside was like walking into a hotbox.

Mamie, already at her typewriter, coffee in hand rather than her usual cigarette, glanced down at me in confusion.

"*Où?*" She asked, taking a sip of her still steaming drink. *Where?*

"*Cours de Français!*"

I mean, technically I wasn't lying to Mamie. I *was* taking French lessons with Valentin. Only I never told her where we were going for them.

She could have asked me why so early. She could have asked me what I was planning on doing. If I was coming back for lunch. But instead, she turned her focus to her typewriter.

"*Ne rentre pas trop tard,*" she said, returning to her work, unflinching.

"What does *Ne rentre pas trop tard* mean?" I asked Valentin, as he opened the door to his house.

"Don't get back too late," he replied with a yawn. He was as his usual casual self, with grey shorts and an orange shirt. I don't think I'd ever see a guy pull off orange before, and yet this random teenager in Provence made it look like it was all the rage. Sunglasses were perched lightly atop his disheveled curls.

"You can take your bike to the garden," he said, "then, we go."

He gave me a weird look as he took in my outfit but said nothing. But there wasn't anything wrong with my bright green gym shorts and my tank top: I mean, what else was someone supposed to wear on a beach hike?

I snuck a glance at his shoes and was glad to see he was wearing sneakers. I had heard somewhere that the French reviled them. At least I was in the clear with my choice of footwear.

We strolled out of his house, the close-knit buildings of the town sheltering us from the sun with their long shadows. A few early birds were having their morning coffees at the cafés as we passed, a smattering of croissants on their tables. My stomach grumbled.

"Do we have time to stop for a pastry?"

"No, sorry," he said, "maybe in Aix."

"Aix?" My heart leapt at the word. "Aix-en-Provence?"

"Yes, why?"

"We're going to Aix." I found myself grinning at the prospect. Aix. The town where you met dad. The place where everything began. The city you never forgot, despite missing it almost two decades.

But I wasn't allowed to feel excited about this trip. I was here to find a treasure, not to enjoy myself. This would be my penance for all the pain I caused you, and it would never be anything more.

The stop was a little post near the castle, with no bench or shade, but it was early enough that it didn't matter. Even so, I could feel the heat rising around me. It was going to be another scorcher.

"The bus should be here in five minutes," said Valentin. The steady chirp of cicada song was already beginning to grow, like someone was turning the volume up on the world.

"Cool," I replied, unsure of what else to say. I still couldn't believe we would be going through Aix. Having only ever heard of it from my mother, it had almost become a sort of fairy tale.

Ten minutes went by, without any sign of the bus. Then, fifteen. My stomach grumbled, my craving for croissants growing with my hunger.

"Crap," I found myself biting my nails, then realized what I was doing and stuffed the hand in my pocket. "It's really late."

"Relax, will you?" Valentin leaned against the bus post, casual as can be. "It will come when it comes. We're not in any rush, we don't have any *rendez-vous*."

"But if we miss this bus, we'll miss the next bus," I proclaimed, "and if we miss that bus, we've basically wasted the day. We should turn back now."

Valentin blinked, slowly, staring at me as if I had just told him my grandmother was a chicken.

"But… we haven't even left the station."

"Exactly, this way we don't mess anything up."

"Jamie," he said, trying as hard as he could to pronounce it properly. Instead, it sounded like he had an awful British accent. "Listen to me. It's going to be alright. You're anxious."

"I'm not anxious, are you anxious?"

"Always. But why do I have to be anxious about busses? They come when they come."

"But if they say they're coming at a certain hour, they should come at that hour, dammit."

"Fifteen minutes isn't late," he insisted, "fifteen

minutes is normal."

"You're kidding me."

"Yes, it sucks, but what are you going to do? Manipulate time? Worry about what you can change and stop getting mad at the things you can't."

"We should call the bus company and complain," I said, "we should see if other people were let down by this driver. I don't know, we should do something!"

"Too much work," he shrugged, "it's just a bus."

"But that's just lazy," I sputtered, "no one's going to get anything done if they think nothing can be done."

He shrugged. "Can *you* make the bus get here faster?"

The bus did eventually show up, a good twenty minutes behind schedule. The driver didn't even apologize as we climbed up, Valentin paying for the two tickets to Aix, end of the line. He marched down the aisle of the nearly empty bus, spreading himself out along the seats in the back. I joined him, taking the seats before his, feeling the exposed skin of my legs rasp against the rough velvet of the seats.

"The bus will take an hour," he said, "but the drive is pretty. I will probably sleep."

"Seriously?"

"Wake me when it gets interesting."

Everything was interesting, but I said nothing. The

long stretches of fields of the countryside as we drove past; the rows of vines, filled with weeds, stretching out on both sides of the road; crumbling old farmhouses and massive estates practically side by side. I drifted off into a trance, watching the world rush by out my window, feeling as if I was watching a film where the only sound was the rumble of the bus and the chirp of the cicadas that chided us along.

The voices swam in my head, reminding me I didn't deserve this. I saw you, struggling to walk because of my mistake. Dad, trying to get the funds together to pay for our hospital bills. Mamie, refusing to talk to me for my entire life and then claiming she had wanted me all along, only to go right back to ignoring me. And here I was, riding lazily along the French countryside, living a dream so many others would never live, while they all suffered because of me.

I wanted to scream. The hunger gnawing at my stomach mixed with the guilt and gave my gut a tight twist. I couldn't be here. I shouldn't.

And then I saw the mountain.

How it had been hiding for so long, I don't know. Maybe I just wasn't paying enough attention, because out of nowhere rose a peak so high it dwarfed the other hills and cliffs. A long crest stretched out before me, all grey limestone and green pines, with a sharp metal point rising from the peak, as if someone had armed the very mountain itself.

"What is that?" I asked. But my mind already knew, recognizing it from paintings in the back of my mind.

"What, the St Victoire?" Valentin grumbled, waking up from his nap.

"That's the St Victoire?" He nodded, and my breath caught. This was it. The mountain you had fallen in love with, Cezanne before you. What had brought you here in the first place. "What's at the top?"

"Oh, it's a cross," he explained, "some monks built it centuries ago."

"That's wild."

"Is it?"

"It must be massive if I can see it from here."

He shrugged. "It's alright."

I watched the mountain grow as we drew closer, dwarfing our small bus. It was magnificent, all long ridges and peaks.

"It's like…" I couldn't find the words. "The spine of a great beast."

"You think?"

It wasn't a judgement. Something inside him switched on, and in a second Valentin went from apathetic to bursting with energy. He sat up straight on his seat, leaning in over the chair to talk to me better.

"It's funny you say that," he exclaimed, "some people have called it a dragon."

"A dragon?"

He nodded excitedly. "When I was a child, my father would tell me the story of the monstrous beast that would attack Provence. Someone brave fought it, and when it died, it turned to stone. I don't know if that is the true legend, but I always thought the mountain looked like a dragon, too."

I turned my eyes back to the mountain and imagined what it could have looked like with massive wings. I could totally see a dragon there.

"Picasso thought it looked like a woman," Valentin added, "painted it all sexy. He loved it so much he bought a castle there, and a lot of land. He's buried at the foot of it."

"He is?"

I hadn't thought of Picasso, of all people, being buried anywhere here. Not that I had even thought about where he was buried at all.

When the bus drove into the station at Aix-en-Provence, I was trying to hold back the giddy feeling in my gut. I was dying to see the town: to see the university where my parents met, to see the art museum with all the original Cézanne's. But my stomach had another thing in mind entirely.

"I need a croissant," I said to Valentin, hopping off the bus.

"We're already late, we're going to miss the next bus if we don't hurry now."

"What? Seriously?"

"Croissant or Cassis?"

I didn't need to answer that. We rushed down the station and Valentin found our bus, and once again we were settling in for a long ride.

"This is going to take forever," I muttered. My stomach grumbled along with me.

"You're the one who wanted to go."

I nodded. I missed having a car, being in control of where I went and when. I hadn't been driving long, but it was enough to get used to the convenience.

"It'll be worth it," he added, with a gentle smile, "Trust me."

He was right. Dad's letter was safely folded away in a paperback in my backpack. If we found these clues, the trip would be priceless. You can't put a price on your mother's recovery.

"So what makes you think the clues will still be there, two decades later?" he asked, as we endured the slow speeds of leaving the city.

"I don't know," I replied, giving the bag a small squeeze on the seat beside me, "hope? I guess?"

"You think your father hid them well enough that no one disturbed them in all this time?"

"I have to."

What would happen if they were no longer there? I mean, I could just give you the single letter and see if that helped any, but it wasn't going to make you better. Not like actual treasure would.

The bus picked up speed as it joined the highway. Pines led our way through the countryside, sturdy, shady umbrellas against the scorching summer sun.

We were riding atop massive cliffs, the ground dropping off so sharply it was as if we were flying. The Mediterranean Sea stretched out along the horizon, deep and welcoming. Gulls swooped overhead in the cloudless sky, intertwining their cries with the chirp of those endless cicadas. My face was pressed up against the glass, itching to get closer.

"We're still in France?" I asked, so in awe that flies could have flown into my mouth and I wouldn't have even noticed. It was like living in a fantasy novel. "How are you so casual about the giant effing cliffs right outside our window?"

"Because I've seen them before?"

"But they're... they're cliffs!"

"Just wait until we get to where your Father wants you to go," he replied, "Trust me. You'll never want to leave."

My excitement faded. I knew he was trying to pump me up for what we were going to see, but there was no point. I was on a mission. I would find the clues, fix you, and go home as if none of this ever happened.

ten

THE TOWN WAS TINY, BARELY EVEN A TOWN - though I was learning that everything really was larger in America. Nestled into a bay between two towering cliffs, it had everything from a crystal-clear coast to a castle, and even an art gallery, All within the span of half a square mile.

I was transported into an impressionist's painting. The houses were all bright colors, around a tiny little inlet of sea, filled with stark white boats in vivid shades of blue. Stores and restaurants lined the port, along with knick-knack souvenir shops, and even two competing ice cream parlors right across from each other.

It was actually kinda funny how I could pick out fellow Americans from the hordes of people meandering around the port: I didn't know if my ears were just tuned to pick up English, but it seemed to be all I could hear. Or maybe that was the American loudness I had heard so many Europeans complain about. Add to that brand name tan sun hats, Hawaiian shirts and large cameras, photographing the port like it was their job, I was pretty sure who had come across seas to see this place.

We switched buses again and were through the town and back up one of the hills. Port Miou hardly was a port, especially compared to the heart of Cassis, but it wasn't that that took my breath away: it was the cliffs. Valentin had been right to use his fingers to describe them: I felt as if I had been swallowed right into the earth. Squeezed right between two sheer cliff faces, it was impressive water made it this far back.

After two hours, two busses, and countless miles, we had finally made it.

Or not, because the first thing Valentin said as we got off the bus wasn't "We're here" but *"Marchons!"* and we walked.

And walked.

And walked.

The path was long, but well maintained, maybe even recently made. It led us up and over the next cliff, while all around us the turquoise sea lapped up against the rocks. Parasol pines provided some shade

Aix Marks the Spot

for the walk, but by the time we reached the top of the hill, I was sweating like a pig.

"Are we there yet?" I asked. My stomach rumbled. It truly was the conversationalist - like my mother's, I realized, the letter coming to mind.

"Tired already, *Jammy*?"

"You aren't?" He shook his head. "Can we stop to eat, at least?"

"Just drink your water. We need to keep going."

I took his advice, chugging most of my thermos and keeping it in my hand for easier access. The way down was easy: stairs carved out of rock, steep and slippery from years of use, but manageable.

The bottom of this calanques was astounding. A beach, under a canopy of pines, leading right up to crystal clear water, almost like a Caribbean dream. Children played in the water as their parents rested on the shore, soaking up the sun.

Was that a boob?

I had heard about European beaches. Been warned about them by my grandma, back as I was packing for the trip.

"Be careful out there, Jamie Martin," she said, as she clutched my bathing suit in both hands, "the women there go topless. Topless!"

It turned out, not that many women were actually

topless, just a few here and there, and mostly grandma's age. Then I realized I was staring and looked at anything else: like the cliffs that courageous, screaming teens were jumping off of.

"Is this the place?" I asked. Valentin shook his head.

"It's the next one over. Not too far, I promise."

"But I'm hungry, can't we stop for lunch?"

"We eat, and then you'll want to nap, and then we'll want to swim, and by then the day is over before we get this clue," he said, "it's your hunt, Jammy: it's your decision."

"Fine," I said, tightening the straps of my bag, "Let's keep going."

The path was thinning this time, leading us up and away from the idyllic beach. Massive bushes rose up on either side, but not tall enough to give us shade. With the cicadas chirping and the stagnant, hot air, I almost felt as if I was in an old western movie.

It made no sense, seemingly leading us away from the cost, limestone slick in places from years of hiker use. If I wasn't already sweating, I sure was now. You could fill the Mediterranean Sea with the bullets that ran down my forehead.

And then, just as dad said, we reached the top, and the world fell away at our feet.

In the space of an instant, we had gone from a stuffy

path to the top of the world. We stood on a towering clifftop, high above everything else for miles, the bright blue sea surrounding us below, waves crashing against stark grey rocks. The pines grew from impossible crevices, dotting the grey with green so bright the contrast hurt my eyes.

"This is the place," I said, feeling the ocean breeze whip at my hair, "this is the place my parents were!"

I was hit in that moment with a feeling I had no words for, though the Germans probably had an incredibly long and complex one to describe it. A feeling of familiarity. Of calm. Of being rooted to the ground, firmly, knowing where I was from and where I was meant to be.

"Nobody shall say of me that I have not known perfect happiness," said Valentin stoically.

"A poem?"

He shook his head. "Virginia Woolf said that of Cassis, the first time she stayed. In the 20's."

Virginia Woolf stayed here? It felt odd to share this place with someone so famous, nearly a hundred years later. I pulled the letter from the bag, rereading the paragraph where dad described this cliff, this view, this moment. It felt as if he was here with me, a hand on his shoulder, guiding me.

"So now, we need to find the old trailhead."

"The old one?" Valentin pointed behind us. The gravel path we had followed up here spread back like the spokes of a wheel, all of them smooth and gentle. Not the climb that intimidated an entire class of masters students.

"I think it was here," he said, striding straight off the path, climbing under the barrier that clearly said, *"do not cross, dangerous cliffs ahead."*

"But..." I stammered. "This is illegal!"

"Do you want to retrace the steps in the letter, or not?" he asked, pointing at a marking on the rock. "Look, it was here. This is the way down."

Hesitantly, I crossed under the barrier, and made my way over to the cliff. It was a short, straight drop, with a dry pine forest below, steeply sloping towards the sea.

Valentin was right, there was a marker here: but it couldn't be the actual path, could it?

"I remember from when I came with my grandparents," he said, turning around and dropping his foot into a hold. Within minutes, he had scrambled down the stone, his feet on the carpet of pine needles.

"Tu viens?" he asked.

"Um, I'm not sure about this..."

And then, out of nowhere, the cutest little dog ran past me, scrambling down the cliff in four swift jumps.

It rushed up to Valentin, tail wagging wildly.

"Jamie?" he called.

"What?"

"You're not going to believe this, but this dog has only three legs."

"What?" I stammered.

"Come and see!"

The odds were uncanny, it had to be a sign. If a three-legged dog could do it…

I tried not to think about the drop, how broken my body would be if I fell. No, I had to do this. This was nothing compared to what I put you through.

On the rock beside me, a tiny painting of a blue man climbing rocks marked this as being at one time the official trailhead. I turned around, grasped the rock, and put my foot down. And then the other.

A few minutes later, my heart pounding, I reached the bottom of the climb. The dog's owners were next, a cute German couple, chatting cheerfully together as they made their way down.

"Valentin?"

"Yeah?"

"This dog has four legs," I said, looking into the eyes of the panting, adorable mutt. It looked back up at me, tail wagging, all four legs comfortably attached to its body.

The owners climbed down, and they continued on their way, dog doing all the guidance they ever needed. Meanwhile, Valentin had this twisted grin on his face, at the same time excited and a little bashful.

"Well, you climbed, didn't you?"

"Yeah, but don't do that, ok? I was really looking forward to meeting a three-legged dog!"

Now we just had to find the cave. Like my parents, almost two decades before me, I followed the trails left by thousands of feet, both human and wild boar, constantly looking uphill for an opening in the rocks.

The cave was exactly where dad had said it would be. We broke off at a fork in the trail, climbing instead of descending. The smell hit us before anything else: cheap beer and old urine. I had to plug my nose just to get close.

"What is this?" I stammered. I definitely did not want to go inside. "Is this it? This gross, dark hole is where my parents had their first kiss?"

Valentin shrugged. "Could be worse. My first kiss was at a bus station."

"Mine was under the bleachers at school."

"Tell you mine if you tell me yours?"

"It was with Justin DeAngelo. He was on the lacrosse team, and I was in the color guard. I can't remember who had dared us, but at the time it had felt like the illicit romance movies we all talked about. It only lasted for a week, when the novelty of it all wore off."

Valentin blinked, slowly, thoughtfully. His hand reached up to cover his mouth, holding back a laugh.

"What?"

"That is the most American thing I have ever heard," he said, barely able to contain the laughter. "Was this real, or on TV?"

"It was real," I grumbled. Lovely. So my life was a living stereotype to this country. "Hey, yours was at a bus station, so it can't be much better."

He shrugged. "We had correspondents in middle school. From Italy. I had a crush on mine. We spent a marvelous week together as part of the class project, and then the day they all went home, we kissed before she boarded the bus. She did not kiss well. I did not either."

"Aw, that's cute, though," I said, picturing a pre-pubescent Valentin trying to understand the mechanics of lip locking with a fancy young Italian girl. In my mind, she was wearing an expensive designer dress, and he was wearing a beret. Two could play at the stereotype game.

"Anyway, shall we find your father's clue?"

The cave was barely wide enough for me to pass, my hands on both walls, but it went for quite a distance into the stone. The tall opening let in a stream of sunlight, even though the pines that guarded the entrance. It was enough to work with: we could see the traces of a campfire in the middle of the floor, flatish stones set up for people to sit on. Valentin lifted one and put it back down.

"No clue here," he said, moving on to the next rock.

I could feel panic rising in my chest. The cave was much, much smaller than anticipated. Taking into account the number of tourists... the almost twenty years since the clue was hidden... the odds of ever finding it were shrinking by the second.

"*Hé*, you going to make me do all the work?"

I shook my head, trying to clear my mind of the thought. No. If I wanted you to have a miracle, I would have to find a miracle.

I stepped deeper into the cave, but it was shallower than I had initially assumed. Much, much shallower. The smell of piss was stronger back here.

I tried to imagine my parents exploring the cave. The way dad spoke of mom's excitement. How could this place plant the seeds of our family? If I hadn't stepped inside, I could totally have seen the lush pine forest and sharp cliffs as being romantic, but this? No.

Valentin brushed past me, raising goosebumps on my skin. I shuddered.

"You ok?" he asked.

"Yeah, just..." I glanced around the cave. There was the entrance, the fireplace. There was the back, and the urine. Not much else.

Until a piece of orange plastic caught my eye.

There was no possible way this was it. Seventeen years, out in the open like this, it would have been snatched up by anyone visiting the cave. I gaped at it, unsure if I even wanted to chance seeing it for myself.

Valentin followed my gaze, seeing the spot of orange at the same time as me. He stepped towards it, rolling the rock that covered it out of the way and picking it up.

"Is it...?" I asked. Could I dare hope?

He handed me the plastic. It was a pocket, the kind you slipped legal documents into to keep them organized at home, but the outside was covered in little notes in permanent marker. I didn't stop to read them, instead slipping it open and grabbing the paper inside.

Two sheets, stapled together. White with black type on them. Notes scribbled in the margins in black ink, pencil, and for some reason, white out.

"Mon Amour," I read. My heart was pounding so hard in my chest it could have exploded right through. "Valentin, this is it. It's the letter!"

My eyes scrolled down the notes in the margins. Some were in French, others in English, others still in languages I didn't recognize. Some were short, saying simply "so cute!" or "adorable," while others were long tirades about love. There was a comically large penis drawn in one corner, though someone else had tried to scribble it out.

"So?" asked Valentin, perching his head so he could see the letter better, "it is really it?"

I nodded, too choked up to speak. I handed him the orange plastic, and he ran his eyes over the notes there, his eyes wide with the same shock I was feeling.

"This isn't normal," I said, "not only did people… dozens of people… who knows how many people… actually find this letter, but they left it here? They added to it? They didn't steal it or rip it or…"

Valentin said nothing, his eyes going to the rock underneath which the page had stayed hidden so long. Neither of us has words for this moment.

"This is a sign," I said, out loud or in my head, I wasn't sure. "The universe wants us to finish this *chasse au trésor*. This needs to happen."

"Well then." Valentin looked back up at me, his eyes bright and - was I imagining this - brimming with tears. "Let's read the clue. See where the universe wants us next."

And we read.

Aix Marks the Spot

Mon Amour,

You found it! You actually found it! I was so worried someone else would get to it first. I had a whole stash of these backup letters prepared to sneak back into place in case you came up empty handed. Now I'm just going to use them to draw pictures of cute cats on them. As originally intended.

Not too hard to find that one, was it? The next one should be easier, though a bit of a trip. That's to get back at you for planning our first date somewhere so awfully remote. Your clue for this one: The Pretty Provence castle. You got it?

I can't remember which one of us decided on it first. After the mind-blowing kiss in Cassis, we both knew this relationship was beyond simple sitting and dining dates. So picking a castle for a romantic trip seemed like fate. Destiny. Whatever. I would slip some symbolism into these letters, but I've done enough of that in all these dissertations, and I think we're both tired of overanalyzing the use of flowers in letters. The author likes poppies, that's it. In this case, the author of these

Sarah Anderson

letters likes you. That's it. You're cute.

You made us take the train to Avignon, claiming you knew of a bus that could get us there. We get there, and of course, no bus. It's mid-November, and the tour groups are sparse, so hitching a ride with them is a near impossibility. So we have to gather our things and hitchhike.

That man was so angry when he heard us speaking English! He didn't even want to let us in his car, he was so miffed. But then you wowed him with your impassionate response about understanding English being the only way to truly capture how much more beautiful French was, and I threw in my agreement, and the man let us in. He was rather sweet, in the end. Just a little fâcheux. Grincheux. Possibly all of the seven dwarves rolled into one.

We had to climb to the top of the mountain, but it was worth it for the view alone. The wind on those castle ruins can be so harsh you feel like you could gust off at any moment. Standing at the railing, holding your hand, letting the wind try to push us off the edge, I felt like nothing could ever tear us apart. The way we laughed, together, in the face at that cold wind, it made me all the surer that this wasn't a normal date. I felt like I had known you since before I was born.

When we got tired of the wind, we slipped back into town, teasing each other about our tussled hair. We grabbed crepes at a local place, and you laughed about mixing cultures. I pointed out we were already pushing it: French and American was a little more shocking than Normandie and Provençal, and you had no answer for that. In fact, I think I scared you a little. So I made it up to you by getting you dessert, too.

It was too early to go home, and too cold to go back to the fortress, so we decided to explore the quarries down below the village. That's where we found the Cathedral, and watched the light show, alone in the dark, our fingers completely intertwined, but our eyes so transfixed we weren't even thinking of being distracted with something so basic as each other.

When we decided to call it quits for the day, we had one small problem to resolve: getting a ride through the valley. It sure was nice to see everything without the tourists, but now

Sarah Anderson

that we actually needed them. we were stuck on a mountain hours from home.

We went to the village's parking lot and waited. And we waited and waited and waited. That's where I hid your next clue: at the very top of the car park. And don't worry: you'll just have to follow the signs.

And this time, have Seb drive you. I don't want you stuck all the way up there in April. The winds are awful this time of year!

So much Love.
Your Pomme Noisette.

eleven

WHEN THE BUS DIDN'T SHOW UP THIS TIME TO TAKE us back to Aix, I didn't even care. The universe had protected the letter, which meant it wanted us to complete the hunt. It was on our side. You were going to get better.

I wanted to spend the day there, swimming in the lagoon blue water, eating the picnic Valentin had packed for us (just how much cheese could one fit in a backpack?), diving off cliffs and soaking up the sun. Even the sky seemed deeper here, deeper than any sky I had ever had over my head, deep enough to swim in, too.

The water had been perfect, the crowd manageable, but my head wasn't there to enjoy it. My mind was thousands of miles away, sitting next to you in the hospital, where you struggled to walk along the little railed path. I couldn't enjoy this until the hunt was over, and you had recovered. I had no right to love any moment of it until I could spend it with you.

So, when the bus didn't show, and Valentin told me we would have to take the train, I could only agree. This is what the universe wanted from us, after all. Even if it meant a smelly, slow trip back into civilization.

We took a tiny bus from Port Miou to the station. All the while, a group of tourists in the back were laughing like hyenas. I couldn't even tell where they were from, they didn't speak a word except to laugh. Valentin cringed, trying not to shoot them glares, forcing his eyes forward on the road ahead.

We flew over a bump, and I practically fell out of my chair. The group laughed again, and I resisted the urge to punch them. Other than Charlie - he deserved it, trust me - I had never wanted to punch anyone before in my life. But that kind of laughter did something to me that urged me to Hulk Out. We were relieved when they got into another car at the station.

The train was a funny looking thing, like an airplane without wings, except the windows were massive. Inside, the seats were blue velvet, wide apart with tables between them. Two people rode this carriage, sitting towards the back where it connected with the next one.

"We got in the wrong car," I hissed. "This is first class, isn't it?"

"No first class on this train."

He didn't even blink, while internally I was cheering our good fortune. I sat down in the direction of the train, and he sat across from me, a little table between us. It was surprisingly cozy.

The train rolled out of the station and down the countryside without making a sound. I only felt my exhaustion when I sank into the blue seats of the TER, whizzing along the Provence countryside at a hundred miles an hour in a dizzying spread of greens. It was almost impossible to keep reading the letter, as the words kept getting tangled in my brain.

"Pretty Provence castle," I said, again, peering up from the letter. Someone had generously circled the clue three times in pencil, which wasn't all that helpful since they didn't share their findings with us.

"Once again, you want me to solve it for you?" he asked, raising one of those gorgeous bushy eyebrows of his.

"Well, you know the region," I said, "so go on. Which castle is the prettiest one of them all?"

"I don't think it's a contest," he said, "I think it's

another word game."

"A word game?" it took me a second to untangle his meaning. "A play on words? A pun?"

"Is that how you say it? I think it's another mistranslation, like your father did with blackcurrant beach. Pretty Provence Castle would become Beau Chateau Provençal."

"And that means something to you?"

"Well, I think he means the chateau of Les-Baux-de-Provence."

"Wait, you mean there literally is a town named 'pretty'?" I wanted to laugh. French town names were ridiculously over the top.

"Well, it comes from *bauxite*, I think," he continued, "and this town is notoriously hard to get to if you don't have a car."

The universe wanted me to find the clues, so that wasn't about to stop me. Stop us, I should say. Valentin and I were a team now, even if he was only here for an autograph.

"It has everything your father put in the letter," he said, "It has the old castle - this one is almost a thousand years old, though it is ruins - and the *Carrières des Lumières*, the light show they went to see. Though it is very popular attraction now."

"I trust you on this," I said, "but how do we get

there? Can we take your scooter this time?"

"No, it's still too far. I will have to check," he said, "But I think we take the train to Avignon... then we take the bus. But there are not many during the day. So we will have to be careful unless we will be... how you say... stranded."

I nodded, but I wasn't worried. The universe was on our side. It was perfect.

I watched as the world flew by our window. Everything had changed today: I had seen a dragon, ridden the bus, a train, and discovered the Caribbean in France. The magic of it would not wear off soon.

"Are you all right?" he asked, suddenly, "have I offended you?"

"You? No," I shook my head, "Why would you even ask that?"

"You look tired," he replied, "I'm sorry."

"I'm just a little... overwhelmed by all this. It's so different from back home."

He broke out one of his patented grins. "It's the train, isn't it? If you think this is cool, you need to take a ride on the TGV."

"It's not..." no, it wasn't the train, although that was really cool, just as he said. It was everything else. Experiencing your world without you was just the beginning.

"Look, if you want to ride the TGV, we'll make it happen," he said, "it's so fast, and so nice, it'll make this train look like an American train."

I nodded. It was better than telling him the truth. Some things I didn't want to share just yet.

We got off at St Charles station in Marseille, and immediately headed to the ticket booth. Even now, the entire station was full of people. Sunlight filtered in from the high iron roofs above, landing on the modern trains and basking them in a warm golden hue. It was made even more surreal when four armed soldiers walked by, brown beret, camo, weapons and everything.

"Go take a photo," said Valentin suddenly, breaking me out of my awestruck moment.

"What?"

"You need an ID photo for your card," he said, pointing at a little photobooth marked *photomaton*. My mind jumped instantly to the scene from *Amelie*. Train station + photobooth = meeting a cute guy with one weird hobby. Irrefutable math. I wondered if Valentin had one: maybe he hid garden gnomes in other people's gardens or created photo collages of tourists in wacky travel outfits.

A minute later, I handed Valentin a very official looking page with five ID pics all arranged. He led me to the ticket sales counter, worked his magic with the man in uniform, and a few minutes later I came out, a few euros lighter, in possession of a funky looking red card.

"Unlimited train and bus," he exclaimed. "So tomorrow when we take the train, you won't have to pay. At least, not as much."

I wanted to kiss him in that moment. Having someone on my side like this was more than my little heart could handle. Instead, I wrapped my arms around him, hugging him on instinct. He seemed taken aback by this. I took it the French were not big huggers.

"Um, er, bus?"

The next two hours passed in a blur, in which both of us were too exhausted to speak. I replayed the views of the calanques in my mind as we reached Aix again, only to hop right back onto yet another bus, practically nodding to sleep as we sped through Provence.

When I finally got my bike back and made my way to Mamie's, the sun was still high enough in the sky that I didn't think anything of it. It felt good to not be melting into the gravel, and that light breeze swimming through the thick air to cool my burning skin felt like a dream. I marched up the driveway to the house, feeling confident.

"Jammy!"

Mamie practically flew into my arms. She held my

head in both hands, kissing my forehead. Then her expression shifted. Whatever tears on her face shriveled up and dried as her frown stretched and grew.

"Where?" She snapped. She held up her watch and stabbed it repeatedly with her index. "Iz late!"

She must have been furious if she was yelling in English, making absolutely sure I knew why she was mad. She sputtered a few words in French out so quickly that they come out a tangled knot which I didn't have the time or know-how to take apart.

Jean-Pascal stepped out of the kitchen then, arms crossing as he leaned against the doorjamb. He was a little too tall for it, his scalp brushing against the frame.

"I called ze *Faures*," she said, ignoring him, "and you not there."

"Valentin and I went to explore," I rambled off to her, and when her brows knotted in confusion, I said it again, slower. "I wanted to see… Provence."

"And you did not tell me?" She spat, *"J'étais inquiete pour toi.* Worried, worried!"

"I'm sorry," I said, "I did have my phone, you could have called."

"So could you."

She spun on her heels and stormed back into the house, past Jean-Pascal as if he didn't even exist. He watched her go into the depths of the house, then turned to me, shaking his head.

"I am sorry," I said, "I hope she knows that."

"*Je suis désolé,*" he replied. "I am sorry."

"You're sorry? For what?"

"*Non,*" he shook his head, stoically, "*Je suis désolé.* You say, to her." And he left, too.

I couldn't do anything right, not even live with my own grandmother. I couldn't talk to my Mamie, even if I wanted to. But there were some languages everyone could speak.

twelve

I HIT SEND, LISTENING TO THAT BEAUTIFUL WHOOSH as the message left my inbox and landed in Jazz's, four thousand miles away. Almost instantly, a notification popped up on my phone.

Got it! She said, *I have to go, we're having drinks to celebrate the end of the camp. Can't wait to read it, though!*

I turned off my data and stuffed my phone into the desk, so I wouldn't have to deal with it. All the excitement I had had from finding the letter had dwindled to a tiny spark now.

I was out like a light. Guilt be damned, the entire trip had exhausted me so much that I forgot to close my windows. Of course, I was covered in those all too familiar itchy bumps the next morning.

Stupid Provence.

Aix Marks the Spot

I desperately wanted to tell Jazz about the treasure hunt, about Dad's old letters, the clue that was still there, and the French boy who was helping me. She would have been all over Valentin. I probably would have been too, if I didn't know about Chloë. But she was too busy for me, and I would just have to accept that.

I was all ready for my hasty Nutella breakfast before heading off to Les Baux, until I ran into my Mamie in the kitchen.

"*J'ai un cadeau pour toi*," she said, a smile breaking out on her face. I didn't like where this was going.

"A what?"

"*Cadeau*. Present!" She handed me a heavy brick wrapped in brown paper. "For you!"

I took a seat at the kitchen table and got to work on the paper. Inside was a book, the words "English to French" printed in big bold letters on the cover. A dictionary.

"Jean-Pascal helped," she said.

I nodded. A dictionary. The lovely gesture felt a little heavy handed.

"*Aujourd'hui*, I want to know you," she said, still not sitting. She beamed down at me like an angel from above. "We shall spend ze day together. Fun!"

I couldn't believe what I was hearing. Mamie actually wanted to spend time with me? I looked up from the book, all my energy going into keeping my jaw from dropping.

"Where are we going?" I asked, and then, noting her disapproval, I added, "*où?*" like a monkey.

"*C'est une surprise,*" she replied, grinning. Oh my god. How was her smile so terrifying? So many teeth. So pearly white. Never reaching her eyes.

What's the catch? I wanted to ask. *Who are you, and what have you done with Colette Martin?*

Instead, the only thing I could ask was, "Are you driving?"

She shook her head. "*Dictionnaire, my puce.*"

Mamie pointed to the thick book, and I found myself groaning internally. She didn't expect me to jump through all these hoops every time I wanted to ask a question, did she? She could very well have a dictionary of her own, too.

"Driving... *Conduire? Qui... conduire?*"

"*Qui conduit,*" she corrected, but her smile was genuine. "*Jean-Pascal va conduire.*"

I wanted to rip my hair out by the roots. Stupid tenses. Nothing I could say would make her happy.

"I'll get dressed," I said, watching as my plans for the day turned to ash before me. "in my room. *Ma chambre.*"

She nodded. "*Jean-Pascal arrive à dix heures.*"

I dragged myself back up the stairs, Nutella-less, day-less. I should have been excited: my Mamie wanted to spend time with me. Finally, I was going to get to know her. But instead I felt like someone had just told me we were going to the dentist to get teeth pulled.

I grabbed my phone and pulled up Valentin's texts. I had missed some from the night before: him spit balling some ideas for finding today's clue, giving me suggestions of what to wear for the castle tour. It made it even harder to send him what I had to say.

"We're going to have to postpone," I typed. "Mamie wants to take me out somewhere."

I hit send, grabbing my clothes to get myself ready for whatever day this was going to be. He replied before I could even start changing.

"Have fun!"

There. He didn't sound disappointed. Did he sound happy, to cancel these plans with me? I couldn't tell, so much meaning was lost over text. Everything about him was so confusing.

I washed up and threw on my clothes, slipping the phone into my pocket as I stepped back into the kitchen. My grandmother instantly reacted by shaking her head.

"*Mais...*" she rolled her eyes, defeated, deflated. "*Mais habille toi comme il faut! Rho lala...*"

I had heard other girls say *Ooh Lala* back home, usually when talking about things that were better not said when parents were present. But this sound... not a word, not a moan, simultaneously neither and both, was enough to remind me how out of place I was once again.

"What's wrong?" I asked, shrinking back, "*Quoi?*"

She gestured at me with a sweep of her hand. Ah, so it was the clothes. I changed out of my pink gym shorts and put on knee length jeans, and a blouse my grandma had packed because she thought I might want to impress the local boys. It was cute, but not something I would buy myself, white with a scooped neck and ruffles around my arms. This time when I descended the stairs, I got a curt nod. I guess that was something.

Jean-Pascal arrived moments later, and I climbed into his car as Mamie locked up the house. He turned back to give me a wide smile.

"Road treep!" he exclaimed, beaming. "Iz good to see yoo, Jammy!"

"*Toi aussi,* Jean-Pascal," I managed to say. Somehow, he beamed even more at this.

Mamie climbed into the car and exchanged quick *bise* cheek kisses with him, and soon we were driving out the gates, Mamie and Jean-Pascal chatting away in the front seat faster than I could even try to follow.

I leaned back into the seats. The beautiful blue sky that had been so overwhelming yesterday was filling with clouds. The countryside looked as if someone had intensified the contrast, the trees sticking out harshly against the hills. It felt like a storm was coming.

"Et toi, Jammy?" said Jean-Pascal, catching my gaze in the rear-view mirror, *"Tu t'amuses en Provence?"*

"Uh…" Thanks for putting me on the spot, JP. It was like being on a quiz show and missing the questions every time.

"Do you like eet 'ere?"

"Yeah," I replied, trying not to offend anyone. "I like it. The cheese is really good."

"Essayes-en Français, Jammy," said Mamie, eyes transfixed by something far, far ahead.

"In French? Um, *J'aime le fromage?* I like the cheese?"

"Lequel est ton préféré?" asked Jean-Pascal. "Your favorite?"

"Le Chevre?" Just saying the name brought back memories of the creamy white spread, the fresh bread turning to crumbs between my teeth. *"C'est très bon!"*

That would be my catch phase in France: it's very good. The only three words I could say with a modicum of correctness, and it seemed like enough of a compliment to just swim by.

We kept driving like this, the clouds getting thicker

as we went along. Sometimes, Jean-Pascal would try to reel me into conversation, throwing me hooks so I could be included, at least a little bit. All the while, Mamie sat stiffly in the passenger side, her fingers drumming on the side of her seat.

The first time I caught the color purple out the window, I thought it was a fluke: it was too vibrant to be natural. But then the road swerved, and I was met with an entire field of lavender, and the jaw I had been holding since this morning finally dropped.

Fields and fields of Lavender stretched on either side of the road, as far as the eye could see. I was driving through the pictures on coffee table books, the actual image that came up every time anyone searched the word 'Provence'.

Jean-Pascal rolled down my window, and I was hit with the fresh scent of clean sheets, the beautiful nasal hug of lavender wafting through my soul. Slowly, I began to relax: the tension I was carrying since our fight the night before started to melt away, basked by the smell of blooming lavender fields.

Another type of flower was growing in the fields: colorfully dressed Instagrammers were taking selfies in and among the rows, some posing in outrageous gowns, shouting to people behind them to move. Others were taking family photos, all in matching white outfits. A woman in a muumuu was yelling for a guy named Sebastian to "take a picture already."

The car slowed, if only because everyone in front of us was slowing as well. Armchair photographers were leaning out the window, while some had just stopped in the middle of the street, forgetting how to cross. Mamie grumbled from the front seat.

We got going again, and the drive continued on. The lavender wasn't our stop: we kept on the road, flanked on either side by the infinite fields, interrupted sometimes by rows of yellow sunflowers, which cast a beautiful contrast with the purple. A feeling stirred inside me, a call to clutch a pencil in my hand and capture the colors as I saw them.

As we drove on, the fields of tourists faded to the background. Out here, the lavender was untouched by the visitors. Weeds grew up in between the rows of these slightly-less-than-picture-perfect fields. The air around us was quiet, smelling of magical flowers. Every once and a while I would spot an old stone farmhouse in a field, left untouched by man or nature. This was the image I had of Provence.

"*Tu aimes la lavande?*" asked Jean-Pascal, ever the conversationalist, "Do you like ze lavender?"

"I do, yes. *Oui*," I replied. I didn't know what else to say. I simply basked in the magic of the beautiful purple.

And still, we drove on. Soon we left the fields behind, much to my disappointment, and the world around us returned to its everyday green. Out of the distance grew a chain of cliffs, grey-and-white stone making an impressive wall of mountain. A tiny village appeared at the base, where a slash split the wall like a giant had taken their axe to it. This, it appeared, was where we were going.

"*Moustiers-Sainte-Marie,*" said Mamie, pointing to the hill. "*Tu vois l'étoile?*"

"*Etoile?*" I asked. Do you see the etoile, whatever that was.

"Ze Star," said Jean-Pascal, as the road became steeper. A series of zig-zag hairpin turns were leading us up the hill to the town itself. Newer homes grew up beside us, right along the road.

"What star?" I asked, scanning the sky.

"Between ze mountains."

I squinted as I looked out of the window, but I couldn't see any star between any mountains. There was only one mountain here, and there were no stars out during the day.

We did one last sharp turn, and finally we were in an open-air parking lot. Jean-Pascal found a spot and Mamie instantly flew out of the car, visibly trembling.

"Is she ok?" I asked Jean-Pascal, as he held open my door.

"She do not like car," he replied.

Oh. That answered a few questions, like why she didn't come to pick me up at the airport. The fact she was willing to endure an hour and some drive to take me to this town made me feel a little warmer towards her, even if I didn't want to come in the first place.

Mamie straightened up and pointed to a spot between the two cliffs as Jean-Pascal ran off to pay the meter.

"You see?" she said, her hand steadfast, *"Tu vois? Là!"*

Neither she nor Jean-Pascal were imagining things after all: because right there, strung between the two peeks like a giant necklace, was a little golden star hung by a chain. I gaped.

"What... *quoi?*" I asked, suddenly able to be dumbfounded in both languages.

"Prieuré," was her only answer, pointing slightly lower than the star. *"Marche?"*

"Marche? March?"

She made a marching motion. Apparently, we were going to march up there, or something. It wasn't the nicest day for a hike, but then again, at least I was finally doing something with Mamie.

Sarah Anderson

The three of us took the old stairs up, breathing heavily at the combination of heat and steepness. We crossed a bridge across a dry riverbed, and followed the stone path, me feeling oddly reminded of something out of Lord of the Rings. Only this, somehow, inexplicably, was real: stone steps up a mountain to a golden star, shrines to the virgin Mary along the way, and my Mamie leading the hike.

At the very top, we found a small church, claiming to be 'Notre-Dame-de-Bouvoir', though there was nothing Notre-Damey about it. It was more like a tiny chapel, dwarfed by the Cyprus trees outside it.

"Twelve century," said Jean-Pascal, practically making me jump out of my skin. No one had dared talk during the climb, lest we waste our breath.

"The star too?" I asked. He nodded.

"A knight," he explained, "came back. Built star."

How a 12th century star could still remain suspended between two cliffs I couldn't possibly tell you. Mamie was already sitting on the edge of the squat stone wall, lighting a cigarette as she stared back at the view. Jean-Pascal looked her way, frowning.

"Do you want to see ze inside?" he asked. I nodded: I didn't really, but it was nice being asked.

The two of us stepped inside, and somehow, it was even smaller than I had first assumed. A few other tourists were already inside, admiring the stone work, each staring at a different corner of the tiny chapel. The only impressive thing about it was its age.

I turned to Jean-Pascal, glad to finally have some time alone with him. I had so many questions about Mamie: about how much he knew about our family, or why Mamie didn't want me around, or why she wanted to even take me out today. Why here, specifically. And what he meant to her, and…

"Jean- "

I clasped my hands over my mouth as the word slipped out. It echoed across the walls, reverberating louder and louder. All eyes turned to me as I shrank back into the shadows. I stepped outside before my embarrassment could grow any more.

At least out here, the view was incredible: the little town below looked like something out of a storybook, tiny houses with tiled roofs lining a river on an impossibly steep hill. From here, I could see terraced hills stretching out into a valley, green pines dotting the landscape, few roads getting in the way.

"On descend?" asked Mamie, stamping out her cigarette.

I nodded, and instantly she began walking down the hill. Oh. I thought she had asked if I liked the view or something, not if I wanted to walk back down already.

Sarah Anderson

It wasn't that I wanted to spend more time up on this mountain, but we had walked so hard to get here, only to turn around and go right back to where we had come from. It felt like a waste. Jean-Pascal said nothing as we followed Mamie back down, and then continued on into the town.

When people speak of sleepy French villages, they probably imagine these towns sans-tourists. We were not the only ones taking in the breathtaking views of *Moustiers*: groups speaking every possible language passed by us as we walked. The narrow streets were lined with pottery shops and souvenir stores, old doors and old stone steps framing our way.

When we reached the main street, the sound of tourists speaking was masked by the sound of a crashing waterfall, and for a minute I forgot I was in France and imagined I was in a little alpine village in Austria, living the sound of music. Water ran right through the town, channeled by large stone walls, only to crash into a glacier-blue pool below. A restaurant hung over the falls, under the watchful gaze of a centuries old clocktower, which struck half past twelve for anyone who cared to hear it.

A small girl skipped by with an ice cream cone, topped with purple scoops. I couldn't believe what I was seeing.

Aix Marks the Spot

"Lavender ice cream?" I asked Jean-Pascal.

"*Français!*" Mamie interjected.

"*Glace...* Lavender?" I asked again. He nodded.

"*Lavande et miel...* and honey."

Oh my gosh. Now that sounded heavenly.

"May I?" I asked, indicating the closest ice cream stall. "*Je... pouvoir?*"

"*Tu peux,*" said Jean-Pascal, smiling.

"*Après dejeuner,*" added Mamie, shooting him a glare. If I hadn't known better, I would have thought they were an old married couple. My Spidey senses were tingling.

"After lunch?" I asked, and Jean-Pascal nodded.

Lunch was at a cute restaurant that overlooked the waterfall, the three of us seated cozily together at the window so we could watch the river down below. It would have been idyllic if it wasn't for the menu in front of me, that was very, very French.

I sat in my chair, frozen stiff at the prospect of ordering. I knew the words, or at least, I think I did, but the problem was they never came out in the right order. And what if the waitress asked me follow up questions? Not to mention the fact I could only get the gist of about half the meals on the menu, and Mamie and Jean-Pascal were chattering away so quickly I couldn't get a question in edgewise.

"Vous avez choisi?" asked the waitress, in a prim white and black uniform, notepad in hand.

Mamie rattled off something in an instant. Jean-Pascal seemed to agree with her about something and handed the waitress his menu. I could only look at her, dumbfounded, as she turned her attention to me.

On the spot, I did the only thing I could: I poked my finger at random in the menu, and smiled, and said, *"S'il vous plait?"*

"Andouilette? Bien sur."

Mamie turned to me and unleashed the most exquisite smile I had ever seen. Talk about beaming, this lady was a beacon.

"Je suis fière de toi, ma puce," She said, as Jean-Pascal gave me a look of pure and utter shock.

Yay me, finally impressing my grandmother! Jamie for the win!

The woman nodded, taking down our orders and heading back to the kitchen. And so passed the longest, most awkward half hour of my life: The food took forever to come out, and I had to sit, listening to the two French speakers go, unable to follow or to join their conversation. So when the food finally arrived, I was hungrier than ever before.

The plate before me was filled with a massive sausage, white and covered with a creamy gravy.

Aix Marks the Spot

Golden French fries, thick and crispy, sat to the edge of the plate, with a tiny salad consisting of three green leaves and a cherry tomato. Relief washed over me: I had won the food jackpot.

Relief turned to dread as I sliced through the sausage, only to see the rolled layers inside. The smell hit me in a wave, so strongly I had to hold back a gag. Old socks left out in the sun too long were replacing the meal I had ordered. Old socks and a men's locker room.

"Bon appétit," said Mamie, before tackling her steak. Jean-Pascal gave me a pitying look. Now I knew why Mamie was so proud of my order, and it had nothing to do with my pointing and thanking system.

It tasted exactly how it smelled. I forced the first bite down, desperate to win her approval. It was like chewing on the sole of a shoe. A little glass cup sat before us, stuffed with single serving ketchup and mayo. I grabbed for the ketchup and spread it over my plate, desperate for anything to mask the taste. The reward came in the form of a French fry, dipped in the gravy – a pepper sauce that actually wasn't all that bad.

Mamie turned up her nose at the now empty ketchup pack on my napkin. Somehow, once again, I had failed a test I didn't know I was taking.

It was drizzling as we left the restaurant. I had heard that meals in France could last hours, but it seemed both Mamie and Jean-Pascal were in as much of a rush to get out of the awkward meal as I was. My stomach churned, unable to process whatever I had just eaten. I think it might have been pork guts or something. And my gut didn't like this gut on gut action.

But I still wanted my ice cream.

"Dessert?" I asked, putting on a French accent and hoping it translated. "*Glace?*"

Jean-Pascal nodded. "*Pourquoi pas?*"

Just then, a rumble of thunder came down the mountain. Mamie looked up the cliffs, then back as us, frowning her familiar frown.

"*Alors là, non,*" she said, crossing her arms over her chest, "*Il y'a un orage qui se prépare.*"

"*Orage?*" That one, I did know. Thank you, Valentin. "A storm is coming?"

The thunder rumbled again, louder this time. The rain started coming down harder.

"It'll only take a minute," I begged, "I really want to taste it. *Je veut...* um... *glace* lavender?"

"*Ça va pas tarder à tomber, et je n'ai pas de parapluie. Allez.*"

Mamie started walking back towards the car, ignoring me. I stuffed my hands into my pockets, my eyes riveted on the ice cream stand. Jean-Pascal gave me another one of his patented pitying looks, and shrugged, his whole body joining into the motion. A definite 'sorry, there's nothing I can do.'

"You said I could…" I found myself whining, my inner toddler peeking out. "I came on this trip. I walked the stairs. I ate the stinking sausage. I only ask for one thing, and you just…"

"Iz not me to decide," he said.

"But you could help!" I begged. "She won't listen to me unless I speak perfect French, and I just can't! I'm trying, but I can't!"

"Rho, mais! Depéchez vous, bon sang!" She yelled back down to us. *"J'ai pas envie de passer une heure mouillée dans la voiture!"*

"Next time," said Jean-Pascal. And even as nicely as he said it, I knew I never wanted another next time.

As Mamie stormed up the hill back to the car, and the raindrops came down harder, I wondered why I ever thought eating a shoe flavored sausage would get her to like me. She wouldn't like me unless I was French.

thirteen

"I THOUGHT WE COULDN'T TAKE YOUR SCOOTER?"

I met Valentin at Mamie's Gate, trying to keep a straight face as I writhed internally. Our 'family time' yesterday had only made matters worse, and the quiet house felt haunted by Mamie's silent presence. I was glad to get out, to get back to Dad's hunt.

Valentin was perched on his scooter, popping off his helmet and running his fingers through sweaty hair as we talked. It felt like weeks since I had last seen him, and just looking at his face made my day shine brighter.

"Not all the way there," he said, and I felt my heart flutter as English poured from his lips. "But we have to get to the train station. Now will you please get on the bike?"

I slipped on the helmet, tightened the straps of my

backpack, and climbed onto the scooter behind him. Slowly, very slowly, I wrapped my arms around his chest. I felt it stiffen.

"Um, why are you holding me?"

"Isn't this how I'm supposed to…"

"There are handles behind you?" he said, flabbergasted, "I mean, sure, hug me all you want, but I'll never be able to drive like that."

"I'm so sorry," I squeaked, my face hot. I let go of his waist and reached back, finding little hooks behind my seat which I could grab onto. "I mean…"

"Don't mention it," he said, obviously uncomfortable. I felt my stomach turn into knots. Not a great start to this adventure.

I gripped on tight as he drove us down the road. He was confident at the wheel, though I was glad no one else was on the road at this hour. If they were, they must have been giving us a wide berth just out of the kindness of their hearts.

I felt like we passed quite a few train stations before actually reaching the one Valentin wanted us to go to. He parked his scooter and I hopped off, suddenly aware of the hot air on my skin. The storm had passed: today was going to be another scorcher.

"Ok," he said, with that deep French accent of his, "this train will take us to Avignon. From there, getting to les Baux will be easy, so long as we do not miss our bus." He opened up the scooter's seat and grabbed his own bag, sliding it over his shoulder.

"Avignon, I've heard of that place, haven't I?"

"Do you like castles?" He led us to the train station, but there was none. Instead, a little cement hut about the size and shape of an outhouse sat on the platform, the station sign larger than the wall itself. A tiny plaque showing a man in a reclining chair with a suitcase and a clock told us this was the waiting room, while it was neither a room, nor had a chair, or a clock for that matter.

"I guess?"

"Avignon is where the pope lived," he explained, "When they split from Rome in the 14th century."

"So it's basically part time Vatican?"

"It was, *ouais*," he nodded, grinning. Valentin was so at ease when it came to telling me stories about France's past. I could see him one day, standing in a museum, telling the world about another great thing France had done which we all took for granted.

"All that is left now are massive walls and the *Palais des Papes*. The Pope's palace. And the city, of course."

"That's so cool!" I said. I knew I wasn't here to sightsee, but I needed something to keep my thoughts off Mamie.

The train slid to a halt beside us and we took our seats, and off we were again, reclining in style.

"Last time I took the train from Philly to Baltimore, it cost me forty bucks each way," I said, as I saw an old tower whiz past us.

Valentin shrugged. "*Pas terrible.*"

"Not terrible?" I translated, "It sucks, man."

"It's how we say that," he said, "*Pas terrible* means It sucks."

"So *Pas Mal*, not bad, would mean 'that's awful?'"

"No, *Pas Mal* means awesome."

"I don't understand your language."

"Neither do I," he replied, with a sly smile playing on the corner of his lips. "*Alors*, how was your day with your grandmother?"

"Honestly?" I said, "*Pas terrible.*"

"Oh?"

Just one sound, and it felt as if I had his full attention. The entire question rolled into a single syllable. I wondered if it was a French thing, not to ask the uncomfortable questions. I had heard the French were closed off, but less than a week ago Valentin was a stranger, and now we were riding trains together, sharing in a treasure hunt as I told him how much it hurt to live with my grandmother.

"Not to stop you," he said, after I had recounted

the awkward car ride to Moustiers, "but the train has stopped, and this is not a station."

As if reading his mind, a voice crackled to life in the PA. It announced something incomprehensible in French, but whatever it was, it turned Valentin's face pale.

"What? What is it?"

"The train is late," he replied, looking like he had just shown up to a test without any clothes on. I blushed as the thought crossed my mind, embarrassed the innocent image had shifted so far.

"But didn't you say that was normal?" I asked, "not to worry about the things I can't change and…"

"This is the only bus to Les Baux for two hours," he said, "if we miss it, we will not make it in time to look for the clue and get back on the last bus."

"Shit," I replied.

"*Merde.*" He agreed.

The train started moving again, but slower than before. America slow. I tapped my fingers nervously against the velvet of my seat, urging the train to move faster, to catch up its missing time.

Valentin threw his backpack on his back and rose from his seat, heading to the door. I followed suit, watching the greenery roll past, nature oblivious to our wracked nerves.

Aix Marks the Spot

It was only when we started arriving in Avignon that things turned ugly. Large walls surrounded the tracks, covered in graffiti, and the train slowed, practically tiptoeing between the buildings.

"Come on, come on," I found myself muttering. I clutched the strap of my bag, my heart pounding. We were ready.

"Dépêche toi! We are going to miss it!"

The second the train rolled into Avignon station, Valentin slammed his thumb against the door release and toppled out onto the platform, ignoring all suggestions to mind the step. I rushed after him, hitting the pavement and following him down stairs only to climb them right back up on the other side.

"Cours, Forest!" yelled some random stranger waiting for his own train, as Valentin yanked open the station doors, only for us to rush right though, pushing past people waiting with their suitcases. The smell of fresh crepes hit my nostrils instantly, only to be ripped away when we burst into sunlight on the other side, right at the feet of a castle.

Well, not an actual castle: the castle's ramparts, extending left and right down the street. I wanted to stop and stare, but Valentin was already running towards a dark architectural mess.

I was out of breath, but he wasn't waiting for me.

He flew down the stairs, rushing into a small waiting room, where people milled around checking bus schedules. We burst out into an underground bus terminal, Valentin seemingly instinctively knowing where to go. My footsteps echoed across the large room as we ran, finally reaching the line that was milling into the bus. We stopped, relieved, neither of us having to say anything, both aware of how close we'd come to missing it.

Well, we were relieved until a man in a polo shirt stepped in front of us.

"*C'est complet,*" he said, hands on his hips, "*désolé. Prenez le prochain.*"

"What did he say?" I'm ashamed at how tightly I grabbed Valentin's arm. "What's he saying?"

"The bus is full." He wasn't even looking at me. Instead, he stared at the people in front of us paying the bus driver, who were pretending not to notice our situation. The driver didn't even make eye contact. The man in the polo shirt climbed into the bus behind the other tourists in their floppy straw sunhats.

"It's full?" My eyes swept the rest of the complex. None of the busses had the same decals as this one, and I realized it really was our only ride out of here. "But the next one…"

This scavenger hunt was bad for my heart. It kept

Aix Marks the Spot

falling and almost shattering on a daily basis.

"So we just wasted a day, didn't we?" I said, feeling quite suddenly on the verge of tears. Being at the mercy of these stupid busses was really bringing out the worst in me. "We have to go back, and call it quits, and…"

"Why do you always panic?" he asked, "it's going to be ok. It's just a bus. We can go tomorrow. We are in no rush."

How Valentin managed to stay so calm, I would never know. There was just something so soothing about the way he spoke, how he never let himself be defeated. Not to mention the way he always pronounced it's as *iz*. I offered up a smile.

"C'est bon, vous avez de la chance, il ne reste que deux places!" Blue polo man announced as he stepped off the bus. Wearing sunglasses indoors, as one does.

"Wait, that sounded good. Was that good?" I asked Valentin.

"It's perfect, there are two spots left," he said, beaming, "probably not next to each other, though."

"I'll survive," I replied, then was surprised to see his smile droop just a little. He turned around before I could make anything of it, hopping onto the bus and swiping his card.

The bus had everything I hated about buses: it was cramped, hot, and crowded. It seemed everyone riding it was a tourist. I had to turn sideways in the aisle to avoid the big camera bags on people's laps, or the sunhats lazily held out past the seats.

Please let the person next to me be cool, please let them be cool, I chanted in my head, scanning the seats for the free space the polo guy had claimed to have found. When I finally spotted it, it was in the middle of the bus, aisle side, next to a middle-aged blonde woman who was fanning herself with the bus schedule.

I cast a glance back, trying to find Valentin. He was in the aisle in the before last, sitting next to a person who could have been my bus-mate's twin. It was impressive how much the two looked the same, down to the heavily gilded fan-waving hands.

The bus pulled out of the station and into the daylight. We were off, an electronic voice listing off stations and stops as we approached them, which was not often. We were going to cover a lot of ground before getting to Les Baux.

I must have been getting used to fading out the cicadas, because I didn't notice the constant background noise of people speaking until we were well underway, and by then it only hit me when I started picking up on conversation.

English. Everyone was speaking English.

Well, almost everyone. I think there was some

German here, Spanish coming from one end of the bus. French was there in pockets. But the massive brouhaha was all in English; American English. Laughing, chatting, making whatever that frat boy 'OOH' sound is called.

The gilded, sunhatted woman turned towards me, glanced me over, said nothing, and went back to looking out the window at the passing French countryside. I stared straight down the aisle, past the hats and the photography kits, through the front window at the road ahead. The abundance of green fields was almost staggering.

"I don't know what she sees in him," the girl in front of me said to her friend, "I mean, he's like, never left his home town. I mean, I get it, some people just like their comfort zone, you know? But I can't be with someone who doesn't get it."

"Preach," replied her friend, "Look, after we get home tonight, I gotta ditch the group. Dad's got his friends over for a business thing, and he wants me to join them for dinner. I keep telling him I want to do this whole European adventure on my own, you know? But he insists on basically stalking me."

"It's so weird," said the other, tisking, "like, why can't he accept the fact that you're on your own?"

"He says since it's his money, he should know

where I am. Is that creepy?"

"My mom doesn't care where I go so long as there's lavender hand cream for her when I get back," said the first, "That's the point of having our own adventure. Our experience. It's like, thanks for the tickets, could you please go now? I'm my own person, thank you very much."

The woman next to me stopped fanning herself for a second and turned to me as if I was a part of their conversation. I just shook my head.

"I just want to soak in the culture," said the second girl, "and I can't do that with dad constantly over my shoulder. I mean, how am I supposed to see what it is to be a local, if I'm eating at Michelin star restaurants every night? Locals can't afford those places. They're not meant for them."

"It's better than the street food I've been forced to have. Not a salad bar in sight. Do you know what they call a Taco in Marseille? I swear, it's a burger inside a burrito. Fries, salad, tomato and all. It's disgusting."

My mouth started to water at the sound of that. Burger burrito? Sign me up! We should have stopped for one on our way through Marseille during the Cassis leg of our mission.

"Ne fais pas attention à eux," said my seatmate.

"Je suis désolée," I said, practically stammering,

tripping over the words as they stumbled out of my mouth, *"Mon Français est très mal."*

"Ce n'est pas grave, Bichette, au moins tu fais un effort."

I wasn't quite sure what she had just said, but it sure sounded like a compliment.

"Tu vas aux Baux de Provence?" she asked, *"ou St Rémy?"*

"Um," I answered, awkwardly. St Rémy I remember seeing on the list of stops this bus too. No Oboes in sight. Wait. Les Baux. Aux Baux?

"Je visite Les Baux," I answered, hoping I had guessed correctly, "The castle. *Le chateau?*"

She smiled gently. *"Je vais aux Carrières des Lumières,"* she explained. *"J'y vais chaque année, mais j'ai pas encore vu celui-ci…"*

"Je suis désolée," I apologized again, *"Je n'ai pas…* words?"

She patted me gently on the arm. "Iz Ok. You have nice day. Must see art show. Iz very good."

An hour later, the bus climbed a hill up to the fortress town of Les-Baux-de-Provence. Valentin had filled me in on the history: that the castle was under siege when the country was torn by religion almost a thousand years ago, that the townspeople themselves had dismantled it as an accord with the king and swore never to rebuild it in order for their town to survive, a promise they had kept for now 800 years.

It was a steep road, but it levelled off in between the two peaks, which is where the bus left us. I stepped away from the crowd, waiting for Valentin to appear. He looked dizzy as he climbed off the bus.

"*Ca va?*" I threw out, "you ok?"

"*Juste*... a lot of talking," he replied, "good practice. But tiring. Exhausting."

My seatmate had been silent the entire rest of the trip, only sighing occasionally when the two girls ahead of us said something particularly nauseating. I watched them climb off the bus now, two almost identically dressed girls, with selfie sticks at the ready.

We stood in the parking lot, which made it rather difficult to take in our surroundings. Up on the right ridge lay the entrance to a small stone town, a lot like Lourmarin, except for the part where it was perched on an actual cliff instead of down in a valley. Down to our left, the road sloped away through what appeared to be a limestone quarry. The rocks were cut too sharp and angular to be natural.

"Is this the place?" I asked, scanning the parking lot. There wasn't another space available for cars in sight, it was that packed. People milled around, tour groups with orange flags on poles, kids chasing each other and squealing excitedly.

"Probably," said Valentin, shrugging, "but I have something to show you, first. Come!"

Along with the flock of tourists, we strolled into town. The place was incredible: tall stone houses rose on either sides of an incredibly narrow and steep street, more than any of the roads I had pedaled over in Lourmarin, tighter and older looking than Moustiers. Stores on either sides sold Gelato and sweets, some toting plastic swords and knight's helmets. It was like a Ren faire on steroids.

Valentin didn't seem to want to stop at any of those. Instead he led me along the long street, up and up and up, until we reached a metal gate that blocked the road.

"We're going to the ruins first?" I asked, "but the clue…"

"Has been there seventeen years," he said, "it can wait another hour. Come!"

We stepped into the visitor's center and Valentin grabbed us day passes, handing me mine and crossing the turnstile.

"When I was a child, my parents brought me every summer," he said, "many times. It is the best."

We stepped out onto a gravel path, the sky so intense and blue above us I thought we might need a new name for the color. We were at the highest point around, nothing to break the horizon but more sky.

Oh, and the catapults in the middle of the lawn.

Two men dressed in medieval clothes were talking to a crowd that had assembled around them. In French, of course, but the way they were pointing, and gesticulating made most of what they were saying obvious.

"Valentin," I asked, reaching again for his arm to support me, "don't tell me we're going to learn how catapults work."

"No, we're not," he said, "we're going to learn how the *baricole* works. By launching it."

And then, in one swift move, he took my arm and lifted it into the air, like I was raising my hand along with the rest of the crowd.

"Oh my god, what did I just agree to?" I stammered.

"You're going to launch the women's catapult. But don't worry, you're not alone. Go!"

He shoved me forward, taking my bag in the process. Me and about five other ladies stepped forward, as the medieval man continued to talk. Up close, the *baricole* was even more massive than I ever imagined, but the trebuchet next to it was even larger. It could have been forty feet tall for all I could tell.

The man was going over safety procedures, but I didn't follow. The other women were pumped, so I just did as they did. We pulled back a crank, turning and turning and turning, until the man told us to step back, and fired. The white-water balloon soared through the air, crashing down well before the man's partner, who yelled something that made the crowd laugh.

The trebuchet didn't even get close to the man. The projectile soared right off the cliff.

"That was amazing!" I said to Valentin as the crowd dispersed. My hands tingled with the thrill of it. "I mean, I'm not sure what the man was saying, but it was epic. I never got to do anything like that before."

This made Valentin's amazing smile grow tenfold.

"Isn't it amazing?" He asked, leading me towards the ruins. Taking up the highest point of the cliff, a massive wall remained, but not much else. "Every summer they do animations for visitors. You ever shoot an *arbalette*?"

"An arbalette?"

He meant crossbow. And no, I hadn't - until today. The line for the shooting range was filled with kids half our height, slipping through the rows to poke their friends, but the guys managing the stand seemed relieved to have us. Valentin hit a bull's eye on the first shot. I was close, surprised by how easy it was to aim.

"Do you want to see the big one?" Asked the guide excitedly, the straps of his leather cap swaying as he spoke.

He led us into a shed next to the stand, and behold,

there stood the biggest crossbow I had ever seen. It was easily larger than me, the arrow itself as sturdy as a sword.

"Armor piercing. Go," he instructed.

We aimed with the crank. Fired. Bull's eye.

There was everything in this town. Jousting, with men in full knight's gear. Different knights demonstrating sword fighting but pounding on each other so hard I thought for sure one would lose a limb. Valentin and I took turns putting our heads through the stocks, all the stress of this morning forgotten.

There was only one thing left to do in the castle before lunch, and that was climbing to the top of the remaining ramparts. The stones were slick with age, and so narrow you had to grab the railings just to make it up.

But dad was right: nothing beat this view.

We stood at the highest point for miles. Around us was farmland stretching in every direction, dotted with towns here and there in the distance. Out far, far away, I could see the Mediterranean, the blue water fading into the sky so that you could barely make out the horizon.

In that moment, I felt completely and irrevocably in love with the world.

fourteen

I INSISTED WE TRY TO FIND THE SAME RESTAURANT my parents ate at in the letter, feeling so pumped up that nothing could stop me. The universe delivered, and on our way back down the hill, we found a corner restaurant which served Nordic crepes. Valentin and I squeezed into a small two-person table, ordered, and finally let ourselves relax.

My heart had been pounding since I launched that first projectile. I had never felt so powerful before, and shooting the crossbow only made me feel bolder. Everything was possible after what we had just done.

"I can't wait to find the clue," I said to Valentin, "I can totally see why my parents loved this place. I want to know where dad sends us next."

"Breathe, Jammy." He poured us water, filling my

glass without even asking. "We will go after food. You have to see the *Carrières*, though. This year's theme is Picasso. You won't believe it."

"The Carrières? Is that the light show my parents went to? I thought dad called it the Cathedral."

He nodded. "It changed hands, has a new name. It is even more amazing now."

"Ok, after we find the clue, we'll do that," I agreed. "I want to see everything dad saw."

First Cassis, now this. Provence was heaven on a plate.

I felt a chill as I remembered why I was here. This was meant to be my punishment: I could not be enjoying it. I needed a way to remind myself to stay on mission, so I wouldn't forget what really brought me here. It wasn't a vacation, it was my penance.

Valentin must have noticed my frown. "Jamie," he said, making a great effort to pronounce my name right this time, "what's wrong?"

"Nothing," I said, shaking my head, "just hungry. Tired all of a sudden."

"Oh, *coup de barre?*" he asked. I gave him my patented quizzical 'what kind of French is this?' look. "That's what we call it when you suddenly… loose battery."

I gave him a weak smile. "Coo de bar, then."

The waiter arrived with our plates then, two

Aix Marks the Spot

steaming crepes folded into squares. Mine had a beautiful egg on top, so lovely I would be heartbroken to take a knife to it. But I still did.

"Tonic water," I hear a voice call. My eyes lift from my plate as I search for the source of the commotion. A woman in a red blouse was confronting a waitress. "I said tonic water, are you deaf?"

The waitress is shaking her head. "We do not have."

"You have to, I mean what restaurant doesn't have tonic water? Do you need me to spell that for you?" She reached for the waitress's pad. The young woman wasn't fast enough, and the stranger grabbed it, ripping the notepad and pencil from the waitress's hands and scrawling on the paper, still yelling. "TONIC WATER!"

"*Mais Madame...* Ma'am, we do not have. I can get you... sparkling?"

"No, I don't want sparkling! Are you an idiot? I want your manager!"

The waitress dashed off, obviously shaken. The woman turned to her husband, who hadn't said a word this whole time. She, however, had a face all puffed up and red, and smoke coming out of her ears. Literally fuming.

"The nerve of some people. She could make an effort, don't you think?"

"Yes, dear," said the husband.

The rest of the restaurant was silent. People went back to their meals, visibly uncomfortable now. I turned to Valentin, but he didn't seem surprised by any of this.

"Does this happen often?" I asked.

"Sometimes. Tourists... the bad ones make it hard for everybody."

After the meal - closed with a Nutella dessert crepe, wrapped in foil to go - we headed back towards the parking lot. Every bite was pure bliss, the Nutella running through my veins and giving my heart a warm squeeze. Love in food form.

I was all ready to scour the place for the next one of my father's clues, when we turned the corner and saw the three tour busses, stuck trying to pass each other. The air was filled with honking, and tourists making mad dashes across the road.

"What the hell?" I muttered under my breath.

The entire parking lot was in shambles. People were trying to find their groups, getting confused between the similar looking busses; while others were just trying to move their cars, but of course the roads were entirely blocked. Drivers shouted at each other and tourists as they tried to untangle their mess. There was no way we were getting through.

"Ok," I said, trying to hide my disappointment, "I guess we wait on the clue?"

"I'd much rather try to find it while the entire world is here." I had to untangle the features of his face to make sure this was sarcasm, but he flashed one of those winning smiles and I knew that it was. "Come on. Let's go see the art."

"Art? I thought it was a light show?"

"It is. Just come on."

He led me away from the parking and the crowd, towards the quarry I had seen earlier. The rocks around us were chiseled and angular, reaching high above the road, as if some large giant had sliced his way through. It wasn't hard to see where we were going: a long line had formed leading down the road and into a cut out section of the rock.

"Dad said it was empty when they went," I said, a little aghast at the crowd.

"It was off season," said Valentin, "and it has grown a lot in the past few years. It's still good, though. Better."

With so many people, it was hard to picture my parents stumbling into this place, the only ones to admire the sharp rocks and the light show inside. The girls from earlier were snapping selfies while waiting in the queue, laughing and having the time of their lives.

I wondered why it made me feel a knot in my stomach.

The tickets Valentin had purchased for us at the castle were valid here too, and we flashed them on the turnstile and slipped through the heavy drapes. I didn't know what I had expected, but it sure wasn't this: the second I stepped inside, instrumental music overwhelmed me, and I was walking through a cathedral of larger than life paintings projected on the walls of an ancient cavern.

The paintings moved and changed to the music, a dramatic choreography dancing on the walls. I didn't have the words to describe the feelings washing over me: I was overwhelmed and awed, completely basked in the pure majesty of light and color.

"I have not seen the show this year," Valentin said, making me jump. I was so absorbed by the artwork that I hadn't seen him approach. His voice was low, like one would talk in a church. He too seemed transported by the display. "But if it's anything like the past ones... it's like nothing else I can describe."

I didn't reply. I couldn't: my jaw was too busy hanging off my face, unable to move as awestruck as I was.

"*Pardon*," said a woman with a strong German accent, and I practically jumped out of my skin. It was hard to imagine anyone else was in this place with us, but apparently, we hadn't even left the doorway.

My trembling knees were making me block the entire entrance.

"There's a good place to watch, over here," said Valentin, and in the near darkness I could see him waving me over.

As we walked, the artwork moved. It spun around the walls in a dizzying waltz, only to settle on a piece, sometimes a single piece repeated across the entire cavern, the music swelling and perfectly matched. Picasso, larger than life, paintings I had seen in books now towering over me. I clutched my hands to my chest, shaking.

"Are you crying?" asked Valentin. I shook my head, but my eyes were hot and full of tears. "Are you all right? Do you need to sit?"

I did. I clutched Valentin's hand for support as we found a stone bench carved into the wall, and sat, becoming pieces of the art as the light settled on us. There wasn't a single corner in this cavernous room that wasn't part of the show. Even the floor was a masterpiece.

I watched the artwork change and move, feeling the music deep inside my bones, feeling... there weren't words for the feeling. But in that moment, I didn't think I had ever known anything more beautiful in my life.

I didn't know when I realized that I hadn't let go

of Valentin's hand, but even when I did, it changed nothing. I was sharing the entire right side of my body with him, my leg against his leg, shoulder to his shoulder. His warmth wrapped into mine as we immersed ourselves in the light and sound, no longer confined by frail human bodies. Right now, we were music, we were art. And together, we transcended.

fifteen

I MUST HAVE WATCHED THE SHOW FIVE TIMES through.

Every time the sequence ended, there was a smattering of applause from the dark people lurking in the cavern, and a short film was projected, more modern and experimental. It was kinda cute, with classic rock and pop art.

Valentin and I picked different vantage points to view. We stood above, behind the railing, seeing down the length of the quarry. We stood below, and let the sheer height overwhelm us. Sometimes we stood, others we sat, and when we got comfortable in the rhythm of the show and music, we walked, trying to find angles we hadn't seen before. From every angle, the experience changed.

When we finally called it quits - I think my heart was just overflowing, I could hardly feel it anymore - my eyes took ages to readjust to natural light. The blue sky from earlier was now cloudy and grey, and the air was hot and sticky. Valentin didn't seem all that happy about this. He looked exhausted, now that we were out: knowing how drained I felt, I could only imagine he was feeling the same too.

I might have been tired, but I felt… good. Like I was the Nutella crepe from earlier, all gooey and warm on the inside. I had melted into something calm, cradeled by music and art and sunshine – though the later was sorely missing now.

We walked back to the village; the parking lot was now empty. Finally, I would be able to go hunting for the clue. Guilt gnawed at my stomach again as I reminded myself that I couldn't lose track of the target: I wasn't here to explore old castle ruins or run around discovering light shows. No, I was here to fix my mistake.

Falling for the French boy wasn't on the list either, but that was happening whether I liked it or not. And I think it fell squarely into the 'liked it' category.

"Water?" Asked Valentin.

"Oui, Merci," I replied, my eyes on the prize.

I felt a drop on my arm. Rain.

Aix Marks the Spot

He walked off to the vending machine as I started towards the now empty parking lot. The thing was surprisingly large for such a tiny town: it covered an entire slope of the mountain, going up and up so steeply I wondered how people could actually park there. It was exhausting just to walk.

"Follow the signs… follow the signs…" I muttered to myself, scanning the lot. There weren't any signs, neither literal nor figurative. The only ones there seemed to be incredibly recent. As in, less than a year or so old.

"Une bouteille d'eau?"

Valentin handed me the bottle, and I took it greedily. The water was crisp and cold against my sweltering skin.

"On dit merci qui?" he asked.

"What now?"

"What do you say when a handsome Frenchman gives you water?"

"Um, *Merci Valentin?*"

"De rien, Jammy, you are welcome."

I finished off my bottle in one go. I wasn't being very smart, drinking as little as I did, but I had bigger fish to fry. Not to mention there was another rain drop, this time on my shoulder. Two storms in two days: and I thought this place was supposed to always be sunny. Maybe I had brought the storm clouds with me from America: the universe punishing me for not staying on target.

"Where do we even start?" I asked him. He could only shrug. "They said follow the signs. But I don't see any."

"It's been seventeen years," he said, "it's possible a lot has changed. I don't remember how the parking used to look."

"Think back, Valentin, think," I said, "we found the last clue. If that one was still there, this one will be too."

He didn't say anything. He didn't even try his usual smile. This was bad news. Raindrops were falling more ferociously now, not singular occurrences but a full-blown event.

"Don't shut down on me now. We need to solve the clue. What would have stood here the longest? Where would dad have put the clue that he was sure no one would touch?"

"Jaime," he said, glancing over my shoulder. I spun around, staring over the edge of the parking lot onto the road below.

Where a bus was filling up.

Our bus.

"Shit." I couldn't help but swear. I threw up my watch and nearly had a heart attack. "We stayed three

Aix Marks the Spot

hours in the show?"

"We need to get on that bus, now," he urged, making towards the stairs, "we'll come back another time. We'll make a plan."

"No, no," I stammered, and for the second time today tears of being overwhelmed started to trickle down my face. Only this time, it was an anxious thing, a raw and painful thing. "No, we have to find the clue. The universe wants us to find the clue."

"Jamie, it's just a game," he said, walking faster, throwing his head over his shoulder. The rain was coming down harder now, and I could feel it soaking through my shirt, the raindrops larger and fatter than any rain I had ever felt. "Your father never planned for it to go so long. The clue is probably gone."

"Why are you giving up?" I had to practically shout now. He was getting so far away. "You were there in the cave! You saw the other clue! Why would this be any different?"

"Because! The parking is new!" He practically spat. He had reached the stairs, grasping the railing with a hand, and through the thick raindrops he seemed to be glaring at me. "Sometimes, you just have to go home. Get on the bus and go."

"You don't ever try, do you?" I spat right back at him, "as soon as things get hard, you what, just leave?"

"We miss this bus, and we have to find our way home in the rain."

"Fine. I'd rather find the clue."

"Ok. Enjoy the weather, Jammy."

And he left.

Whatever feelings for him I had, evaporated in that moment. Poof. The rain washed them clear off me. I spun on my heels, not even wanting to look in the direction of that French coward. Maybe the stereotype was right about these people. It explained why so many of them wore those stupid white shirts.

I tried to forget about him as I went to every sign in the parking lot. The rain pummeled down on me as I turned every *no parking, handicapped only,* and *no right turn* sign upside down. Up and up the hill I climbed, stopping every meter to check anything that might be of interest.

Nothing.

"Excusez-moi, mademoiselle," said a man in a very official looking tan uniform, holding an umbrella to keep the rain off, *"mais… je peux vous aider?"*

I blinked my confusion at him. Oh crap: the way I was wandering around, lurking, he must have thought I was casing the place. A tiny teenage car thief.

"Mon Français is *tres… mal,"* I said. At this, he rolled his eyes, but said nothing. He was waiting for me to

continue. *"Chasse au trésor?"*

"Comment?"

In my limited French, I told him. I was looking for signs. He looked as confused as I felt. But when I pointed to my backpack, he put the umbrella over me, so that I could pull out the letter.

"Lettre... secret? Hidden?" I pointed to it, then to the parking lot at large.

"Caché?" he made the sign with his hands, of things being under things. I nodded: now we were getting somewhere.

"Où est..." I struggled to find the words, per usual. "Oldest sign? Old?"

I imitated walking with a cane, much to his confusion. But he got the picture. He held the umbrella over my head and pointed up the hill.

Without another word, he led me up towards the cliffs. I probably should have been worried: it was naive as heck of me to follow him in the first place. But there, at the very top of the hill, the castle ruins melded with the parking lot. I couldn't tell if it was rock or if it was a wall. We didn't go there: instead, we turned towards the lower end of the castle, towards a single *no parking* sign.

"C'est le plus vieux," he said, pointing at it. "Ze oldest!"

I was shaking - again - as I approached the old sign. It was dented and faded, seemingly older than I was, maybe even older than the man who had led me here. It was bolted to the wall with a single lead pipe, closed at the top, and...

My fingers fumbled. Open at the bottom. My heart nearly stopped when I felt the smooth film of plastic inside.

The letter was still here.

sixteen

Mon Amour,

You should have seen the look on the parking guardian's face when he found me snooping around looking at all his signs! I told him I was doing an art project, and he seemed to buy it. Filled up a whole roll of film with pictures of stop signs from odd angles just to cover my tracks. I know you're going to find them, somehow, you snoop, but I have time to come up with a compelling lie. Maybe a dog took my camera.

But I digress: it's time for your third clue. You've signed up for a treasure to hunt, and so a treasure you will find. Your next clue:

Sarah Anderson

the most Romantic theater.

You'll remember it when I tell you it's where we had our first fight.

We had only been dating two months at this point, and the end of the semester was fast approaching. We needed a day off, so the plan was to get out of town, take the train, and visit all the roman ruins of the city. The new museum had an incredible collection and we took pictures of ourselves standing behind the crumbling statues, as if we ourselves were roman nobles. We ate lunch near the arena, starting to feel the chill of winter, and we talked about the bull fights and concerts that were still held here, two thousand years after the structure was built.

You asked if our relationship would last that long. If we would still be together after a hundred years, if people would talk about us in a thousand. Your way of gaging if I felt the same way about us as you do.

And I panicked.

We spent the afternoon exploring the theater, but the entire time we were arguing. Every hiccup in our relationship was dug up, turned over, and put on display, like the marble chunks that lined the park. I brought up how your mother hated me, and you threw it back in my face, saying that I hadn't even told mine about you. It was true. I was afraid of what she would say. She never liked foreigners.

We ended up getting so loud that we had to go to the back of the park, where the grass met the wall, where our ancestors would have stood if they too were booed out of the theater for making too much noise. The argument boiled down to the biggest hurdle we had faced: our lives were just too different. Everything was against us: the Atlantic Ocean, the end of the year fast approaching, parents, and those deathly annoying tropes on television. We were simultaneously living stereotypes and avid deniers that those same stereotypes even existed.

"We like the same cheese," you said, and I laughed so hard I fell back, hitting the wall. A brick fell out.

"Oh, look at you, destroying cultural heritage," you said, petting my shoulder in a soft mock-slap. "Shame, shame!"

And all at once, the fight was over. We put the brick back in the wall and left the theater hand in hand. It didn't matter that our worlds were so different. We both wanted the same thing.

Find the brick we put back. Your next clue is there. I swear I didn't purposefully destroy any more nationally valuable property.

Love you,
Your Brioche

Valentin was waiting for me at the bottom of the parking lot, taking shelter near the vending machines. The rain was already coming to an end, turning into a hot drizzle. The man in the uniform - the parking guardian who played coy when dad came to hide the letter - was going on and on in French, still completely befuddled. I couldn't blame him. I was awestruck too.

Valentin, however, looked disappointed and drenched.

"What are you doing here?" I asked, "weren't you going to take the bus?"

"It was full," he said, rolling his eyes, "I shouldn't have expected any less."

"Well, now we're both stuck," I said, "but I at least have the letter."

Valentin snorted so loudly something shot out his nose. The rain washed it away.

Aix Marks the Spot

"C'est un ami à vous?" asked the guardian.

"He asks if I'm your friend," translated Valentin, raising an eyebrow. "What do you think, am I?"

"The man who ran off and was fully intending on leaving me here asks if he's a friend?" I crossed my arms over my chest. What he was playing at, I had no idea.

"Look, I'm sorry, I really believed that you would follow."

"Yeah. You just wanted to get home."

"Exactly," he replied. Obviously not the reaction I was hoping for. He seemed to realize this, frowning. "What?"

"Bon, je vous laisse, les enfants," said the guardian, *"rentrez bien."*

"Attendez!" Valentin shot right past me, planting himself in front of the man and spit balling in rapid French. I couldn't follow the sounds coming out of his mouth, let alone the words. All I could do was wait, arms crossed, feeling the rain fall, making my clothes cling to my skin.

When he finally turned back to me, he had the most neutral expression on his face. Oh my god, Valentin had a resting bitch face.

"He says he knows someone who can give us a ride to St Remy, and then we can take a bus to the station from there."

"Seriously?" Relief was an understatement at this point. Having a way home suddenly took the weight of the world off my shoulders. Even though it meant basically hitchhiking with a stranger.

He let us wait out the rain in his little station, though it was much too small for the three of us. He kept an eye on people who came to pay their parking, and we stood in the corner - though it was more like we took up the other half of the room - reading Dad's letter over and over again.

"This one is easy," Valentin kept repeating, "it's not even a challenge. It's Arles. That town has really cool Roman ruins. The theater is still used for concerts and shows, believe it or not. We can go there Monday."

"Because tomorrow's…"

"Sunday. Everything is closed Sunday."

Which meant I had to spend an entire day with my Mamie, or more likely, without her. Being in her home without being in her presence. Lovely.

Finally, the parking man's friend knocked on the door of the tiny office. Imagine my shock when I realized I recognized her: long dreadlocks, bandana artfully holding them back, baggy shirt and pants - even though I was too tired to really notice her on my first day in France, there were only so many people who could pull off that look.

Aix Marks the Spot

The shepherd. The one who had barked at Jean-Pascal.

"Valentin?" she said, her eyes falling on Valentin, *"Qu'es-ce que tu fais la?"*

The two launched off into excited chatter, losing me before I could even try to pick up on their words. Valentin's hands were flying around the room like crazed birds let out of their cage. Even the guard had to take a step back, not that there was anywhere for him to go.

"This is Jamie," he said, pointing to me, "she does not speak French, yet."

"Maëlle, enchanté," she replied, "nice to meet you!"

I reached a hand out to shake hers and was pulled into the bizarre kissing dance of the French.

"Jamie," I replied, *"enchanté."*

"I love your accent," she said, grinning sheepishly.

"I do, too. Yours, I mean."

We laughed. There was something about this girl that made you instantly want to be friends with her, something about her laugh that pulled you right in. My worry about missing the bus and needing a way home melted right away.

"Maëlle will bring us to the train station, so we can pick up my scooter," said Valentin, "since she's also going that way."

Even better. I silently thanked the universe for once again being on our side. "Oh my gosh, thank you. *Merci*... how do you say thank you a lot?"

"*Merci beaucoup*," said Valentin, and Maëlle waved us off.

"Please. It's my pleasure."

Her car was ridiculous: we had to fold down the front seat, so I could clamber into the back, and when I was there the seat was covered with muddy hiking boots and old clothes. Maëlle had quickly pushed them aside to make room for me to sit, but nothing could be done about the state of the seat itself.

The sun was already low on the horizon as Maëlle drove us down the hill, careful to avoid the massive tourist vans. I looked back behind us at the fortress as it shrank in the distance, a castle literally standing - in states of disrepair, but still - a thousand years. It seemed like so much in Provence was built to never change. Maybe time itself stood still in some pockets of this place.

Time. Oh shit.

"Valentin," I said, "can you translate for me, for a sec? I just need to call my Mamie. Tell her I'm going to be late."

It was probably the most nerve-wracking experience of the entire day, and I'm counting watching the bus drive away - seemingly with Valentin on it - in the middle of the rain as I was searching for a long-lost clue. Every ring was another twist of a vice around my gut. Finally, she picked up.

"Allo?"

"Mamie?" I said, putting the phone on speaker. *"Je suis désolée…"*

I told her I was going to be late tonight. To not wait up on dinner (though I knew I was going to be hungry), to save any punishment she wanted for me, but I was going to be home tonight, just late. No, I had not been drinking. Like I would ever, ever again. No, I had not been doing drugs. She seemed more worried about the drugs than all the drinking, but overall, she didn't seem to care.

When she finally hung up, Valentin's eyes were wide, and he was smiling the least reassuring smile I had ever seen. Holding his gaze was like soaking up an apology.

"What?" I asked.

"I'm having a barbeque with friends, tomorrow, if you want," he said, so much pity in his voice it was dripping out into the car, "You should meet them. They do not speak English, but they are good friends. You will like them."

"Really?"

Being invited to Valentin's, to meet his friends? Sounded like perfection. Better than dealing with my sullen Mamie all day, by far. I hadn't seen anyone my own age except Jazz and Valentin since the accident.

And maybe… if it wasn't for the pitiful look in Valentin's eyes, I could have imagined he wanted me there for more than just raising my spirits.

"So good for you!" I watched Maëlle grin through the rear-view mirror. "Is good way to make friends in the corner."

"Area, not corner," Valentin let out a laugh, "though Jamie should be the one correcting you!"

"Oh yes," she nodded eagerly, "please correct me. I want to learn to speak better."

"Me?" I scoffed, awestruck she'd even ask. "You should hear my French! I have no right to comment."

"But how else will I learn?"

The rest of the way home, she made herself speak English. But not for my benefit: for hers. It was astonishing how good it felt to be better than someone at something for once. I forgot all about my awful French, and instead wowed them with my use of English, a good old turn of phrase, some fun idioms and expressions.

"Here we say *'mêle toi de tes onions,'* but I don't think 'mess with your own onions' is the right saying?" she asked. Valentin nodded enthusiastically, looking back at me.

"It means to look at your own problems," he said. This one took a minute to catch.

"Oh! Mind your own business?"

"That's how you say it!" Said Maëlle, slapping her leg. The car shuddered for a second. "This is your stop, Valentin."

"*Merci pour tout, Maëlle,*" he said, as she pulled up to the station. I hadn't recognized the trip since we were riding in the car instead of the train. It didn't help with how dark it was getting, either. The sun was so low, the shadows made it look like it had already set.

"Jamie, you come up front, I drive you home," she said, patting the now free passenger seat, unhooking the latch that held it down. Valentin was already making his way towards his scooter in the dark: when had I missed this conversation?

"Really?"

"Iz on the way. Come."

I stepped out of the car only to get right back in. The front seat was almost as bad as the back, with mud cracking the carpets under my feet. Now long dry, the dust covered my once black sneakers.

"So..." I asked, as we pulled away from the station, my hands poised on the seat, "Woof?"

"Oh! You know WHOOPH?" I shook my head. "I am doing internship. I am apprentice with farmer. I take care of sheep and I get free bed and breakfast. Iz fun!"

Well, that explained the barking part. She fixed her eyes on the darkening road ahead, hands getting so tight on the steering wheel that her knuckles started to turn white.

"Jamie," she said, suddenly stoic and low, "you need to be careful with Valentin."

"What?" the way she had said it, her voice... it was like a whole different person was suddenly in the car with me. My hands dug into the old foam of the seat, unsure of anything that was going on now.

Already, we were reaching the driveway of Mamie's house. All too soon. She parked the car off the side of the road, so I could get out, but issued a last warning before I did.

"You will leave France soon: before, do not get too... close. It will hurt him." She ran a tongue over her suddenly dry lips.

"Um, sure," I said, nodding slowly. Every word out of her mouth was English, but I couldn't understand a thing.

I walked home even more confused than when I started. Mamie was waiting for me in the kitchen, a plate of now cold chicken before her. I knew this was a serious when I saw the French to English dictionary under her fist.

"Jamie, we must talk," She said, pushing the plate towards me. The smell of feta and green bean salad filled my nostrils, turning my stomach.

"Pas faim," I said. Not hungry. She nodded, took the plate, and put it in the fridge. The glass of water, though, I took eagerly, drinking as much as I could.

"Two days now, you gone until late," she said, carefully enunciating every word. "I am worried. Your parents warned me…"

"Oh." I realized what this was right away. This was meant to be a punishment, after all. Sending me away so I could not hurt you again. The exile of Jamie: fun was not part of the package.

And the fact that Mamie was suddenly speaking English was a worse sign than everything else combined.

"I called ze mozer of Valentin. She say she never see you."

"Yeah, because we've been having my French class outside," I said, then realized there was no way she could follow. Indignant, backpedaling Jamie spoke too fast for her own good. That was ten times too fast for someone who didn't follow English. "We are outside. All day."

"I am worried," she continued, seemingly not hearing, "zat you are hurting yourself."

"Me?" I stammered. "Hurting myself?"

Her eyes were wide, and she tightened her grip on the big fat book. I took the glass of water, swinging it back like a shot, forcing it down, trying to remain calm. I don't know what game she was playing, but it wasn't one I wanted to be a part of.

"Mamie, I am fine," I said, *"J'apprends le Français. Je fais amis."*

Her eyes sparkled: either at the announcement I had just made (two new friends really hardly counted at all, and my French classes were more of just overhearing others speaking French) or the fact that it had been in actual French.

"I want you to be ok," she said, "I want you to be… happy."

"Well, that's pretty hard if you don't fucking talk to me."

The word slipped out before I could think. My hands flew to my mouth, trying to stuff it back in, but it was too late. At home, dropping the f-bomb in front of my mother meant no phone privileges for at least a week. In front of my dad? Grounded for a month. But Mamie just blinked.

"Bon," she shrugged, whatever sparkle she had

gained from my French fading just as fast. *"C'est ta putain de vie."*

I didn't know there was a p-bomb until today, but I sure didn't like being on the receiving end of it.

seventeen

THAT NIGHT I CRASHED IN BED WITHOUT OPENING my windows, but I was tired enough to sleep through the stuffy night nonetheless. It was only when I woke up the next morning that I realized I was suffocating.

When I finally made it down to the kitchen, my English to French dictionary out on the table, waiting patiently for me to put it to use. I poured myself a cup of coffee from Mamie's press and sat down in front of it. There had always been one of these in my parent's house – well, French to English - but I had never used it. It was for translating obscure French poetry and old paperback novels about depressed women that I never had the urge to read either.

Not to mention I had an entire wealth of knowledge in the phone in my back pocket. Which I pulled out now, remembering excitedly that today was the day I would finally meet other human beings I could – potentially – talk to.

I missed talking to people.

"*Salut, ça va?*" I texted. Hi, how are you. Not too intimate, not too aloof, right? How were girls supposed to text in France? Oh god, please don't let me have just accidentally booty called my only friend in the entire country.

"I'm good. Coffeeeee." He replied, almost instantly, way too many 'e's at coffee just to emphasize how tired he was.

"*Tu ne vas pas te baigner?*" Mamie stood at the doorway, coffee cup in one hand, iPad in the other.

"*J'ai pas...*" I flipped to the page for want. "*Envie?*"

"*Allez, ça te feras du bien.*" She sounded disappointed.

The dictionary was taking too long. I opened up a translator app on my phone and started typing, trying to get the spelling right. At least she spoke slowly enough for me to make out the individual words. Apparently, swimming would make me feel good.

"*Tout à l'heure,*" I said. Later. She nodded.

"*Pratique, ton truc,*" she replied, glancing over my shoulder at the translator app. "*Quel appli?*"

I never thought I would bond with my grandmother over phone applications. I never thought my grandmother would own an iPad, either. Maybe it was this whole view of France I clung to in my head, this idyllic world caught in the past, unchanging, or maybe it was just how un-tech savvy my other grandma was but downloading apps with my Mamie in the cool of her stone kitchen had never even crossed my mind.

As she watched me play around with the app, my phone buzzed. A new text from Valentin. I didn't have time to hide it before Mamie caught a glimpse.

"*C'est ton copain?*" she asked. Is it your… I didn't know the last word, so I ran it through the app. Two translations came up for it: friend, and boyfriend. My face went red.

"Valentin," I answered, trying to avert the question. "I am going… *je vais… manger?* To eat? Barbecue."

"Oh…" she replied. Just like that, our moment was over. She took her coffee and turned around, heading back up the stairs. To her tower, I assumed. She was a paradox: she neither wanted me, nor wanted anyone else to have me.

I wish she would just talk. Tell me what she wanted from me. How I could be the granddaughter she wanted me to be. I could only guess that speaking French was on the list of criteria, but what else could have been on there, I didn't know unless she told me. And she told me nothing.

I opened Valentin's text. The prospect of getting away from here, from her, made me smile: though I was terrified of having to speak French to his friends. So long as there was food, I think I could make the most of it.

"Come to my home at 11:30," he said, "Maman will drive us both."

My mouth watered: hot dogs and burgers, dripping with cheese and ketchup and relish. Lemonade and iced tea. I couldn't wait. I wanted to leave right away.

I wasted my morning by trying to draw again. I took my sketchbook out onto the patio, and tried to draw the house, to no avail. Every time I put down a line, it seemed disjointed and out of place. The straight ones were all crooked, the climbing vines too large. Whatever artistic skill I'd had had – or thought I'd had – before the accident, it was all gone now. It took everything in my power not to toss my sketchbook into the pool.

So it was with relief and relish that I watched the clock strike 11:15 and that I got on Mamie's old bike. It felt like routine, biking to Valentin's, kissing him on both cheeks - forcing my blushing back down as I did so - and parking my bike in the back garden as his fat cat watched me with judgy eyes. What wasn't routine was getting right into his mother's car, sitting in the back as she excitedly drove us away from the village of Lourmarin.

"Valentin tells me you two went to the *Carrières des Lumières* yesterday," said Mathilde, "Did you like?"

"It was amazing," I replied honestly, "we spent hours there."

"Last year's was better," she said, "but every year is spectacular. I'm glad you are getting 'im out of ze 'ouse."

"*Maman*," Valentin hissed.

"'ave you met Maxence yet?" she asked me, ignoring him. "Valentin and 'im have been friends since they were babies. 'is mozer makes ze best beans. She is from Madagascar. Have you been?"

"To Madagascar? No."

"*Maman*," Valentin insisted, "*pourquoi tu la poses toutes ces questions?*"

"My son thinks I ask too many questions," she said, "you tell me if I do, yes?"

"Sure?"

"Oh, I am sorry, zen."

"Wait, no, I didn't mean…"

Crap. Even when I wasn't talking, I was managing to screw up conversation. I didn't even have time to correct myself, because it was then that she pulled the car into a small side road, and all words were ripped from my mouth.

We drove through an open gate to the largest house I had ever seen. It wasn't a mansion, or a castle: maybe something in between. An imposing block of a home, somehow older looking than Mamie's, all old brown stone and red shutters. Large trees like the ones that shaded the roads led our way to their front door, ushering us to rugged luxury.

Mathilde parked long enough for us to get out, then drove off again, not staying for lunch. I wondered suddenly if I should have brought something: back home I would have figured out something with the drinks, but here, I hadn't even asked.

"Relax, Jammy," said Valentin, catching my gaze, "you look stressed."

"I may have seriously overestimated my readiness for this," I muttered in reply, but my stomach's rumble drowned it out. Valentin laughed.

"Food will make all things better," he said.

"True. I haven't had a burger for ages. I can't wait."

"Burger?" He tilted his head to the side, like a confused puppy, "we are having barbecue, not burger."

"Are you telling me that barbecue doesn't mean the same in French?" I had been so excited to scoff down meat ever since he I had gotten the invitation last night. I felt my heart sink to a new low.

"The French invented barbecue," said Valentin, somehow smug through all this.

"No, they didn't."

"Ever wonder where the word came from?" He asked. I shook my head. "Well, I tell you. It was from the roast pig. You know, the one that turns?"

"You mean, a pig on a spit?" I made the gesture of rotating the meat, and he nodded.

"The stick went from the *barbe* of the pig, the beard…" he pointed to his chin, "to the *cul*."

He pointed to his rear, and I didn't need a translation for that. I burst out laughing.

"You can't be serious!"

"Ho! Mais vous attendez quoi là? Je ne suis pas votre valet!" A guy about Valentin's age appeared at the doorway of the majestic home, shaking his head at us. *"Mais rentrez, m'enfin, il fait trop chaud pour être au soleil."*

Valentin darted inside the house, so I followed, not sure of what exactly was going on. But they were embracing before I could even ask, kissing both cheeks, laughing about something incomprehensibly French. The guy turned to me, and I was struck by how handsome he was: his dark skin was sharp against his bright blue eyes, and oh my gosh, now he's kissing my cheek, and I need to kiss him back, and I…

"You are ze American?" He said, enunciating every

syllable, "My name is Maxence. What is your name?" He sounded like he was reading out of a textbook.

"Hi, um, I'm Jamie," I replied.

"Hello Jamie, nice you meet you."

We shook hands, even though we had just kissed. Somehow, this seemed weirdly more intimate. His hands were smooth and soft, except for his callused fingertips.

"*On est les premiers?*" asked Valentin, scanning the room quickly. We stood in a kitchen much like my own grandmothers, but highly modernized, clashing with the outside façade of their old home. Big bundles of garlic hung from the ceiling, filling the room with their heavenly aroma. One of the walls was covered with the same insect made out of glazed pottery, dozens of them, painted in bright vibrant colors.

"*Chloë est dehors,*" he replied, pointing out the back door, "*Pierre et Charlotte arrivent dans cinq minutes. Ils viennent de m'envoyer un texto disant qu'ils partent.* Oh. I am sorry. I do not speak English good."

"And I... *mon Français est très mal.*"

"Mauvais," said Valentin, turning to me, "your French is bad, not sick."

"Oh, thanks for that."

"*Et toi, tu ne parles pas Anglais très* well," he said to Maxence.

"Heh ben, Fuck you, *mec."*

He threw it out so casually, like it was just any other word. It seemed all the French would swear in English more readily than they ever did in their own tongue. Did swears have power, when they were not understood?

"On met la table?" asked Valentin, as his laughter subsided.

"Deja fait. Sors, y'a l'apero."

Maxence practically shoved us out the back door, where the table was already set under the shade of a willow tree. The cicadas out here were louder than anywhere I had ever been before. Out on the edge of the dining area, where gravel gave way to big bushes of laurel, blooming in pinks and reds, Chloë was on the phone, hanging up as she saw us.

"C'est Jammy!" she exclaimed, beaming. *"Comment ça va?"*

"Ça va!" I replied. "And you?"

"Am good, am good." She exchanged kisses with Valentin, then leaned towards me. I wondered how on earth the French could tolerate such a long and arduous greeting. Kisses here, kisses there, it was like it was never going to end.

It got worse when two more guests arrived, one carrying a box of rosé wine, the other a bottle of *limonade*, and the kissing started all over again. Hi to Pierre, a tall, string bean of a man with a mop of black hair, like an elongated Harry Potter; and his sister, Charlotte, a petite, round girl with wavy hair. They didn't look anything like siblings. She positioned herself by Chloë like she owned her, despite being half her size.

"Apéro!" shouted Maxence as he came out of the kitchen, tray in hand. We made our way to the table, and then the kissing commenced again, as Maxence's parents came out of the house.

Oh crap. They told me their names again and I missed it and by reflex just nodded and smiled... It's fine, I guess. I didn't really need to know their names if I wasn't going to be able to talk to them anyway. We have Maxence's dad, the French guy lighting the tiny grill, and Maxence's mother, who's showing us the marinated meats, placing them next to the grill, saying something that makes everyone laugh. I laughed awkwardly along, not even sure why.

At least, it seemed, that our barbecues were not all that different. There were sausages, one kind red like it was dumped in paprika, and there were skewers of peppers and pork, or lamb, it was hard to follow with Valentin missing a few words in translation, turning to me and throwing out French words and not realizing, saying things to Maxence's mother in English, making her laugh when she realized he wasn't doing it on purpose.

He sat between Maxence and me, across from Chloë and Charlotte. The two were going on about something that was apparently both thrilling and not exciting at all, making them in deep conversation but quiet and contemplative at the same time. Maxence's parents took the other side, putting me at the furthest point from Harry-Potter-Pierre, who seemed as out of it as I was.

Now Chloë was serving us all rosé from the box, and Maxence's parents weren't saying anything about it. I couldn't understand them – well, I already couldn't understand the language, but the culture was ten times more confusing. Maybe the wine would help. Or… make it worse? I wasn't quite sure.

Oh. I wasn't supposed to drink it yet. Everyone is toasting something. I throw in my own hand, but Valentin puts a hand on my shoulder before I can clink my first glass.

"You do not cross arms," he said, insistently, like I had just stepped on a landmine. "And you make eye contact. No crossing. Look them in the eyes."

"What? Why?"

"Or seven years bad sex," said Chloë, reaching out her glass to me. "Now look in my eyes…"

I was blushing red as I did, but we clinked glassed properly, and she nudged me to reach out for the rest of the table.

"Then you do not put down your glass until you take a sip," Valentin added, "or again, bad luck."

"Bad sex!" Chloë insisted.

"Do not tell her... eh... *sotises*," said Maxence's mom. "*Valentin. C'est quoi le mot?*"

"Nonsense?"

"Do not tell her ze nonsense."

I took a sip of the wine, smiling, pretending to like it. I wasn't a wine drinker, and the rosé was cold and bittersweet, a little acidic, like grapefruit juice. It wasn't as sweet as I had expected it to be, and somehow was weirdly refreshing. I could sorta see why people called it summer water. I filled my water glass with the lemonade instead and was slightly disappointed to see it was some kind of Sprite. Whatever: it still tasted comfortingly common.

"Jammy, where are you from?" asked Maxence, leaning over the table. "In America?"

"Philadelphia," I replied. Charlotte nodded across the table, as if I were describing the weather. "It's in Pennsylvania."

"Philadelphia, close to New York?" she asked.

"It's not that close, but I guess?"

She nodded again, but this time, I don't think she understood me. I guess I wasn't the only one to nod and move on at the table.

Luckily, Maxence started passing food around, and the awkward conversation was over. Valentin pulled a slice of cantaloupe off the plate, passing it along to me. Dried Parma ham and balsamic topped it off, like something at a fancy restaurant. This wasn't at all the barbecue I had expected: a handful of friends sitting down and eating, with actual courses, wasn't at all the meal I had in mind. But dang was that melon good.

"What's an *Apéro*, exactly?" I asked Valentin, as inconspicuously as I could.

"Snack before the meal," he explained, "chips, nuts, drinks."

"Melon?"

"The entrée."

"Oh," I said, confused. I thought the meat was the entrée. None of this made any sense. If you saw tears coming out of my eyes, I wasn't crying: it was literally my brain melting in frustration.

I needed a distraction. I listened to the conversation, picking up words here and there, as I ate my melon and nibbled at the snacks. There was a thick green olive paste which I spread over dried bread like hummus, so salty it was addicting. I was probably putting on fifteen pounds just by sitting at this table. Halfway through eating a jar of it all by myself I suddenly picked up words in English.

"Does it make sense to you?" asked Chloë, sipping at her wine.

"Does what do what now?"

"*Verlan*," explained Valentin, "when we speak *à l'envers*. Backwards: Ver-Lan."

"I already don't understand French," I sputtered, "if you started speaking backwards on me, I probably wouldn't notice."

He relayed this to his friends, who seemed to find this hilarious.

"So if we wanted to say bizarre, we say *Zarbie*," he continued.

"Why are you telling me all this? What did I miss?"

His face fell. "You haven't been following anything since we got here?"

I shook my head. I wanted to bury my face in the wine glass. "*Non*."

"Oh," he said, solemnly, forcing a smile, "we were joking about how you didn't pick the best place to come to learn French. In the south, we have our own languages. Provençal, the original tongue, isn't spoken much, but there is an accent. And our vulgar words are different from Paris. And we have verlan, too."

"Here is my English," said Pierre suddenly, from the other side of the table. He cleared his throat. "Where is Brian?"

All at once, like a wave of sound, they answered in unison, "Brian is in the kitchen!"

My eyes went wide in what could only be called terror. I needed to warn the Americans right away: France was brainwashing its people to know where some guy named Brian was currently standing. Or maybe there was a guy named Brian in *their* kitchen? I glanced over at the door. It didn't look like anyone was in there.

"Did you take French class in *lycée*?" asked Charlotte.

"High School," corrected Chloë, "like ze musical."

"I did," I replied, "but it's just my first year. Did you take English?"

"We all take English," Charlotte replied, "Since primary school. I take Spanish as my second. Did you have to pick French name for class?"

I smiled at this. "I did! I am Amélie. Like the movie?"

"*Amélie Poulain?*" she said perfectly, "I had to pick American name. Say hello to Stacy."

"I am Tracy!" Chloë raised her hand. "And I am pom-pom girl!"

"You mean a cheerleader?"

"We did a project where we had to pretend we were

an American student," said Valentin, "I was Josh."

He threw out the name like it was a wave crashing on the beach. Somehow, it sounded like the most angelic sound when it washed over his lips. I wanted to sink into it. He looked far too sophisticated for a simple Josh. No offence to any Joshes present.

Instead, I unleashed the most un-sexy snort in the history of snorts. The idea of a classroom full of 'Josh's and 'Tracy's was so weirdly hilarious I couldn't hold back my laughter. Golden age Americana invading the nation.

"He and me, we write story how we are football players," explained Maxence, "and we were, as you say, popular. We got very good mark."

"Qui veut des merguez?" asked Maxence's father, pulling the reddish sausages off the flame. He passed the now overflowing plate to his wife, who slipped two onto her plate and passed them on.

"Be careful, these have spice," said Valentin, as the plate reached us. "They are hot."

"You no have merguez in America?" asked Pierre.

"No, I don't think so."

"They have burgers," said Chloë, before turning to me, "Can you say Burger?"

"Um, Burger, why?"

Her grin exploded on her face. "Ha! Buuurger. I

love it. Your accent is *adorable.*"

Her comment didn't exactly hurt: no, it was different from that, because part of me liked hearing her like something about me that I had no control over. But the other part, the one who lived with Mamie, tutted in the back of my brain.

"And what about my accent, Chloë?" asked Valentin, wagging his eyebrows at her, "do you find it *adorable* too?"

"I find it *zarbie* as hell," she replied, and the table burst into laughter.

"Le beau est toujours bizarre," said Valentin proudly, "the beautiful is always weird."

"Baudelaire," agreed Maxence's mother.

I realized in that moment that none of them cared how I spoke. I had never noticed Valentin's accent or even Chloë's when they spoke to me, I was just so relieved to understand them. Ok, that was a lie: I was in love with Valentin's accent. Maybe that was too strong a word, but the more he spoke, the more I found I adored the sound of his voice. As he translated the conversation for me, bringing me in from the sidelines to include me; as he tripped and stumbled over words, or corrected me as I butchered his; as he repeated words to make sure he got them right, or I did, I realized that the words leaving his lips were more beautiful than any I had ever heard before.

I didn't think it was possible to fall in love with someone's voice before. For an accent to be an actual accent, worn proudly like a golden pin. I found myself listening more to how he said the words, than the actual words he said, nodding and agreeing along until I was a living bobble head.

But maybe I wasn't in love with the voice. Or the words. Maybe, just maybe, I had fallen for the man who spoke them.

eighteen

LUNCH IN FRANCE WASN'T MEASURED IN MINUTES. It was measured in hours and bottles of wine.

Meat after meat came off the grill, each more flavorful than the last, Maxence came out of the kitchen with a heaping plate of cheeses and an armful full of fresh bread. Around the table, we ripped off pieces of the crispy baguette, no cutting board required. Cheese was sliced and passed as wine glasses were refilled.

It didn't end there. We had somehow forgotten the salad, so out came a bowl of fresh green leaves topped with balsamic and olive oil, and another of the sliced tomatoes and basil. At this point, we barely had room for more, but Maxence's mother came back out with bowls of fresh cut strawberries and whipped cream for dessert, and none of us could say no.

By the time my glasses were empty, Maxence was bringing us tiny cups of coffee, shots of pure espresso. I was going to need it: the food had made me so tired, I felt like I was dozing off right then and there. A new equation entered my mind: wine + food coma = negative language skills. Even Valentin seemed to support that theory, drifting deeper and deeper into um's and *hein*'s as the meal came to a close.

"*Ca vous dit une partie de Boules?*" offered Maxence's dad.

"*T'es pas serieux...*" the son muttered, patting his belly.

"*C'est moi qui a fait toutes les grillades,*" he insisted, getting to his feet. "*Allez. Quatre equipes?*"

"What's going on?" I asked, as everyone on their end of the table griped and groaned. Valentin looked a little dazed. More than a little: he kept patting his belly like it was a dog that needed reassurance.

"It looks like we're playing *pétanque*," he said, "François insisted, since he did all the cooking."

Ah. François. I told myself to remember the name, but in my post-feast state, my thoughts were fading fast. How anyone in this country wasn't fat I had no idea. We all had to waddle to the front side of the house, where the gravel path was spacious enough for cars to park, though none were here now.

"And what exactly is *pétanque*?"

"Iz for old people," said Chloë. "*Charlotte est dans mon équipe!*"

"*Maxence!*" Pierre nodded at his friend, who responded with an equally curt nod. "*Gros!*"

Wait, I knew that word. Did he just call him a fatty?

"My team?" asked Valentin, making my heart soar. I knew we were the only ones left not yet paired up, so of course we would make a team, but still there was something about hearing him ask that made me all warm on the inside. The Nutella crepe feeling returned.

I nodded, maybe a little too eagerly, before realizing what I was getting into and forcing myself to stop.

"I've never played before," I said, "I'll drag you down."

"Don't worry, we're only playing for butter."

"For what? Butter?"

"He says the game is for no," said Chloë.

"Don't you have a teammate to stand by?" he snapped at her playfully. "You already stole Charlotte, do not rub it in my face."

"Wow, you talk garbage in English," she said, caught between awestruck and sarcastic.

"You mean the trash-talk?"

She turned around and trotted over to Maxence, who was pulling out pouches of shiny metal balls, checking them for who knows what before handing them out to the newly formed teams.

"So what is this game?" I asked, feeling dizzy from the heavy meal and the gentle hint of alcohol I had ingested. Come on coffee, do your stuff.

"It's easy, in principle," he said. "We throw a little ball, the *cochonet*, out into the field. Then we take turns throwing the balls as close as we can to it. The team with the most closest wins."

"That does sound easy," I said. It also didn't sound like much fun, like a French corn-hole. It was fun for maybe one round, but then people always seemed to want to do the same thing for hours.

Maxence handed me my metal balls, and I was shocked by how heavy they were. The shiny spheres had rings embossed around them, each set slightly different so they could be better told apart. The tiny yellow ball was thrown, landing about fifteen feet away, and the game began.

It was astonishingly slow, but we were so full of food that it didn't really matter. Time had somehow slowed down for all of us, even the beats between cicada chirps seemed to be stretching out. We took turns throwing our balls, trying to get close to the little cochonet. Maxence was amazingly good at this, somehow hitting opponents spheres so they busted out of the way.

"So is this... um... some kind of national pastime?" I asked, my palm sweaty against the silver orb.

"Maybe in the south," said Valentin, "people joke it's an old person's game. But I learned it in primary school."

I tried imagining little Valentin and other kids, armed with heavy metal balls and instructed to throw as hard as they can. That couldn't have ended well.

After everyone had thrown, we scored points, and began again. Over, and over again. But it didn't seem like the point was to play the game: we were all just standing there, together, chatting and laughing, though I only picked up half the words that were being said.

Still, half of the words was better than where I was at when I first got here. I was slowly getting the gist of conversations, thanks to Valentin's help.

"*Une dernière partie?*" asked François, as he picked up the *cochonet*.

"*Allez,*" said Maxence. Everybody nodded.

"One last party?" I asked. Valentin smiled.

"One last round," he replied, "we're one point behind with Maxence right now. What do you say we beat him?"

"What? We're second?" I couldn't believe my ears. The scoring system was so confusing (why was there even rope involved?) that I hadn't followed that part at all.

"We make a good team," he said, picking up our *boules* and handing mine to me. "Let's show them evidence of international cooperation."

One by one, we threw our boules. Silence fell over us as we concentrated on our last throws. My heart raced as my first one landed not even an inch from the cochonet. Valentin cheered, which only made my heart beat faster.

His misbehaving curl swung across his forehead, which he diligently pushed back into place. I wanted to tell him to leave it there: he looked so good, even those tiny flaws made him more perfect. He caught me looking at him, and I watched as his smile stretched wider across his face, those perfect lips spreading with joy.

I found myself wanting to touch them, to press my lips against his, to see how soft they really were. But then Chloë was stepping up to throw, and I had to move away, and the moment vanished.

"A kiss?" she asked, "for good luck?"

I turned just in time to see Charlotte reach up on tip toes and press her lips against hers. My heart fluttered: not just at seeing the cutest couple I hadn't realized was actually a couple, and marveling at how perfect they were together, but at the realization that Chloë wasn't at all who I thought she was. For some reason, I had imagined her a competition, when neither of us had been competing at all. Why it was ingrained in me to immediately think a gorgeous woman was someone to beat, I did not know, but I hated myself for it.

And loved her for setting my heart free.

Her throw landed her close to the cochonet: closer than any other one but mine. So I guess she was competition, after all.

They played their last hands, until the ground was littered with metal *boules*. The last throw was mine, but there was no chance I was getting any closer than Chloë's. My brow furrowed in concentration.

"You're going to have to push that one away," said Valentin, his voice lowered to a whisper, despite the fact that we were playing the last move. Maybe I should have asked him for a good luck kiss, though that would probably make me feint instead of win.

"I'm not sure I can aim that accurately," I replied, my voice lowering to match his. My eyes were riveted on the little silver ball with two concentric rings around it. The only thing between us and victory.

"You need to throw like this." Valentin reached for my hand, turning the wrist so it was upside down, holding the ball from above. "You can do this. I believe in you."

His fingers were warm against mine, more than warm. The electricity of his touch ran up my arm and filled me with a flutter I had never felt before.

No way I was throwing accurately now.

"You want to take my turn?" I asked him.

"*Hé!* Your turn. You play!" said Maxence, "*Allez!*"

Valentin stepped back, and it was like all the breath left me at once. I had to play, I had to throw now, before I couldn't breathe any longer. I clutched the ball tightly, pulled back my arm like I was bowling, and launched it into the air.

Time stood still as it vaulted through the air. It arced over the gravel, spinning and spinning until it came down with a hand crash. It rolled and rolled, until it came up on Chloë's, only to slightly tap it.

"Is that it?" I asked, "did we win? *Nous a… gagné?*"

"*On a gagné*," said Valentin.

"*Non!*" Maxence interjected, somewhat indignantly. He stormed up to the boules and pulled out the measuring string for scoring. "*On ne sait pas!* We do not know!"

"*Je la corrigeais, Max.*"

"Ignore the boys," said Chloë, "that was good throw. You play good, for American."

"She played excellent," added Charlotte, "you jealous."

"Jealous, impressed," Chloë grinned, "You cool, America."

"*Merci*," I replied, "*les filles.*" Thanks, girls. They smiled, enough of a congratulations to go around.

Meanwhile, Maxence and Valentin, along with François, were crouching over the balls, intently measuring them with the strings.

"*Celle de Chloë est plus près,*" said Maxence, "*un point, donc égalité!*"

"*Non, celle de Jammy est plus près,*" said Valentin, "*deux points, on est les champions!*"

"What is happening?" I asked the girls. Charlotte shrugged. Apparently, shrugging was just as integral to French language as actual words were.

"*Deux points!*" called François, standing. "*L'équipe Franco-Américaine remporte la Victoire!*"

"*La vache,*" said Charlotte.

"The cow?" I spun around, but the only animals in sight were the horses in a nearby pasture. "Where?"

"*Non, la vache,* it means…"

"It does mean cow, but, wow, cow!" said Chloë.

"We win!" said Valentin, and before I knew what was coming, he lifted me in the air, spinning me around before my weight caught up with him and he had to put me down.

"We won?"

"We won!" I couldn't believe it. I had beat them at their own game. Though I felt like I had won for another reason. Valentin stood so close to me, I could feel his breath against my skin. "Beginner's luck?"

"Americans! They come to France, they take our games!" Said Maxence, obviously pleased with himself.

While time had stood still for our game, it had to catch up with itself to make up for what we had missed. The rest of the afternoon passed in a blur. It was suddenly four o'clock, and a blink later, it was six, and then again, it was eight. None of us were hungry anymore: we had all eaten well, and snacked on melon or cheese, whatever hadn't been devoured at lunch, unwilling to say goodbye.

Even when Valentin's mother showed up, we didn't leave right away. She meandered into the garden, kissing everyone, grabbed a glass of wine and sat down with us.

"Jammy, did you like ze food?" she asked, reaching for a strawberry.

"*Très bon*," I replied, "and the company was even better."

The afternoon had been perfect. For the first time since arriving in France, I felt like I belonged. Not perfectly, not by a long shot: but somehow, I was fitting in, and people actually seemed to like having me there. Maxence's parents metaphorically wrapped their arms around me and made me feel like family, making me miss my own even more.

I wondered if this is what it was like for you, when you came here on your year abroad. If people took you in, if Aix welcomed you with open arms the way Lourmarin did me. How the people here taught me to speak and listened to what I had to say, how our cultures started to tangle and mesh, finding similarities and laughing at the differences.

Then I remembered Mamie waiting for me in her large, empty home, and everything fell backwards yet again.

We said goodbye, exchanging kisses and Facebook friendships. I didn't know how to ask when we would hang out again: I craved their company now more than ever, and it seemed like they at the very least found me mildly entertaining. Maybe, just maybe, that would be enough.

Mathilde drove us back to her house, apologizing for not having picked me up from Mamie's in the first place. She went on and on about my bike, though I'm not sure what about, because my tired – and still a little teensy bit tipsy - mind couldn't make heads or tails of her accent. I didn't mind. Buoyed by bubbly feelings in my chest, she could have told me they were amputating my arm and I would have smiled and nodded.

"Give me a minute to find mine," said Valentin, as I rolled my bike from out of his yard.

"You don't have to do that," I said. He shook his head.

"I'm taking you home, whether you like it or not. There might be boar on the way, after all."

I laughed, but he remained dead serious. Oh. Were there actual boar around these parts? Like in Dad's stories?

"I'll race you, then," I said, running on the high I had from such an amazing day.

"Ah! Traitor! You turn on your team like this? My heart, it breaks!"

He found his red bike, an old, dusty thing, covered in mud and scratches. The only part of it that didn't make a sound was the bell. He got on the creaky old thing and, before I had a chance to mount mine, pushed off towards the road.

"You cannot catch me!" he exclaimed, "I am the unbeatable!"

I did catch up with him, but before I could pass him there was a car and I had to slow to let it get past us. Then the race was on again, the two of us neck and neck, flying towards the setting sun.

When we reached Mamie's gate I didn't want it to end. My heart was pounding in my chest, and not just from racing. It might have been from the beautiful disheveled hair of the cute Frenchman before me, feebly attempting to rein it back into place as he dismounted his bike.

"It's a tie," I said, trying not to breathe as heavily as my body wanted to. It wasn't a good look for me.

"No, it's not," he said. With on swift move, he touched the gate of her estate. "I win!"

"I got off my bike first, so I win!" I replied.

"Fine, it's equality," he said, "but I get points for having to go back."

"Agreed."

Neither of us knew exactly what to say next. It was odd, this feeling inside me, one where I just wanted to blurt out everything that was going through my head: how happy I was he had invited me into his circle of friends, how proud that we had won the weird lawn bowling game, how thankful I was that he had taken me home.

How handsome he looked, with the setting sun casting him in shades of pink. How I could see his Adam's apple bob when he breathed, and how much it made me want to press my lips to his neck. How I wanted to run my hand through his - albeit sweaty –

mop of hair, feeling his curls around my fingers.

"I, eh, I will go," he said, grasping the handlebars of his bike. His knuckles were white against his skin.

"Wait," I said. Now was the time to say it. To say everything. To tell him that there were feelings bubbling inside me for which there weren't words in any language.

"Yes?" he asked, and there was an eagerness to his voice which I must have been reading into.

"The cicadas have stopped."

And negative a thousand points for Jamie! There goes all my experience with flirting, not that there was anything to begin with. Even so, Valentin was smiling his oh-so-familiar smile. It wasn't big and toothy like the guys at my school back home. His smile was a line, revealing nothing, except maybe, just maybe, that he wanted to stay, too.

"Valentin," I said, slowly, gripping my own bike so tightly my fingers went numb. "Thank you. Thank you so much for today. For everything."

"It was just a barbecue," he replied, with that whole-body shrug of his. "And I didn't even cook."

"You brought me to meet your friends," I said. Something caught in my throat: oh god, I wasn't going to cry, was I? I wasn't that emotional. "You helped me understand them. You helped them understand me.

You gave me a voice, Valentin, in a country where I have none."

"You always had a voice, Jamie," he said, and my name rolled off his tongue perfectly, no jam attached. "I might have just helped you find it, but it was always there. And I love your voice."

"I owe you one hell of a good autograph from Mamie," I muttered, rolling his words through my mind, biding myself time to process what he had just said.

Loved. Loved. *Loved*.

We moved into another language, then. A language where lips didn't say words but connected one to one. A language where tastes and smell were more important than sound and sight. One where I finally felt that hair of his, just as I had been wanting to since the first moment we met.

He held me gently pressed up against him, one hand on my back, the other gently cradling my head, as mine wildly grasped for his. His lips were soft against mine, welcoming discussion, tasting of melon and sweet summer wine.

I could have kissed the sun from the sky, the way I was kissing him. I wanted him on my skin like I wanted sunlight in my life, drinking him in, soaking him in.

When we came up for breath, he ran his fingers through my hair, gazing at me with a look I had only dreamed of ever being on the receiving end of. The same look in his eyes that I saw when we went to Cassis or even when Jean-Pascal drove me to the castle on the very first day I was here. It wasn't a look of fiery, passionate adoration, but a warm, overwhelming look, one of a bond deeper than roots in soil. The same look I am sure he was seeing as he looked into my own eyes.

The look of coming home.

nineteen

PEOPLE WHO THINK THAT PARIS IS ROMANTIC have certainly never been to Provence before. There is simply nothing like kissing a French boy under a pink sunset, as the cicadas wrap up their daily sonata, rosemary and lavender wafting in the air.

I pushed my bike up the hill to the house, too wobbly to bike on my own. I was past feeling bubbly, now, I felt like dessert, sweet and melty and warm in the middle, like the Nutella crepe in Lex Baux. No other words fit: I didn't know how else to describe the feelings in my chest, confusing and comforting all at once.

Valentine liked me. More than liked me. And he kissed me: *he* kissed *me*. After thinking I was going mad, seeing things that weren't there, projecting onto him what I wanted to see, even after all that, I wasn't imagining any of it at all.

My hand rose to my lips, the tingle of his kiss still there. Pure magic.

It was getting dark, twilight descending on the little Durance valley, and so Mamie wasn't in her tower. Nothing to worry about, especially since she didn't want to see me, anyway. I half expected to run into her in the kitchen, but the room was empty when I got there, even the heavy dictionary cleared off, making it look abandoned.

She had probably simply gone to bed early, I shouldn't have been worried. She had her schedule and I had mine. But as I stepped over the threshold, all the warmth from Valentin's kiss was washed away by a frigid cold. Something was dreadfully wrong.

"Mamie?" I called out, sweeping my eyes over the small room. "Mamie? I am home!" And then, just to be sure she wasn't going to play her French card, I added my new vocabulary for good measure. "*Je suis la!*" I am here!

Nothing.

I took the stairs up to the landing, scanning my eyes over the living room. The front door was wide open, letting in a gentle evening breeze. Strange, she always kept it closed.

Panic was beginning to rise in my gut, filling the hole

left by the now missing warm fuzzy feelings. I dashed across the room to the door, throwing it open all the way so I could see the garden. Nothing. Not even a ripple in the pool. I closed it behind me, struggling with the handle, all the worst possible things running through my head.

I had left her alone, and someone had attacked. Burglary gone wrong? Kidnapping the acclaimed author? I didn't know, all I knew was that it was my fault, again, and I…

I shouldn't have jumped to conclusions. As I turned around I saw her slouched on the couch, one hand cradling a now empty bottle of wine, the glass sitting on the table a good distance away.

She had been sleeping, but my slamming of the door had inadvertently woken her. She grumbled something under her breath as she pushed herself up to a sit. Dizzy, she brought a hand to her head, the other one still clasping the wine bottle.

"Qu'est-ce que tu fais là?" she muttered. What are you doing here?

"I came home," I replied, "from the barbecue, remember?"

I had never dealt with a drunk person older than myself. Heck, I had never dealt with a drunk person *when* I wasn't drunk myself. Taking care of a wasted senior was not part of the job description.

"For a minute, I thought you were *ta mère*," she said. Your mother. Half the words came out English; the other half, French, strung together in a drunken slur.

"Mamie, what did you do?" I asked, "what happened?"

"*Rien*, nothing happened," she said. She tried to push herself up to a seat, failed, and fell back on her elbows again. I reached down to take the bottle from her hand.

"You need to get to bed."

"And you need to speak French!" she snapped right back, eyes shining with the glimmer of tears, "I know what you're doing with that boy, and it's not classes. You're just like your mother. You bring your stupid American ways to this country and expect everyone to follow you. No. I will not let this happen again."

"Again?" I froze, still holding the wine bottle. Slowly, I sat down on the couch beside her, putting the glass out of her reach.

"Every year, they come. Students. Au pairs. Tourists. Wanting their perfect French man. They come, they take what they want, and they wash away thousands of years of history, just like that. Your mother was no different, and neither are you."

I should have taken her words as the blabbering of

a delusional drunk, but they stung deep. Her English was better than when she was sober. I slid away from her, sudden scared of the small woman.

"What did you say about my mother?"

"American whore," she spat, tears now running freely down her face. The words chilled the blood in my veins. *"Espèce de pute!* She comes to this country. She takes our food. She takes our wine. And she takes my son."

Mamie was shaking now, and so was I. I wanted to run, screaming from this room. I wanted nothing more than to fly back home and forget this woman was even related to me. But before I could even move, she thrust a bony hand and grabbed my wrist tight.

"You belonged here," she hissed, "she should not having taken you away from me. You are my blood. The waters of Provence run through your veins. You are wasted in a country so disgusting."

Her words ran together in a twisted Frenglish. I struggled to understand her, though I didn't want to. I wanted to get her far, far away from me.

"That American Whore as you call her, that's my mother," I said, the word tumbling out of my mouth like vomit. I ripped my hand from her grasp, but she was stronger than she looked. I could feel my heart beating in my wrist, claw marks up my forearm. "And she was there for me every second of my life. Which cannot be said of you."

"Your mother decided to take you away." She flicked her wrist into the air. "I told your father that if he were to leave with her, he would not be welcome back. He chose her. He chose her over me. He wanted the fancy American, with the fast cars and big houses. She seduced him away. Even his own mother could not save him."

She brought her hands to her eyes, sobbing wildly into them. Mascara ran down her cheeks, turning her hands muddy and black.

"If it was not for her, my son would still be here. She poisoned his thoughts. That's the problem with you Americans: you take what you want. You think everything belongs to you. Mark my words, when she gets tired of her French man, she will take someone else. Spit him out into the garbage."

"That's not true!"

I was standing now, blood boiling. Her words were sharper than glass, cut deeper than anything I had ever felt before. It took all of my willpower not to spit at her.

In that moment, there was no one I hated more than this woman who claimed to be my blood. I saw nothing of my father in her. I didn't want her anywhere near me.

"My mother did not come here to take from you,"

I spat, "she came here to learn from you. And you closed your door on her and turned her away. You want to know why my father chose her? He chose her because you pushed him away!"

"No. He chose her because of you."

If the room was cold before, it was colder still now. I was standing in a freezer, my blood boiling and ice cold all at once.

"Your mother told him she was pregnant," she said, and she was smiling now. No, sneering. "She came to the house. I told him she was using you as a way to tie him down. That if she were not with child, he could not want her near him. She tricked him. He went for you. He chose her, *for you*. And I never saw him again."

Me, me… it was always my fault. Since before the day I was born, I was here, ruining lives. I caused the rift between my grandmother and my father. I'm the reason he chose my mother over his own blood and left his homeland for good.

Me.

My fault.

Always my fault.

"Do not make the mistakes I made," she said, her sentence punctuated by a small hiccup, "your heart belongs to Provence. Do not be seduced by America. All they want is for the world to be their theme park.

They don't care about the people who live anywhere else. They don't care about our culture. All they care about is themselves."

"Mamie, please, you're scaring me," I said, taking a step back.

"Go back where you came from," she hissed, "I don't want to ever see you again. Tomorrow I want you out of my house, I want you gone. You are no blood of mine."

Maybe I proved her point by leaving her alone. Maybe I did care more about myself and my breaking heart than my mad old Mamie sobbing drunkenly on the living room couch. I ran up the stairs to my room and locked the door shut, heart racing.

Trembling, sobbing, I picked up my phone, turning on the data and dialing the only number I knew by heart. Jazz. Jasmine always knew what to say. Even after the accident, she had been there for me.

But the phone went to voicemail after a single ring.

She had hung up on me.

Even my best friend didn't want me. I was spoiled goods, born rotten. A curse to everyone I met.

I was the reason everything was wrong with my world.

twenty

THE RIDE TO ARLES WAS A SILENT ONE.

I was getting used to the buses now. Admittedly I was liking the trains better, but these rides weren't far off in terms of comfort. I would even have been enjoying myself if it wasn't for Mamie's voice signing circles in my head.

Just like my mother… just like my mother… I'm the reason my father never saw France again…

I had stuffed odd clothes in my backpack, along with my computer and a toothbrush. I would have to find another place to sleep tonight. Maybe I could reach into my savings, find a hotel, or an Airbnb, something, anything. I couldn't go back to that house: I didn't know what Mamie would do to me if I went back, if she would even let me on the grounds.

What did she tell you? Was she sending me back? Returning me, for not matching the description?

If Valentin had noticed something was off, he didn't say anything about it. He was good when it came to silence. He never had to fill awkward moments with words. One hand resting lightly on his lap, the other hanging in the aisle, he stared out through the window straight ahead, letting me have my moment.

I wanted to wrap myself in his arms and sob. If our kiss the night before had meant anything, he should be here for me now. But I couldn't ask that of him, not after every bridge I touched burned to ash. I had been destroying lives since conception.

The bus stopped, and instantly the quiet was broken. Three teenagers stepped onto the bus, the guy in a Hawaiian shirt and the two girls in practically see-through white blouses and mini shorts. Sunglasses and sunhats snugly on their heads, nothing about them walked by without screaming 'tourist.'

And that wasn't counting the actual screaming.

"I'm getting so good at paying the bus drivers," said one of them, leading her friends down the aisle of the bus. Valentin straightened up, retracting his arm. She brushed past him.

"Still, it's like, so dumb we have to haul all these coins around. Hello, paper money exists, people!"

Sarah Anderson

They took a seat near the end of the bus and we got back on the road. I thought that would be the end of it, but no: they just somehow, unbelievably, got louder.

"God, I hope there's a Starbucks in Arles," said one of them, "like, the coffee here sucks. Mom said we needed to stop at a cafe but all they have are these ridiculous tiny cups!"

"It's like drinking coffee sludge," said the guy, "and it's like none of them know what a latte is! It's summer? Can you not put ice in coffee for me? It's that easy!"

Valentin's hands tensed into fists. His eyes never left the road, but I could see them bulging in their sockets even from here.

"When I get to Arles, first thing I do, I'm going to find that Starbucks," said the first girl, sighing heavily, "I need to wash that taste out of my mouth."

"Sasha, they don't have one there," said the other girl.

"No Starbucks? What is this place?" she said, her voice somehow rising a higher pitch. "Look, if I have to have another one of those disgusting little cups…"

"Just ask for a café creme," said the guy.

"I can't drink cream. It's bad for my complexion."

"It's not actually cream, it's milk," said the second girl.

"Then why the hell do the call it cream?"

I sank lower into my chair. The more outraged she was, the more shrill her voice became.

I wasn't the only one having trouble with her, though. The people around me I could tell were tensing up too. Cringing, if I could say so. Valentin's fists were tight as lead.

"I have to say something," said Valentin, turning to me.

"Please don't," I mumbled, "It's not worth it."

He climbed out of his seat, making his way to the back of the bus. I leaned forward, breathing deeply. Hopefully they wouldn't see me if I was hunched over like this.

"S'il vous plaît," he said, calmly, *"on n'entend que vous."*

"What?" one of the girls laughed in response, "piss off. We're not bothering anyone. Speak English, dumbass."

"I do speak English," he replied, "which is more than I could say for you. Now please, there are other people on this bus, could you tone it down?"

"OOOOH!" the guy of the group sounded like Valentin had just dropped an epic rap burn. "Shorty's got attitude!"

"Shorty has no patience," said Valentin, "please. There are other people here than just you."

"Yeah!" yelled someone from up front. A girl

clambered over her seat, "keep it down back zere!"

"If you don't like it, get a car, loser!"

"Next time you want to see France, go to ze EPCOT, you'd 'ave a better time!"

She sat back down. My face was hot, red with embarrassment.

Stupid American, stupid American... my Mamie's voice danced circles in my head. I needed to be anywhere but here right now.

"Bon, Merde, passez une bonne journée," said Valentin. He slipped back into his seat beside me, having changed absolutely nothing. He was fuming, though. While my face was red with shame, his was hot with rage.

"I just had to say something. I couldn't hear myself think."

"I know," I replied, half wishing they would keep speaking in their obnoxiously loud voices. At least I wouldn't have to hear the words in my own head.

"Are you doing alright?" he asked, then. "You look a little…"

"I'm fine," I lied, "I don't think I was ready for *merguez* quite yet. I just… feel ill."

"Do you have a *gastro*? Do you need *smecta*?"

I shook my head. I didn't need anything. Just to be left alone.

Maybe so I could die under a rock.

The bus dropped us off and we piled off, trying to get as far away from the loud trio as possible. Luckily, you didn't need to be a bat to echolocate them. I kept my head down as I shuffled through the town, hands stuffed in pockets. I was the reason you couldn't come back, so I didn't deserve to see a single thing here.

"You shouldn't have said anything."

I don't know where the words came from. At first, I didn't even think I had been the one to say them. We stopped, and I finally looked up, only to see ruins rising from the earth behind the tall iron fence. I preferred to look at them than make eye contact with Valentin right then.

"Why not?" he asked, opening the door to the visitor's center of Theatre Antique of Arles. Air conditioning hit us in a wave, and for a second I was able to relax just a little. Then I saw his face, and the nerves came right back.

"They were annoying, but you didn't have to confront them about it."

"*Deux moins de 18 ans*," he said to the grey-haired woman behind the desk. I flashed her my driver's license, and she nodded. We paid cash, argument on hold until we dealt with the fee.

Outside, the sun was back with a vengeance. But who cared about the sun when two thousand years of history stood before you? Argument on hold indefinitely. Fuming placed on pause. There was nothing I wanted to distract me from this.

A semi-circle of stone seats rose up towards the sun in front of a raised wooden stage. Two columns were all that was left of the original back, but they stood beside state-of-the-art sound equipment. I didn't know what impressed me most: the fact that the entire semi-circle was still intact, or that the stage was still being used, two millennia after it was built.

"Look," said Valentin, "most of the time, I am fine with tourists. They are cool. But today they just… what is the expression? Got under my skin. They annoyed you, too."

"I don't want to talk about it," I muttered, climbing over a carved piece of rock. The park was strewn with chunks of the theatre, ruins with no place to go.

"What happened to you?" he asked, "yesterday you were happy. And now…"

"I said I don't want to talk about it!"

I marched off in the direction of the larger chunks of stone, hoping to leave Valentin behind me. Not a chance. I could hear him still on my tail.

"Was it something I did?" he asked, "it wasn't what I said to the tourists, was it? You would have said the same if the situation were backwards."

Aix Marks the Spot

"No, it's not you, ok?" I said. This wasn't the place from the letter: the edge of the property was another fence like the one at the entrance, so no brick wall here. The hunt just was not happening today.

"Was it because I kissed you?" he asked, earnestly. He seemed to sink into the earth. "Because the last thing I wanted to do was hurt you."

"No, no," I replied, shaking my head, the phantom memory of the kiss dancing on my lips. Any other day, it would have made me smile. But today there was just too much.

"Then what? Jamie, I'm worried."

"It's just..." I didn't know how to ask it. How to ask why my grandmother thought calling my mother a whore was the right way to go about things. How to ask why I felt so ashamed of my heritage when I was here. Why I was embarrassed to be from America, when I shouldn't have cared.

"Why do you all hate Americans?" I blurted out. "I mean, you're nice to me, but then you seem to hate everyone else from my country. I'm not different just because my dad is French, ok? I *am* an American."

"I know that, Jamie..."

"But seriously, why?" I stuffed my hands into my pockets gingerly. "Last night, my grandmother went on a rant – more than a rant - about how we were all trying to destroy her home. My own grandmother. I just... I don't understand, Valentin!"

Just then, I heard a voice I recognized bounce off the wall. Well, three voices. On the stage, the three tourists from the bus were laughing, their voices amplified by two-thousand-year-old perfect masonry. I would have been impressed that the acoustics withstood the test of time, but now the girls were taking towels out of their bags and wrapping them around their chests like togas, urging their guy friend to do the same.

"Oh Romeo, oh Romeo, wherefore art thou, Romeo?" said the girl who just really, really needed her Starbucks.

"I right here, right here, I just stepped in a pile of shit!" replied their friend. The three burst out laughing.

"You want to know what we hate about Americans?" said Valentin, pointing at the stage. "We get hundreds of thousands of tourists here every year. But the ones who treat the place like it's their own personal theme park tends to be *them*."

He marched towards the stone ring, and for a second, I thought he would call the Americans out again. But instead he stormed up the seats, making his way to the very top of the seats. I followed him, trying not to hear the butchered lines of Shakespeare flowing behind me.

"You see these seats?" he asked. "My family is

Provençal. All the way back. Which means my ancestors sat here, once. My back-back-back-back - who knows how far back - parents came here to see plays. Plays I learned in school. You're half French: your family is local, your ancestors would have been here, too. When I come to see this place, I see it as my heritage. I see it as a history my family built, and I will continue to build. I see it as something I can proudly say belongs to my *patrimoine*, and that I must try to be worthy of it."

He turned to stare down the theater at the stage, shaking.

"And then tourists like them come here," he said, thrusting his arms wide to scoop up the vision of the three teens in their towel togas, running after each other on stage, "and they think is all for show. That this place was made for them. That we are all animators for them to play with. When I was a boy, a woman asked me if I was an actor because I lived in Lourmarin. She thought the entire place was a ghost town, and the locals were hired to fill the set. Actors! I was eight years old!" He was breathing heavily now. I couldn't help but feel a little scared: I had never seen him like this before.

My eyes fell off him, fell off the edge of the seats, and I saw it: a wall of bricks, lining the homes behind the theatre. The place my parents had had their own fight. The place my father had hidden the clue.

But I couldn't leave now. Valentin was still on the point of exploding, and I had to defuse him before he got any worse. Not that I got the chance to speak; he was already moving through to his next point of contention.

"You know why I learned to speak English?" he asked, "because I wanted to watch your series. I wanted to watch *Game of Thrones!* I wanted to play your video games and understand your memes. I want to go to university to study poetry, and there is no chance I can afford your American schools. Not that they will take me: I had a friend with 17 on their Bac and they were told *everyone* had a baccalaureate. No! So I will go to school here, learn to speak English because everyone must. I speak English, French, and Spanish: I have online friends in America who haven't even tried to learn French. So you know why I am mad at Americans? Because they are so *annoyingly* entitled. To everything. To my home, to my food, to my culture. They do no appreciate it, they simply take it, and I…"

"Please, calm down." A man in a grey uniform stood on the steps, hands raised. My heart leapt to my throat.

"Je suis calme," Valentin smoothed down his shirt, wiping his sweaty palms off in the process. The

Americans were nowhere to be found.

"Je dois vous demander de partir," the man continued, *"vous perturbez la visite."*

"Sérieusement?" Valentin snapped. *"Nous, nous perturbons la visite? Et eux, alors?"*

I carefully stepped away. I didn't want to know what was going on. The guard guy didn't seem to care about me, anyways. As he and Valentin argued about who knows what, I left through one of the theater's exits, arriving before the old brick wall. This was it: this is the place my mother and father almost called it quits. This is where a turn of fate might have stopped me from existing. Which would probably have been better for everyone at this point.

I wondered if it was worth it, me continuing to hunt for these ridiculous clues. I knew, deep down, that they were just pieces of paper. There was no such thing as a miracle cure, especially not for what you just want through. And I am sorry, sorry every day for what I did to you.

I can't yet fix what's wrong with us. I will figure it out as I go. I'll never stop trying.

The walls were tall, so I tried to imagine what it would have been like to fight here, instead of up on the arcade. Where would you have leaned, where would dad have pushed. Where would the grout be crumbling from centuries of use. Where would your letter be…

Guesswork wasn't working. So I pushed.

I blocked out all other sound around me and focused on the wall. I pressed and jiggled every brick on that wall, as my phone vibrated itself into oblivion in my pocket. Valentin must have been trying to call me. I didn't care. Call me the entitled American, but I needed this time to myself.

As the brick came out in my hand without resistance, I wasn't surprised. I wasn't happy, or sad, or relieved: I was past that now. I was calm, resting in a place beyond emotion, too exhausted to really care. Because even if I did find it, it would change nothing. But there it was, hope or no hope: Wrapped around that brick, folded over a million times, was the letter I knew would be there.

```
Mon Amour,


Woah, you're halfway there - wo-oah, living on
a prayer! That's not part of the clue. I just
wanted to let you know you're doing great, my
darling!
 Anyway, back to the adventure on hand. Your
next clue is: 'X' marks the spot.
```

Aix Marks the Spot

It was so hard to pick a hiding place for this clue. I mean, every street corner here holds a dear memory. Remember the day we came home, drunk as skunks from the end of exam party, and we took off our shoes and climbed into the Four Dolphins to cool down? Or the time we were exploring the cloister at the cathedral, and they accidentally locked us in? That poor priest was terrified when we showed up at his office and asked to be let out of the place!

But I wanted to give you a real challenge, and, in turn, gave myself the challenge of finding our most memorable day there. And I think I found it: it was that concert, right?

Let me set the scene: Manu's little sister, the cello prodigy, is about to have a concert. Nobody wants to go since we've never met her before in our lives, but Manu has promised us all pizza and drinks if we show up to support her. Free food is always good, so we show up like the good friends we are.

The conservatory is in an old, old building. It's got this smell so many other local buildings do, like most of our classrooms, of old wood and earth, a little churchy. It's already dark out, and we're all lamenting how early the sun sets now that it's winter - though it has been winter for literal months already - when a woman lunges at us.

She demands our tickets. We don't have them, Manu does, and she's telling us to turn around, to go away, that we need to stop trespassing. Finally Manu comes down with the tickets, and then she starts railing on him, telling him that they are not a tourist beach for people to come and go as they please.

She eventually lets us go up, but she's still mumbling under her breath in the corner. She lights up a cigarette. Seb needs a smoke, but he isn't about to ask her, so he turns to the closest smoker in the room, who just happens to be Manu's little sister. Manu is stunned. He had no idea she had picked up on the habit. He starts railing on her now, and she's shouting back, telling him it's her life, and she can live it however she wants to. Her professor breaks them up, so the concert can begin.

And it's true, that girl is talented. She played a piece so lovely that time itself stood still. We sat and listened, hands intertwined between our seats, feeling like we were part of the haute-culture by being here tonight.

Aix Marks the Spot

That's when Seb yells "Au feu!" and we see the smoke.

Not sure who dropped their cig – I think everyone was smoking in that room – but one of the old carpets was on fire. The sister flies from her cello. The professor runs to the window, throws it open. Five people are stomping out the flame.

There's a moment of calm as we all realize the danger has passed. People are looking at each other, wondering if this means the concert is over, or . . .

And then a pigeon flies in through the open window.

It perches happily on the old brown desk in the corner of the room. Well, I say happily: it's hard to tell with pigeons. But now the entire room is staring at it, and none of us know what to do.

That was the evening we witnessed an entire group of well-dressed people chase an uncooperative pigeon around a fancy antique room. Refusing to talk to each other, each trying to be the hero, they would lunge and send the bird flying to the other side of the room, confused, and nowhere near the window.

Sarah Anderson

Around and around and around they chased it, so Manu's sister got bored and started to play the rest of her concert. A few people sat back down, while at least five guys kept chasing, determined to flush the bird out.

So she plays the Benny Hill theme. Of course.

I had never been so impressed with a sixteen-year-old before. I snorted out laughing so hard that I had to cover my mouth. I had to walk away, just to get it all out. Which is when I spotted the bird poo on the Victorian desk, looked up, and got another dose of it smack dab in the middle of my forehead.

So I hid the next clue in that brown desk. Ask for Monsieur Henri, Manu's sister's teacher. I warned him you were coming. I didn't tell him where I hid the clue, and be warned, he teased about having to quiz you before letting you through to find it anyway. Be warned. Come prepared. Maybe a nice bottle of rosé.

Good luck,

So much Love,
The Pigeon hater,
Your Crepe a Go Go.

twenty-one

VALENTIN STOOD OUTSIDE THE VISITOR'S CENTER, leaning against the wall. He dropped the phone from his ear as I approached, making mine go silent. To my right, I could see the city's amphitheater, a tiny version of the colosseum that was astonishingly still in use. Valentin's words came back to me: my family had been there when it had been built. My ancestors belonged to this city as much as I did. I might not have deserved to be here, but part of me was still allowed to call this place home.

I didn't want to talk to him. The look on his face was hard to decipher: his eyebrows were light, his lips neither smiling nor frowning, as if he were caught between any and all emotions. I could very well have turned and gone back to the bus station by myself, fuming silently.

But I was scared. Scared of being alone. Scared of losing the one person who I could speak to, here. Maybe everywhere. Jazz still hadn't called back, or even attempted to. I guess that was over as well.

"You didn't get in too much trouble, did you?" I said.

"Well, I cannot see any other ruins today," He said, full body shrug on cue. "So that is disappointing."

"I guessed the next clue by myself," I continued, "So I'm going there next, and you're free to join me if you feel like it. But just because I'm American, don't think I'm entitled to your presence, you know."

The lips curled into a light smile. It wasn't strong, but it was a start.

"Sure," he said, "though I guess it depends where it is."

"It's in Aix-en-Provence," I replied, "it's the city where my parents met. Where they fell in love. And Dad told me exactly where to go."

His eyes went wide, but still, no smile. He reached for the letter, but I clutched it tight, unwilling to let it go. It was my letter. It wasn't for sharing.

"Are you… are you sure?" He asked.

"What do you want me to say? That I need you to double check it? Because I don't need you, Valentin.

I'm not trying to manipulate you into spending time with me, though I guess the autograph kinda was a... crap. I'm doing exactly what Americans do. I'm coming here, and I'm taking over, I'm speaking English and stealing their French men..."

"*Ho-oh-la*, wait?" Valentin threw up a hand, eyes going wide, "what the hell are you talking about? This isn't about what I said back there, is it? Because I didn't mean it against you, not at all. I meant it against..."

I couldn't hold them back any longer. I burst into tears, exhaustion and shame flowing freely down my cheeks. There was just no winning with these people. Kicked out of America, rejected from France like a bad transplant. I would never belong. I was cursed to ruin lives and stand out like a sore thumb everywhere I went.

Valentin wrapped his arms around me, and I didn't have the strength to push him away. I sobbed into his shirt, salty tears mixing with his musky cologne, letting his heartbeat try and calm me. He hushed me soothingly, stroking my hair, calming and warm.

"What did I say?" He asked, his voice gentle and low, "what happened?"

"I'm awful," I blubbered, "despicable. The scum of the earth."

"Jamie."

His hands retracted from the hug, only to grasp my

shoulders. He held me there, tightly, grounding me into the ancient earth.

"Jamie, you are not any of those things. You are one of the bravest people I have ever met. One of the maddest, certainly. Who else would follow a treasure hunt older than they are, and manage to actually find the clues?"

I shook my head. "That's not bravery. That's... stupid. I'm a dumb, naïve girl who thinks the universe is magically going to heal her mom when she finds these stupid clues. Talk about stupidity, I'm the dumbest girl on the planet if I thought for a second that would actually work."

"Not stupid," he insisted. "Maybe a little... weird, granted. *Le cœur a ses raisons que la raison ne connaît pas.* The heart has its reasons which reason knows nothing of. Pascal."

"You're quoting poetry at a time like this?"

"Poetry from a scientist, sure. You really care about your mom; you love her. Her injury is out of your control, so you try to make it something you can manage. That's not stupid. That's just human."

"But I broke her," I muttered, "I'm the reason she's hurt. If I wasn't so stupid, she would be here with me right now. Instead, I've been kicked out of the home of the only family I have left, because I…"

"You got kicked out?" Valentin stammered. "Jamie, this is serious! Why didn't you tell me?"

"I don't know you," I shook my head. His hands crisped against my shoulders, his sweaty palms sticking to my shirt. "I like you, so, so much. But I don't know you. I don't want to… I didn't want to… I already ruin everything; I didn't want to ruin… this."

"You are staying with me tonight." He dropped his hands, staring intently into my eyes, and there it was, exactly what I didn't want to see looking back at me: pity. I didn't need pity. I needed to get out of here. I needed to fix myself so I didn't break everything I touched. And this was going to break something: my heart, his heart, or maybe both, I didn't know.

"I can't ask that of you," I said, my voice so low I didn't know if I even managed to say them. "What would you mother say? And didn't we just talk about entitled…"

"There's a difference between being entitled and being in need," he said, shaking his head, "I was just angry at the tourists for being loud, alright? I don't even mind American tourists: to be honest, Parisians are worse. But you need to have a place to stay. Please. I have a couch. And my mother? She will be happy for the company."

"Are you sure?" My body didn't know if it needed to

stop crying, or double down. I was caught between a sniffle and a sob, like a sneeze that didn't want to leave.

"No question. There is no way you're going back there. She's your grandmother, she has no right to kick you out."

I nodded, slowly. She did have good reason to hate me, seeing what I did to her family, though I wasn't going to tell him that. The thought of having someplace warm to sleep tonight was already lifting my spirits.

"We should wait and go to Aix tomorrow," he said, "the day is already half gone, and you want to be able to see more than just the clue."

"If you say so." I extracted myself from his arms, wiping my soaking wet face on the edge of my shirt. The air was a relief on my sweaty skin. "Let's go home."

"Not just yet. I have a place I want to take you first. To cheer you up."

"I'm fine, Valentin."

"No, you're not. Come with me. I promise you'll like it."

"Is it food?"

He laughed. "It's not food. But it's better."

"That's a lofty promise, Mr. Valentine."

"Lofty? I don't even know the word."

Whether he did or not, it did not matter. He took my

hand and slowly we set off, heading away from the roman ruins and further into the heart of the town. The roads were thin, the old buildings so close together that I probably could have touched both walls if I stretched my arms far enough. When it widened, it was to reveal medieval houses and strangely modern cars.

The town was a labyrinth of these streets, worse than Lourmarin. At least there you didn't really have to share the road with cars. It was as if the sidewalks here were completely arbitrary. But finally we turned to face a modern glass building, oddly out of place in the midst of the ancient stone, and Valentin was right: I liked the surprise.

"You said you liked art," he explained, "but you haven't been to a single museum here yet. I hope you like Van Gogh."

twenty-two

THE FIRST TIME I HAD SEEN STARRY NIGHT, I HAD been probably eight years old. You were hanging it in the doorway of our new suburban home, giving our new stairway a welcoming, elegant look.

You didn't know this, but you had just changed my life forever. I stood before the painting for hours, mesmerized by the swirls of light and color. I was transported across the globe, to a little Provençal hillside in the dead of night, watching the stars swirl above me.

"I've been there," you said, coming back to straighten it again. You were never happy with how it hung there, it was never perfect.

"You have?" I had asked you, wide eyed and impressed. "Does it really look like this?"

"A little," you replied, "Van Gogh – the man who

painted it – could see things we can't. He painted the night sky as he saw it. I saw it during daytime, and it's different now."

I nodded, pretending to understand. "But why didn't he paint it the way it really is?"

"You would have had to ask him that, Jamie," she said, ruffling my hair, "But I like the way he sees the world. It's more beautiful than how I do."

That had been the day I had picked up my first colored pencil with a purpose. Before then, I had only scribbled. But that day, I wanted to show people how I saw my home. How I saw the plants and the trees and my goldfish.

I drew every day since that moment, filling sketchbook after sketchbook with glorified doodles until I could confidently draw what I wanted to draw. It wasn't perfect, it never was: I was still learning, and I kept wanting to do more.

Jasmine had been with me since the beginning. We had met in art class in third grade, when the art teacher had paired us together for an portrait challenge. We realized we both loved drawing over anything else in the world, and soon, the only thing we loved more was each other.

It took me years to learn how to draw what was in my head, and only seconds to lose it. Since the accident, nothing I tried to draw came even close to how I saw it. My hand would cramp before an image was even close to be finished, and worse, most days I couldn't even sketch at all.

I tried not to think about Jazz as I stood in the museum, staring at a Van Gogh I had never seen before. A snow-white field with a city in the distance, an abandoned plow in the middle, crows gathering above. Every brushstroke was deliberate, making the image so alive despite the frozen winter setting. I ran my thumb over my ticket stub, thinking of you, wondering if you had ever seen this picture too.

"He painted this in Provence, in St Remy," said Valentin. It was the first time he had talked since we had paid for our entrance. "We passed it on the way to Les-Baux, in a bus."

"I would never have guessed." My voice was barely higher than a whisper.

"You probably know all this," he continued, "but when he was alive, people didn't really like him."

I scoffed. "That's an understatement."

"He ended up being institutionalized in St Rémy as well. They now offer art therapy classes there. But we have to go visit the village, you would love it. They have signs telling you where everything was painted. Former fields are now playgrounds. Some things have changed, but the others…"

"I would never recognize them either," I said, moving on to a painting of a wheat field lines with purple irises. It was hard to imagine Van-freaking-Gogh was the one to put those strokes on Canvas. "He saw the world so differently than I do. The landscapes would never be the same."

I loved this awestruck version of Valentin. Going to massive cliffs, old castles, and ancient ruins were just his every day, but Van Gogh could still blow his mind.

"It's incredible to see how he could take all that pain, all that confusion, and create something so beautiful with it."

"He's my favorite artist," I said. I didn't need him to tell me anything about him, but hearing his voice, his enthusiasm… he could have kept talking for years and I wouldn't have stopped him. "Some days I wish I could travel back in time and tell him it's going to be ok. See how much more art he could create. But how much beauty he could bring into the world."

"Like that Doctor Who episode," said Valentin.

"You know Doctor Who?"

"Part of why my English is so good," he replied, winking. "But you're right: I wish I could do that, travel back in time and tell our past selves that it's all going to be ok."

"Too bad we're stuck in the present," I replied, "roughing it out."

We moved onto another room, finding the man himself: Van Gogh's self-portrait hanging on the wall, though smaller than I had expected. He wore his hat, his rough blue jacket, his cropped orange beard. I wanted to laugh: it was the same hat that Jean-Pascal cherished.

It hit me in that instant that I was actually here. Two different men in Provence, two heads, a century apart, bound by the love of the same hat. I tried to imagine Van Gogh walking through Arles, the same city I was in now, easel on his back. In that moment everything became real, the world exploding into technicolor, full of color and depth. Because this was the place: this was where the artists I loved painted their art, real landscapes around them.

"The say the sky in Provence is what brought all the artists here," said Valentin, as if reading my mind. "It's a shade of blue you never see in nature. It creates a contrast with the colors they all wanted to capture. Some managed better than others."

I nodded, eyes still riveted on Van Gogh's portrait. I would never be able to capture that blue, no matter how I tried. Post-accident Jamie would have to find a new passion. She would never have the skill I saw before me.

The museum was large, with more than just the Van

Gogh collection, even if it was my favorite part of the whole thing. We left out the giftshop, and I had to admit, I was feeling a little better. It hadn't solved the problem of my Mamie kicking me out, but she wasn't all of Provence. I was still here, exploring where dad's roots had been ripped from the soil. I didn't need Mamie to plant me here, I was doing very well on my own.

"Are you hungry?" asked Valentin. We passed a familiar café, and I did a double take: yellow awning, tables and chairs outside… the sign before it confirmed I was right. It might have been daytime, but I recognized Van Gogh's café scene.

"Oh my gosh, can we actually eat here?" I begged. To eat at the place where the artist himself once sat? The place had been renamed café Van Gogh in honor of him, and I wondered if they had appreciated his patronage when he was still alive.

I was falling right into the habits Valentin hated, sounding just like the loud American I knew I was. For the umpteenth time that day, I felt shame roll through my bones.

"You are going to make me broke." Valentin patted his pockets down, proving how light he was. "I've got better."

His better was three-euro paninis from the tiniest store you had ever seen. He grabbed us cokes from the fridge as the woman rang us up, and in a few minutes, we were strolling down the street with our melty, cheesy messes.

"No wonder you guys don't do Micky D's when you've got this as your fast food," I said. The pesto and mozzarella were perfect together.

"What is a Michey D?"

"McDonald's."

"*Oh, Mac'do!*" He exclaimed, "it's too expensive."

"Too expensive?"

What the heck even was this country? Paninis where cheap and McDonald's expensive, it was completely upside down and backwards to boot. Come to think of it, there wasn't a Wendy's or Chick-Fil-A anywhere in sight. I wondered if the tourists from earlier had ever found a Starbucks, because I sure hadn't seen one.

Oddly enough, I didn't miss my chains. I was happy with my melty panini and my mind full of art.

twenty-three

WE SPENT THE AFTERNOON JUST WANDERING around town, seeing as how Valentin couldn't get into the other ruins. He suggested a certain blue museum, but we didn't have the time: eventually we just had to call it quits and catch the bus, arriving in Lourmarin just in time for dinner.

His mother didn't seem at all surprised to see me there. She gave me the *bise* and told me to set the table, so I did, taking the plates and setting them out on the tablecloth. It was as if I was family: I hadn't even had the time to put my bag down yet.

"You should put that in my room," said Valentin, carrying a salad bowl to the table. "I cannot believe my mother has you doing work."

"Oh, I'm happy to," I said, "I kinda want her to like

me, you know."

"Like you? She loves you. We all do."

"Really? Why?" I asked, trying to ignore the fact he had just said they loved me. HE loved me. Maybe I was just reading too much into it: we hadn't even talked about last night's kiss since, well, last night.

"Why me?" I continued, "I thought you guys didn't like Americans."

"I told you, we don't like loud Americans who have nothing interesting to say, with fake smiles and tans," he replied with the familiar Valentin smirk. "But most aren't like that, and you always have interesting things to say. And a nice smile."

"Thanks." I didn't know how to answer that. Maybe with a compliment in return? Think, Jamie, think. Is this supposed to be flirting? "Your smile is nice too. I like how your teeth are straight and white."

Well, that went well. But he was beaming, so that had to count for something.

Valentin led me to his bedroom, one floor up and overlooking his small garden. It was a cozy room, about half of what I had back home, but it fit everything in snugly. His bed was wide, his desk in the corner was taken up entirely by a massive computer. The shelf between the bed and desk was full of the same white paperbacks that cluttered Dad's room back at Mamie's.

Aix Marks the Spot

"You can put your bag here," he said, pointing me to the desk as he rushed to pick up strewn laundry and shove it into his closet. Leo must have been sleeping on one of his shirts, because I heard a disgruntled meow before seeing a tail bob out the door.

I plopped the backpack from my shoulders, relieved to have the weight finally off me. It set me free to explore the small room, picking up details I hadn't noticed before, like how the wall hidden from the door was covered in posters of random video games (were those giant rabbits?) or how a big black book on Napoleon sat on his bedside table, bookmarked three quarters of the way through.

"Uh, dinner?" Valentin's voice plucked me out of my snooping, and I looked up to see him twitching nervously.

"Yes, sure, yeah."

Back in the dining room, Mathilde was just finishing pouring us water. She looked back as we entered, putting down the carafe.

We sat down together for chicken cordon bleu and salad. The leaves were lightly tossed in a homemade vinaigrette, and I could have eaten that for my entire meal. The chicken was even better.

"So what did you see today, Jammy?" asked Mathilde, ripping off a neat chunk of baguette to soak up the leftover vinaigrette on the table.

"Valentin took me to Arles," I replied, taking the baguette and imitating her. I could get used to ripping my way through a loaf of bread. "We did the Theatre Antique and the Van Gogh foundation."

"Oh, I love that museum!"

"It was amazing!"

She wanted to talk about nothing but art after that. Van Gogh this; Cezanne that; what did I think of Picasso, genius or weirdo? Neither of us had all the perfect words, but Valentin did an amazing job filling in those gaps.

After devouring a plate of fresh cheeses, we called it quits on dinner. I helped tidy up, all the while Valentin quizzing me on my knowledge of French kitchenware, and I was surprised that I knew most of what we ate off of, though I was still on the fence about the gender of a spoon.

"So they teach you to talk about plates and forks, but not about asking for directions?"

I shrugged. "Admittedly, I wasn't in the best program."

"By the time you go home, you had better be fluent," he said with a wink, "American English is exhausting. So much smiling and arm waving."

"We have arm waving?" I scoffed. "You French use

your whole body to shrug. You don't just use your hands, but your shoulders and chest and whatever else. I could never learn that."

"*Rho*, you will," he said reassuringly. "So long as you don't pick up Parisian habits, we'll understand you fine."

I sure hoped so. I liked it. Being understood, I mean. Though I liked everything else to do with spending time with Valentin, too.

Mathilde leant me pajamas and pointed me to the shower. Oh heaven, the shower was normal! I had spent over a week now learning to clean myself in what amounted to that tank from Empire Strikes Back. Now I had my feet in a tub, and the rain shower relaxed my every muscle.

Clean and now dressed in soft PJs, I almost forgot that this was a result of Mamie kicking me out. It could almost be a normal slumber party.

With a boy.

That I liked.

A boy who was now standing in the hallway, taking in my towel-turbaned hair, holding his phone out to me.

"What?" I asked, confused.

"I thought you might want the *whiffy* password," he explained, "You probably miss civilization."

"Oh god. Gimme."

I practically ripped the phone from his hands and barreled into his room, grabbing my phone from the desk and typing the password in lickety-split. Not that I had actually missed anything: a message from Jazz, but nothing I wanted to hear.

"Hey girl," she said, *"Sorry I couldn't answer last night, I was out. I didn't even hear the phone ring. Talk later?"*

Yeah, right. I had seen her hang up. I wanted to call her out on it, ask her really why she wasn't there, but I stopped myself. I had restraint. I would wait until I was no longer mad at her to answer… if that day would ever come.

"I'll be on the couch tonight," said Valentin suddenly. He was making it a habit to break me out of my trances, it seemed. "If you need anything, you wake me, ok?"

"Oh no, I can't ask you to do that!" I replied, rising to my feet. I handed his phone back. "Please. I'm the one crashing here. I'm not going to push you out of you bed."

I glanced at the comfy double bed, hoping I would still somehow get to sleep in it. It looked so wide and nice: as much as sleeping on the couch was the right thing to do, it didn't mean I didn't want to stay here.

And then I saw the box on his bed side table.

Oh.

"*Merde! Merci, Maman.*" He flew to the small blue box, picking it up and throwing it into the nightstand in a flash. I didn't know whether to laugh or back out of the room slowly.

"It's not every mom who would leave a box of condoms out for her son," I replied.

"I'm so, so sorry about that," he said, his face so red it could have been on fire.

"I guess that means she likes me?"

He brushed his hair away from his forehead, laughing the most uncomfortable laugh I had ever heard, wobbly and weird. And I laughed too: Mathilde was so like you, and yet so different. I wondered if all French moms were this chill about their teenagers sharing a room – though chill seemed to be an understatement. When Charlie and I were dating – if you could even call it that – I don't think his mother even knew I was in his life. I don't think I told you much about him, either.

My gut churned at the memory of us in the back of his car, his hands parading over grounds I had never shared before, mine reaching for places I had always wanted to explore. How could I ever have believed it was anything more than just that. How disgusted I had felt after I saw his phone, that night at the party.

"I'm really sorry," he said, catching my attention, "I

really didn't mean..."

"It's fine, Valentin." I took a seat on his bed, reveling in the comfort of soft clean sheets. "It's not you I'm struggling with."

"Your Mamie?"

"I guess. Her, and a lot of things. Is it ok if I just... sit here? On the internet?"

"Sure," he replied, "I will be in the living room if you need me."

He turned and heading towards the door, and I felt guilty for pushing him away. The box of condoms hadn't bothered me: only the memories they brought back did. He looked deflated, defeated: it broke my heart.

"I don't mean to kick you out," I stammered.

"Don't worry, I understand."

"No, no..." Come on Jamie, this is English! The words shouldn't be so hard when it's the only language you know! "Why don't you stay with me? I'm just going to be on my phone. I won't be good company but I'm not trying to be a bad guest, either."

"It's fine," he replied, "I can do the same downstairs."

"Please stay?"

His eyes lit up, and I had never seen something as beautiful in my life. He sat down on his bed beside me, keeping a polite distance – I hadn't mentioned the bed, but I wasn't going to push him off now. I mean, it was *his* bed - between us, he took out his phone, too.

I scrolled down the old messages I had never tried to answer. Downloaded the emails that were clogging my inbox, deleting the spam. Turns out, some apps get oddly clingy when you don't open them for a few days: I deleted most of them right away. I didn't like how they fought for my time.

"Thanks for letting me use your Wi-Fi," I said, turning to Valentin. His eyes went wide.

"It's wi-fi?" he stammered, "*Merde!* I've been saying *whiffy* for years! You never corrected me?"

"I thought it was kinda cute."

"Cute? It's an abomination of the English language!" he said through a thick grin. "You are supposed to say when I speak wrong!"

"And lose your accent? No thank you. I like the way your speak."

"Good luck getting my help with your French," he chided, "you'll be stuck with your accent forever."

"No! The horror!"

"Bon courage pour me comprendre."

"What now?"

"Good luck understanding me if I *parle comme ca!*"

"Merde! Putain! Sacrebleu!"

"Wow, you can speak Marseillais. Good job!"

Stalemate. We grinned at each other like our lives depended on the width of our smiles. And god, was his smile beautiful.

"Thanks again for today," I said. "I haven't felt this - I don't even know the word. Included? At home? - Since I got off the plane at Marseille airport."

"My pleasure," he replied, "you're in Provence: anything less than a warm welcome would bring shame upon my family."

The last time I had been so close to him, I had tasted his lips. He had kissed me so deeply it had sucked all the homesickness right through my chest, if only for a moment. Was he leaning in now, to make it all go away again? Was he going to ask where I wanted this to go?

I thought of the little blue box in his nightstand, and blushed. If that option was on the table, I wasn't sure what I'd say.

But he didn't lean in. He didn't try to kiss me. He simply went back to his phone, back to scrolling through memes. Was any of this flirting, to him? He was French, he would know better than I did. Maybe it was all just a normal day for him. Maybe yesterday's kiss was just a... really enthusiastic goodbye.

Wow, French was really, really confusing.

"I think I'm going to go to bed now," I said, almost robotically, dare the confusion take over my entire brain. I pulled back the covers and slipped under them, though it was much too warm for sheets in his room, too. He reached over and turned on a rotating fan without having to ask, and the air breezed over us, instantly relaxing me.

"I'll go," he said, "let you get your sleep."

"You don't have to leave," I muttered.

"Are you sure? You said that you wanted to go to bed, no?"

"I didn't say you had to go. It *is* your room."

So, he stayed. I curled up on my pillow (his pillow, smelling gloriously of him) and closed my eyes, letting sleep begin to peacefully wash over me. But in the quiet, my mind began to churn. It started off with the mental weight of the meaning of that kiss, but then it drifted off to what had happened after: Mamie's breakdown, her drunken insults, her throwing me out, and everything that came with it.

"Are you alright?" asked Valentin.

"Mm-hum."

"You're not," he insisted, "Did I do something wrong?"

"Why do you always assume it's you?"

He didn't answer. I peeked open my eyes to see him still scrolling in the dark, memes tiny on his screen. It was astounding to think he had wasted his time learning English for that.

"I don't know what to tell my parents," I said, "about Mamie."

"That Collette Martin is a drunk and you're not safe with her, maybe?"

"I'm sorry this means you won't get your autograph."

"Please. I don't care about that anymore. She's not worth it."

"You sure?"

He nodded. "You read someone's books, and you think you know them. But books are… they're for the reader, not the writer. So I was really only seeing myself when I thought I was seeing her."

I nodded, though I don't think he could see it in the darkness of the room. When he had shut off the light, I didn't know. He still sat atop his sheets, hairy legs stretched out along the bed, lit blue in the glare of his phone. A spooky, hairy ghost resting beside me.

"I'll call my parents tomorrow, after we come back from Aix. See if we can work something out for me to stay back home. There's no room at Grandma's house, but maybe someone from school won't mind me living with them."

"And leave Provence?" he stammered, "You can stay here, if you want to. My mother understands, she would be… delighted."

"You mean it?"

Would it work? Would my parents approve of me staying in a stranger's home, instead of Mamie's? Valentin was far less foreign to me than she was.

"You said you wanted me to stay," he said, quietly, his voice a low whisper. "Jamie, I want you to stay too."

And I fell asleep there, in the bed next to him, his words running on a loop in my mind, warding off my Mamie's words like a magic charm.

twenty-four

WAKING UP NEXT TO SOMEONE IS A SERIOUSLY underrated activity.

I don't think there's anything quite like opening your eyes to someone else's sleeping face. To see the look of peace there. Seeing a person without their mask on, the lack of tension, no veiled emotions, only them.

Valentin might have had a stoic face during the day, but in the morning, before he woke up, he was soft. His hair rested in waves around his face like a halo, and he breathed softly in my face, filling my nose with the scent of gross morning breath.

Good moment over.

I sat up, realizing one of my feet was wrapped around his legs, and pulled it back sharply. Oh god, I had slept with a boy. Not slept-slept, but shared a bed, let him see me in my ridiculous baggy pajamas, *touched his foot with mine.*

Skin to skin contact.

That happened.

I flew out of bed, grabbed my clothes, and got changed in the bathroom. Breathe, Jamie, breathe. It meant nothing, and he would wake up without even knowing any of that happened. Because nothing did happen.

I trotted down to the living room, feeling out of place. I was hungry, but didn't know which cupboard to open, or even if I should: it wasn't my home, and I was definitely the intruder here.

"*Ah, salut,*" said Mathilde. She was leaning against her counter, coffee in hand, reading something on her phone which she put down when I walked in. "Are you 'ungry?"

I nodded. She pointed to the coffee machine and I nodded: I was developing a real caffeine habit in this country.

"You're awake early, did you not sleep well?" she asked.

"I slept great," I replied, "I'm just used to getting up early."

I remembered then that this woman thought Valentin and I had spent the night together, in the truly religious sense. I cringed, thinking of what

Grandma would say if she ever met this heathen who encouraged premarital sex. She was still on my mom about me being born out of wedlock, and that was almost seventeen years ago.

How was I supposed to talk to her, exactly? Short of yelling "I haven't had sex your son!" I didn't know how to approach the topic. But it didn't matter, because she didn't seem to care. She handed me my coffee and I thanked her, inhaling the wonderful scent of roasted beans.

"We can get pastries," she said.

"Really? That would be amazing!"

She slipped on her shoes and grabbed a tiny brown change purse, and we set off across the street. It was the same bakery I had explored my first day at the market: the friendly baker chatted amicably with Mathilde as I scanned the various rows of treats, my eyes falling once again on the glazed bun I so wanted to try.

"What would you like?" asked Mathilde, as the baker grabbed a twisted chocolate rope for Valentin.

"Um, what is that?"

"*Brioche Glacée,*" she replied.

"*Je voudrais un brioche glacé, s'il vous plait,*" I said to the baker, "*Merci!*"

She said something back to me and I nodded, not sure what I had agreed to. She threw something out to

Mathilde and she replied the same, excitedly bobbing her head the whole time.

When we returned home, our arms were full of pastries and fresh bread, still hot from the oven. Mathilde didn't even wait to walk through the front door before ripping off a steaming chunk of bread and devouring it.

"Goute," she said, handing me the loaf, "it's the best when iz still hot."

She was right, it was heaven. I never believed that bread could be so heavenly and full of flavor. I wanted to eat the entire baguette right then and there.

"Pauline says your French has improved since last week." She put the pastries down on the counter, reaching in the fridge for milk. "She's impressed, you learn fast!"

"Me?" I scoffed. "I only know how to order food."

"That's all anyone really needs to know, isn't it?"

She heated the milk for us in the microwave, filling cereal bowls with cocoa powder. By the time she was done, she had made each of us massive amounts of chocolate milk.

"Can you tell Valentin breakfast is ready?" she asked, "I have to go to work soon."

It felt weird coming back into his room after last night. The space had become entirely his again, and

I wasn't meant to be in there, certainly not while he was sleeping. Luckily, he stirred as I opened his door, glancing over at me through tired, squinting eyes.

"Um, breakfast?" I squeaked, and when he didn't immediately reply, I threw in, *"Petit dejeuner?"*

"J'arrive," he muttered in response. He was coming, he said, but there was no telling how long it would take.

"There is hot chocolate," I added, "if you don't come now, it won't be *chaud* no mo'!"

"Quoi?"

I darted out of the room before I had to find an explanation for my terrible rhyming. Way to make things awkward, Jamie.

Mathilde was already halfway through her croissant by the time I came back down, bowls of chocolate on the table in front of her. She dipped her pastry and ate the soggy end, her eyes riveted on her phone until I stepped into the room.

"I never make breakfast," she said, "it's nice having you as a reason to."

"You didn't have to," I replied, taking a seat across from her, "I don't want to be an inconvenience."

"This isn't an *inconvenient*," she replied, "it's nice to have you."

Valentin wandered past us then, still squinting, groggy. His hair stuck up in every which direction.

Aix Marks the Spot

He glanced at us for an instant, grunted, and shuffled into the kitchen.

"Quoi? On ne dit pas bonjour?" His mother chided.

"Café!" he called from the kitchen, and she shook her head.

"He usually never wakes up until after 10 o'clock," she told me, "he must like you very much."

I said nothing, instead sipping at my chocolate. It was surprisingly weird to sip it from a cereal bowl, like I was a child breaking the rules.

"So where are you going today?" she asked.

"Aix-en-Provence," I said, reaching for my Brioche Glacé. "My parents met there, and I've always wanted to see the city."

"It's a fantastic town," she replied, "the best in the world."

"Not Lourmarin?"

"Lourmarin is the prettiest village. Aix-en-Provence is more special than that. It is not the most beautiful, or the most cultured. But when you are there... it's a city with a voice. If you're lucky, it speaks to you."

"That's... poetic."

"You'll see. Maybe."

The brioche was even better than I imagined. The sweet bun was not too sugary, and the icing was thin enough that it added the perfect flavor, plus a gentle, gummy texture that clung to my teeth. I felt like a child when I ate it, but that relapse was worth it for the taste.

Valentin sat down with us and muttered a hello to us both, before chugging down his coffee. Only then did he move onto food, and a few minutes later, to conversation: mainly about how weird it was to be chatting with his mother in English.

"When did you learn to talk so good?" she asked.

"Last summer, *avec papa*," he replied. At this, she went cold, putting her coffee cup down on the table a little harder than needed. He forced a smile. "He was at work the whole time. He wanted me to show Paris to the son of one of his colleagues. The son was American, and we talked a lot."

"Oh, I remember," she nodded. "I am impressed. Your accent is much better than mine."

With that, she cleared her place and left for work, in a slightly worse mood than she had started. Valentin didn't say much, blaming his lack of coffee. He said nothing about our night together, even now that she was gone.

"We still going to Aix today?" I asked, just to be sure. He nodded into his hot chocolate bowl.

"As soon as I get dressed. And there's a bus. Ok?"

"Hell yeah."

He grinned at this, picking up his twisted chocolate

pastry and smiling so wide it dwarfed the sun.

The bus deposited us right into the heart of the city, though the station wasn't all that big. It had been the same bus that had been the first leg of our journey when we came to Cassis: barely a week ago, if even, but a lifetime ago now. This time, I was in Aix to see Aix. I was finally here.

This was it: the place my parents had met and more, Mom's home away from home, the place she clung to in photographs and postcards from before I was born. Giant plane trees shaded the streets as we left the station and headed in the direction of the conservatory. It was refreshing in the hot sun to have the cool breeze waft down the roads.

We reached the end of the road and were met with a towering fountain: Three tiered and reaching to the sky, water flowed out of lion heads from beneath the feet of three women, into a copper basin where the water now flowed out of heads. Giant fish and cherubim on swans blasted jets out over the heads of mighty lions, as cars drove around the gigantic ensemble, clearly not impressed.

"La Rotonde," said Valentin, "Aix is known for its fountains, and this one is the biggest. Maybe the most beautiful, but the others are amazing as well."

I couldn't reply: my breath had been taken away.

Sarah Anderson

We walked through rows of fancy stores in crisp clean buildings, where it seemed the entire world was out shopping. Past them, and we were hitting an even more modern part of the city, passing buildings with architecture I had only ever seen in futuristic films. Valentin led me to a silver-grey thing that looked like the ship from Interstellar, landed on earth and ready to take off.

"This doesn't feel right," I said, as we reached the entrance. At least, I think it was the entrance. It was hard to tell with everything going on: a massive triangular piece of glass, rising at an off angle, like someone had sliced the bottom corner off the building itself. Valentin held it open and we stepped inside.

Instantly, I knew this wasn't the place. The smell was that of fresh paint and metal, not the old church smell my dad has described.

"This isn't it," I said.

"But it's the conservatory," he replied, "isn't that where the letter said to go?"

"Yeah, but it's too new," I said. "Dad said it was an old building. This one looks younger than either of us."

"Je peux vous aider?" asked the man at the desk. "Can I help you?"

"Yes, is this the *conservatoire*?" I asked.

"Yes," he replied, "are you here to sign up for

Aix Marks the Spot

classes?"

I shook my head, "I'm just wondering. Was this the conservatory seventeen years ago?"

"I do not understand," said the man.

"The building is new, isn't it?" I urged.

"Oh!" His eyes widened as it clicked for him. "We had a smaller building. Where the Musée Caumont is now."

"Can you tell us how to get there?"

The man kindly pulled out a map on his phone and showed us it was only a few minutes away – though everything in town was just a few minutes away. We ended up retracing our steps back through the city to the massive fountain.

"Are you hungry?" asked Valentin, quite suddenly, as we reached the crosswalk.

"A little," I replied, "why?"

"Just come with me."

He led me only a few steps from the fountain, down some stairs into what I thought would be a metro stop, but no. The stairs led under the street and right back up the other side, with three shops in between.

And from one of them wafted the heavenly scent of dough and melted cheese.

"Crepes!" I exclaimed, before throwing my hands over my mouth.

I took one with cheese, ham, and a whole egg in it, watching as they spread the batter onto large black rings, melting the cheese and cracking the egg right there on the same plate. They folded it up, wrapped a paper plate around it, and that was how I was served my meal.

The first bite was pure bliss. Valentin and I climbed back into the light of day with cheese dripping down our fingers, and big, bashful grins on our faces.

There was no clean way to stuff your face with crepe while walking down the street and eating with the Frenchman proved it. By the time we were done, settled on a bench in front of the massive glass Apple store, both of use were covered in strings of melted cheese.

"You have egg," said Valentin, "here."

He reached over with his napkin and dabbed at my chin, and all at once my nerves were back. I found myself inching away from him on the round bench.

Still, no mention of our night. I wished he would just tell me what we were, now. If he considered us more than just friends, or if this was just... what could it even be, a fling? A bit of summer fun? I found myself blushing as we stood up again, my focus on the mission wavering in the breeze of his on-again off-again affection.

We passed the crepes place again, climbing up the

other stairs, emerging on the other side of the street in a neighborhood so different from the last. Here, the buildings were old: the trees were larger and shadier, covering a wide main street with fountains at every intersection. A man selling shaved ice sat at the corner, under a parasol. We walked right by him, following the main road until we took a sharp right.

"At the end of the street, there, that's where Cezanne went to school," said Valentin. I couldn't tell if he was joking.

The Caumont Museum was in a magnificent old building partway down the street. Massive iron gates towered over us, larger still than the ones in Arles, or anywhere else I'd been so far. A tour group outside was receiving a talk about them, but in Italian so I couldn't even try to follow.

Sometime in the past ten years, the old conservatory had been transformed, fully renovated into an art museum. The actual conservatory had been moved to the ultra-modern building in the more architecturally modern part of town, leaving the Museum to grow and become a cultural hotspot. I had never been to Paris before, but it made me think of all the pictures I had seen of museums over there.

We stepped into the visitor's center, and Valentin began speaking to a woman in rapid-fire French. She scratched her head, glancing the two of us over, and ran off. Valentin turned to me.

"If she asks, the desk was really important to your grandfather," he said.

"A cover story. I like it."

The woman who came back out was dressed exactly as I imagined every gallery manager to dress. Tight cigarette skirt and a cute white blouse that made her look like she was working in the Louvre, and not a small museum in the south of France.

"Je peux vous aider?" she asked, and Valentin launched into his rapid-fire explanation of our story. Well, a little bit of a twisted story. From what I was able to tell, my grandfather had been a piano prodigy here, and then - I don't think I got this right - he had gotten attacked by an elephant and lost the ability to play. Ok. And then he married…

Oh. He was throwing in Mamie's name. I mean, there's not many other things that sound like Colette Martin. The manager's eyes bulged.

Whatever she said back to him wasn't good, though. She slapped her hands on the sides of her thighs in a way that was more defeatist than anything I had ever heard or seen before today. Then she went back to her office, holding up a finger for us - wait.

"Let me guess," I said, "the desk is gone."

"They got rid of a lot of the old furniture when they took over," he explained, "but she has the list of where they sent them all for us."

The woman had gone above and beyond. When she came back, it was with a thick stack of printed paper, with a photo of each piece of furniture, accompanied by the people who purchased them. The auction list.

"J'espère que ça puisse vous aider," she said, handing me the stack. I trembled as I took them.

"Merci," I replied.

I was thankful. I really was. But whatever help the universe had been giving me had dried up the second we arrived here.

I thought Aix was supposed to be special. Instead, it was going to ruin everything I had been working so hard to accomplish. I could almost imagine it laughing.

twenty-five

WE WENT ACROSS THE STREET WITH THE STACK OF paper, finding a table in the bookstore there.

I was so overwhelmed with the whirlwind we had just been through that I didn't notice at first how much English I heard around me. Not loud, tourist English, just… English. The books around me were in English; the staff would ask for drink requests first in French, then casually in English; signs and merchandise were in English. The place itself was called *Book in Bar*, and I didn't need a translator to tell me that.

"What can I get you?" one of the staff came up to us next with a tray.

I ordered a lemonade, and Valentin an iced tea, though my mind was not all there. No, my entire focus rested on the stack of text in my hand, the pile of furniture printed in black and white where my father's last clue was somehow hidden.

"Do not panic, Jamie," said Valentin, "We will find the desk. It is here."

He patted the stack of paper in front of me, and I tried to hold back the bitter taste of disappointment. For all I knew, the desk could have been sold for scraps at this point. The clue could have been destroyed long ago.

The waitress came back with our drinks, placing them on the small wooden table along with a small cookie each. Valentin took the stack of papers, splitting them in half, retrieving a pencil case from his backpack.

"If you find a wooden desk, you circle it," he said, handing me one, "and then after, we find out which desk is the right one."

He made it look easy, but on the first page alone there were three desks. We moved through the packs, drinking our drinks and trying to ignore the people meandering around us.

But the books had a calming effect on me: Books were the most soothing surrounding in the world. I found myself simultaneously mad and calm, a paradox only literature could explain.

"I have fifteen," I said, once I had finally gone through my stack. "You?"

"Only six. What does the letter say?"

"About the desk?"

He nodded. I pulled out the letter, carefully stowed away in my bag, and together we scoured the text for every single little detail.

"Well, dad says it's old," I replied, "Victorian, even. So we can discount these two desks which are rather modern looking."

"And brown?" added Valentin, "quite a few are black, and this one is white. You see? We are getting there."

He was right. The more we dug into the letter, the more we cut out impossible furniture. Until, finally, we only had one left.

"You see?" he said, with that warm smile of his that usually made my stomach flutter. Instead, my stomach did a quite ungraceful belly flop. Plop.

This is why the clue wasn't here, I realized, as I stared into those eyes that I had fallen so hard for. I had gotten distracted. The universe no longer wanted to help me with this quest, seeing as how I was losing focus. If I hadn't started falling for Valentin, the clue would probably found its way here now.

"It seems we have to go to *Isle-Sur-La-Sorgue* for this one," he explained, tapping his long finger on the image of the single desk left. "We can still do that today, though there's so much more of Aix you need to see. Shall we go tomorrow? Finish the day here?"

"No," I insisted, shaking my head. "We go today. I'm not here as a tourist: I need the clue. It's more important."

"The clue has been there for seventeen years; can't it wait another day?"

"No."

He opened his mouth as if to ask why, then snapped it shut again. I was rather relieved he wasn't pushing the question: if he had, I don't know what would have spilled out of my mouth.

We paid for the drinks, him grabbing a paperback for the train on the way out. Outside the door the weather was sweltering hot, and the soothing effect of the books lost their magic. I was alone again, and mad.

And so, we made our way to the train station, bought our tickets, and rolled out towards the mysterious Isle-sur-la-Sorgue, my hand clutching the little desk printout the entire time.

Valentin said nothing. He stared out the window along with me, in silence. Was he waiting for me to speak first? If so, this was going to be a long ride. He was actually quite terrible at speaking, come to think about it: he hadn't brought up our kiss yet, at all. So even if I did want to know where we stood – which I no longer did, no, I had to stay focused on the mission – he wasn't going to be the one to tell me.

I watched the scenery out the window instead. I was starting to get used to the typical Provençal village. To the old homes with their bright shutters and terra cotta roofs. The narrow-cobbled roads with plants shooting up this way and that. But nothing had prepared me for Isle-sur-la-Sorgue.

I had never been to Holland, but I could imagine this is what Dutch cities would look like if I had. Canals running through the streets, great massive water wheels turning and spraying droplets on bright flowers. Rushing water spewing down, stairs leading to the edge so that locals could drop their feet in - or wash their clothes, at one time, I suppose. Even this late in the day people were sitting with their feet in the current, washing their cares away.

I also hadn't expected the number of antique dealers. Every store was either selling antiques or fancy interior design, modern and ancient beside each other in the same displays.

"Hurry, they're going to close soon," said Valentin, the first words he had said to me since we had boarded the train, leading me away from the water and into a small courtyard. It was a place dropped out of time: a gravel square surrounded by old stores on all sides, elaborate antique statues sitting next to hundred-year-old trunks and uniforms from another century. I wanted to step into every store, be whipped away to another time. But time was the one thing we were lacking.

Valentin spun around on his heels, his eyes darting from door to door. He held the paper up, then put it down, then lifted it up again.

"*Merde,*" he swore, "Where is she?"

I ripped the paper from his hands and darted to the café. One of the waiters was picking glasses up off the table, placing them on a precariously large tray which he held over his shoulder.

"*Excusez-moi,*" I said, probably butchering the pronunciation, "*pourriez-vous m'aider?*"

He turned, still balancing his tray, a smile flashing on his lips. I held out the paper, pointing at the name, struggling to hold it steady as I trembled.

"American?" he asked. He glanced over the paper, squinting slightly. I could see the exact moment when his face fell. "I'm sorry. So sad."

"What? Why?"

"Go talk to ze woman over zere," he said, pointing at a white tent with his free hand. "She speak better English."

"*Merci,*" I replied, but my nerves were shot now.

Sorry meant bad news. Sad? Worse news.

Valentin looked about how I felt: pale, exhausted. But he said nothing as we made our way to the white tent. Every step felt like forcing my way through thick water: slow motion cast upon me, though my heart beat faster and louder than ever before.

The woman at the white tent was sitting smartly in the shade of her tiny antique stand, fanning herself with a piece of her own brochure. She was surrounded by stools of all shapes and sizes: some dark and in terrible shape, in serious need of some love; while others were metallic and stark, clean and new. She nodded at us as we approached.

"*Messieurs - dames,*" she said, "*que puis-je pour vous?*"

"*Parlez-vous anglais?*" I asked.

"A little bit," she replied, "how can I help you?"

"We are looking for this woman," I said, holding out the piece of paper and pointing to the name beside the desk, "can you help us find her?"

"Oh, *Joelle.*"

Like the waiter before her, her face fell. What had been a professional customer service smile was now replaced with heartfelt chagrin. She stood, and I realized she was much taller than I had pegged her for. Her blonde hair almost touched the roof of her tent.

"I am so sorry," she said, "but Joelle died last year."

My heart shattered. I felt it happen through my chest, the millions of tiny shards flying everywhere and lodging themselves into my soft tissues. Dead. So blunt, so final.

"I'm so sorry for your loss," I said, unsure of how to react. The way the woman looked, it seemed as though she had lost a dear friend.

"I'm sorry I could not bring you good news," she replied. "May I ask, why are you looking for her?"

I unfolded the paper and handed it to her completely. She looked at the desk and shook her head.

"I have not seen this piece," she said, "We have been helping her family sell her stock, but I do not remember seeing it here. It must have been sold before she passed."

"Can you help us find who bought it?" I urged, "please. It's a matter of life and death."

I regretted the words when they came out of my mouth. For me, the letter meant the world. Finding the clue and completing the hunt would save you, would put you back on your feet. If I could save you, maybe I stood a chance myself.

But this woman had actually lost her friend: dead had already been a fact, here. Even so, she did not react to my poor choice in words.

"I'm sorry, I do not have access to her records," she

handed the paper back to me, unfazed. "But if you go inside, there are many other desks similar to this one. I am sure we can help you."

"No," I snapped, "it has to be this one."

"Jamie," said Valentin, reaching for my shoulder. I shook him off. "It's over. We need to go."

"No!" I felt the heat in my face, the rush of blood through my veins. "No! I need to find this desk! You have to help me!"

"There is nothing I can do," said the woman.

"Please!" I fell to my knees, unable to hold myself up any longer. "Please, it's for my mother. Please. It could save her life."

"I do not know what to say," the woman replied, curling her lip in disgust. She glanced at Valentin, practically begging him to drag me away. "I cannot do more. Now please. It is time for me to close."

"Please," I said, *"S'il vous plaît.* Help me. Help me!"

Valentin took my hand, stepping away from the tent, hoping I would follow. But the day was hot and I slipped my sweaty hand from his, rushing at the antiques dealer again.

"S'il vous plaît madame!" I pleaded, *"Aidez-moi!"*

"C'est fini, Jamie," said Valentin, interposing himself between me and the now terrified stall owner. "It's over. We have to go."

Aix Marks the Spot

"And you!" I snapped, placing my hands squarely on his chest and shoving him back. "You're such a defeatist. No wonder they say all French men are cowards: you never try anything. You never do anything."

"That's not true," he said, righting himself. "Look, can we talk in the train? We need to go. You are causing a scene."

"Me?" I stammered. It was hard to see anything other than Valentin's stupid face through the tears that were streaming out of my eyes. "Everyone should be causing a scene in this fucking country! Nobody does anything! Oh, you need to find a desk? A simple freaking desk? No one even lifts a finger!"

"Enough, Jamie," he said, stepping forward. I had never been afraid of him before, but in this moment, there was something in his voice that made me want to cower back. And maybe I should have: maybe, the rational part of myself said, maybe you need to get a grip. But the rational part of my brain was still impaled by the shards of my now shattered heart, and it wasn't having any of it.

"Whenever things get hard, you give up," I snarled, poking him in the chest pointedly, "You never do anything. Every time we got close to finding a clue, who was the one who ran away? You. If I had listened to you, I would never have come this far in the first place. So shut up and help me!"

"*Bon, ca suffit!*" The woman was suddenly between us. "*Dehors!* Out! Both of you!"

The entire square was silent as we left. The only thing I could hear was the ringing in my ears, the pulsing anger I had towards them all. A country of whiny quitters.

I would not give up.

I couldn't give up.

But the rational part of my brain said it was over, nonetheless.

And then, the only thing that could ever make this worse came crashing into us, quite literally. Valentin shoved me into one of the warehouses, my nose instantly overwhelmed with the smell of old wood and musty attics. He stared out the door, eyes wide in terror, as a group of men in suits, dressed far too hot for this weather, walked by. They didn't see us, laughing as they passed. His face turned red.

"What the hell, Valentin?" I stammered, shoving his hands off me. He had pushed so hard I half expected there to be a hand-shaped bruise on my chest.

"*Chut!*" he snapped, fingers to his lips.

"Don't shush me in freaking French," I said, stepping away. "What just happened?"

"Will you be quiet for a second of your life?"

Aix Marks the Spot

I had never seen him so mad before. Even in the dim light of the antique warehouse, I could see his face, red and hot. But definitely not in the attractive way, no, far from it. His hair stuck to his forehead, slick with sweat.

"Tell me what's going on," I insisted.

"Because you're actually going to listen for once?"

"What is that supposed to mean?" I snapped, putting my hands on my hips. Not that it made me feel any better. "Is that a quip about my country again? Look, I'm sorry I got loud, ok? I guess it's my American genes. You think I'm different because my dad is French? Because my grandmother is some kind of icon to you? Let me make this very clear: I'm not French. I'm American, just like those girls you openly mock. And I'm mad because I'm angry, not because of some stupid cultural stereotype!"

"Just shut up!" he said, "you are starting this again!"

"Starting what? A scene?"

"You just have to always make it about you, don't you?" A salesman walked passed us, staring, but did nothing to step in. "For once, can you just please do as I say and be quiet? Because that's my father who just walked by out there, and I'm trying not to let him see me, *d'accord*?"

"Your father?"

I stared out the door at the courtyard behind, trying

to find which of the tall, dark haired men could have been the man I had heard oh-so-little about. I thought he was meant to be in Paris: what he was doing here, down south, at a random antiques fair, I didn't know.

Was that really your dad? Why was he here? Didn't he tell you he was coming? I wanted to understand what was going on, but it didn't feel like the time – or place. I did what he asked and kept my mouth shut, as we watched the men leave the courtyard.

"Didn't you want to say hi?" I asked; no, squeaked.

"He didn't," Valentin shrugged, "or he would have called. Come, we have a train."

"Hold on," I said, as he turned to the other exit to the warehouse, heading towards the station, his hands stuffed deep in his pockets. Talk about fuming, I could practically feel the frustrated heat that radiated off of him.

"No."

"No what?"

"No, I don't want to talk about it. I just want us to be quiet, ok?"

"Not ok," I replied, trying to catch up but practically having to run. His stride was so long when he wasn't adjusting for me. "You can't just shove me in the dark and expect me to be ok with it. What happened back there?"

"What happened?" Still, no eye contact. We crossed the street, waving at the cars to stop and let us by. "What happened is that you made a scene. That my father saw. And maybe, he saw me there, with you."

"So you don't want to see him, and you don't want him to see you, but you also want him to call you and see you? What?"

"It's complicated."

He didn't say another word to me as we took our seats across from each other. Our train pulled out, and we once again silently stared out our windows.

The countryside rolled past our windows. Green fields stretching out along the horizon, capped by stubby mountains. I watched them with an intentness rivaled only by my need to not look Valentin in the eyes.

"It is a shame you did not get to see the town," he said, suddenly.

"Hold on, aren't we going to talk about what just happened?" I asked, staring out the train window, still avoiding eye contact, even between our reflections.

"You mean, you screaming in the middle of the antique market?"

"No! About you casually avoiding your dad!"

"Don't change the subject."

"Isn't that exactly what you're doing?"

I've heard it said sometimes that tension was thick

enough to cut with a knife, but right now a knife wasn't enough. Maybe a sword would do, but I wouldn't count on it.

"My father lives in Paris," he said, shrugging, "he sells antiques to rich Americans who want to furnish their New York apartments. Sometimes he comes to the south for a good find. It's nothing to talk about."

"So, you hide."

"When the girl I am standing with is screaming and scaring me? Yes, yes I hide."

"I was scaring you? You were terrifying! That hurt, you know!"

"I'm sorry."

"Are you though?" I scoffed, "I'm not just talking about a bruised collarbone. What you said… You blame me for not listening, but you never say anything! You never told me about your dad. And then our kiss, our night, and… you never spoke of them again. It's like none of it even happened."

He said nothing. Like always. Hallmark of his life.

"I came here because my parents kicked me out," I continued, staring at my knees. My voice came out so shaky all of a sudden. "and I'm not wanted here either. No country wants me. Nobody wants me. So if you're just trying to mess with me, stop. Just stop right now and never talk to me again."

Aix Marks the Spot

The silence in the train was deafening as I shut my mouth. Valentin's eyes were wide, fixed on me in a way no one had ever looked at me before. His mouth, perched somewhere between open and closed, didn't seem able to make a sound. But he didn't look away. He didn't blink. He watched as I wiped my eyes with the edge of my palms.

"Don't say that," he said, his voice low.

"But it's true."

"Your parents kicked you out?"

I nodded, slowly. The tears were pushing their way back through again.

"Of the whole country?"

I nodded again.

"Why?"

"Because," I took a deep breath, steadying myself. The words I was about to utter I had never admitted to anyone but myself.

"Because, I almost killed my mom."

twenty-six

MY FIST MET WITH THE GROUND BEFORE IT MET with Charlie's face. Though I had been aiming to take a swing at the jerk, I had only managed to find thin air, and kept going, collapsing on the floor face first.

The worst part now was that the asshole was laughing. I couldn't tell up from down the way my head was spinning and gripped the fibers of the carpet to keep the dizziness from making me sick. Each guffaw hit my head like a jackhammer.

"Don't even look at her, you douchecanoe," said Jazz, her arms taking my shoulders and helping me back up to a seat. The light was blinding up here. "Jamie, honey, are you ok?"

I tried to tell her that I was, but all that came out of my mouth was a single, thick sob. She wrapped her arms tighter around me. Charlie was nowhere to be seen, but then again, the fog around my eyes made it difficult to see anything.

"What an asshole," she said, and I nodded, hiccupping another sob. I leaned into her chest, inhaling her scent, equal parts rose perfume and cheap beer.

"I'm going home," I blurted out.

"You sure? The night can still get better!"

"No, no," I pushed myself up off the floor, leaning on her for support. Teetering on my wobbly knees, I focused on getting the room to stop spinning. I was fine. I was alright. I was good.

"You're not good," said Jazz. I hadn't realized I had said any of this out loud. "I should get you some water…"

"It's ok, it's fine, I'm fine…"

I found myself with my head in a bush, somehow outside, alone. Where Jazz had gone, I had no idea. How I had gotten outside, I had no idea. My mind was still spinning. Charlie's crass grin swam into my vision.

I had to go home.

I dunked my fingers in my pocket and fished for the keys, but the pocket was empty and I came up dry. Panic started to rise in my chest. The car had been my sweet sixteen gift: dad's first purchase in the US, sixteen years ago, bought off somebody's front yard when his broke down on the way to the hospital to meet newborn me. I had promised to take care of it. Losing the keys was not part of the deal.

I fell to the ground again, dizzy and disoriented. Dad was going to kill me when he found out. I couldn't let him know. I would have to walk home, but that wasn't possible, it was clear across town. And I didn't want anybody here to see me like this, not even Jazz. Where was she?

"I'm not angry, I'm disappointed," dad was saying, lights flashing by the windows wildly. Somehow, I was now in his car, a bag in my hand stuffed there hastily by mom in case I had an accident. I knew that much, I could remembered the feeling of plastic pushing past numb fingers, the touch of mom's hand on my shoulder, as she helped me into the back.

My skin was slick with sweat, sticking to the seats. I wanted to be anywhere but there right now. Especially with Dad raving in the front seat, his voice somehow raspy and shrill at the same time. When he was mad, his French accent came bursting through like an uninvited guest.

"Seriously, Jamie," he spat, "you told us you were going to a sleepover! You realize this means you're grounded, right? You should never have been drinking, not this much, not this late... what would have happened if someone called the cops?"

"I'm sorry," I muttered. My tongue tasted of acid and tequila. Or at least, I think it was tequila. "Why are you here, mom?"

"Dad's here to yell," you said soothingly, "I'm here to make sure you're ok."

"Thanks, mom."

"Thank your father. You deserve to be yelled at, too." You turned back to face the road, grinning sheepishly into her reflection. "But I'm glad you called us, I..."

I was on the ground now, this time, the lights around me blinding, flashing. I couldn't remember how I got here, either. Unlike the other memories of the night, which were fuzzy, vibrant, spinning dizzily and wildly in my head, between here and then there was only darkness.

And cold.

I found myself crying out as I pushed myself up. A piece of shattered glass had pierced my palm, though where it had come from, I couldn't possibly tell you. There was a ringing in my ears so loud I couldn't even hear myself think.

There was an arm on my shoulder, both gentle and hard. In a daze, I turned to look at the stranger, shocked to see them in uniform. Bright fluorescent yellow stung at my eyes. He was saying something, his lips moving, but no sound was coming out. I blinked the confusion from my eyes, offering him my hand, not sure what he was looking for. He nodded, a single, curt nod.

"Over here," he said, his voice getting louder, "Ma'am? Ma'am? Can you tell me your name?"

It took me a minute to conjure it, but the man was patient. He waited as I sorted my brain, trying to push the fuzziness away from my carefully organized facts.

"Jamie," I said, my voice salty on my tongue, "Jamie Martin. What happened?"

He's not the man who answered me. Instead, the answer I received was in the form of an earth-shattering scream. The ringing burst back into my ears as the entire night was swallowed in a single, horrifying, "Monica!"

I was in a hospital bed now. My racing mind was finally beginning to settle, but nothing was making any sense. I couldn't find my parents, but then again, I wasn't allowed to move in the first place. The glass had been removed from my skin, every gash stitched up and bandaged. If you were to look at me, you might think I had fallen off my bicycle.

But I hadn't fallen off my bike. I didn't know what had happened to me. I couldn't make the pieces fit together in my head, everything come out in a shoddy jumble.

Finally, dad walked in the room, bandaged even less than I was. His skin, however… I had never seen it so pale before. Ashen might have been the proper word. It was so devoid of any color, he looked out of place in the real world, as if he had stepped right out of a black and white film.

"Dad." I would have run to him like a toddler if I wasn't pinned to the bed by my IV. He closed the door and collapsed into the chair in the corner, staring at the floor. With a deep breath he folded forward, laying his head in his hands, muffling a scream.

"Dad, is mom…?"

I didn't know how to ask it. I didn't know how to say it. My worst fear, his worst fear, our nightmare playing out on the other side of that door. My heart was racing, while my mind refused to process it.

"She's alive," he said, throwing himself back into the chair and staring at the ceiling now instead. Grief has a funny way of not allowing you to experience it comfortably. "She's still alive. But her legs, Jamie, her legs…"

That was the first day I saw my father cry. And in the next few months, it wouldn't be the last.

twenty-seven

I TOLD VALENTIN EVERYTHING. I TOLD HIM ABOUT moving into my Grandmother's house, so that you could recover and go through physical therapy. I told him about the supposed 'lack of space' and my father calling up the one woman he had vowed never to speak to again, in order to get me out of there. In order to get me away from you.

"And now Mamie told me the truth," I finished, "the truth that I'm the reason they stopped speaking in the first place. That dad ran off with my mom in order to raise me, because she didn't approve of him dating my mom. Dad threw me out just like he should have done seventeen years ago."

"Jamie…" Valentin reached a hand forward, taking mine gently. His fingers were soft against my skin.

Aix Marks the Spot

"It's not your fault."

"It is," I insisted, "everything is. Mamie and dad would still be talking if it wasn't for me. And mom would..."

"Jamie. It is not. Your. Fault."

No one had ever said that to me before. No one had ever told me those words, so clearly, so sternly. For a second, I half imagined Valentin's voice was coming from all around me, from the land itself, but too quickly that moment was gone.

"You don't know anything," I snapped, pulling my hand from his, "you don't know me. We met what, a week ago? Ten days? You do not know me."

"I know you well enough," he said, reaching a comforting hand and placing it firmly on my knee. I didn't know what to make of it: but the hand wasn't moving. It wasn't pushing. It was solidifying, rooting me to down to the train.

"You need to call your father," he said, his eyes wide and pleading, "you cannot go on thinking that everything is always on you."

"But it is," I said, "and I know - I just know - that if I find the treasure at the end of Dad's hunt, everything will be better. Mom will recover. Dad will ask for me back. And Mamie..."

"The hunt won't help anything, don't you see?"

Valentin practically snapped, "you are distracting yourself. Trying to find a quick fix to a problem that is much bigger than you. You cannot fix your mother, there is nothing you can do to fix her. It is outside of your control. You need to accept that."

"Says the man who is always giving up," I said, pulling my knee away.

"I do not give up," he said, "I choose which battles to fight. Some of them are not for me."

"Then you never do anything new. You never do *anything*."

"And maybe I need to. But you need to stop feeling guilty about the things you cannot change. Because it will - as they say - eat you alive."

"Like you would know."

"My father left because of me, and he as much as said it to my face. I wouldn't wish that on my worst enemy, and you are… the opposite of that."

Silence fell upon us once again. The train rolled on, the only sound in the cabin that of gentle wheels on tracks. Valentin stared at his feet, and I stared at his hand, still on my knee, not knowing whether move it or not.

"I don't understand," I said, "how could someone do that?"

"He didn't want to be a father anymore. He didn't

want to live in the south. From one day to the next, he picked up his things, and moved to Paris."

"That's awful," I stammered, "what kind of human being does that?"

"Cowards," he said, "so when you called me one earlier, I… no. It doesn't matter."

"But it does. It does matter. You can talk to me."

"Can I?" He snapped, removing his hand, "because it doesn't seem to me like you listen at all. If you weren't doing your stupid hunt, if you weren't so… mad, I don't know, he wouldn't have seen us together, he wouldn't think…"

"My stupid hunt?"

My hands were shaking, so I clutched them into fists, but it did nothing to help. What had been sadness a few moments before unfurled into anger.

How could he give up like that? How could he think things were over? The universe had proved it wanted us to finish this hunt. His refusal to follow through was burning through me like a forest fire.

"This hunt means everything to me," I spat, "It's my dad's love for my mom. Proof that maybe he might have made the right decision following her to the US. That maybe I wasn't totally screwed up from birth. It was going to make everything better, and you call it stupid?"

"But it wasn't going to change anything," he said, "The letters, they're pieces of paper, Jamie. It never was your job to fix your Mamie, your father, or your mother. The accident was not your fault. And here you are, not listening again. I was talking, about my father, and you just brought everything back to you."

"Back to me?" I stammered, "You insulted me! And you're avoiding your own problems, blaming everything on me!"

"You shamed me! In front of my father!"

"A man who didn't even tell you he was here!"

"He's still my father! And you're not listening to me!"

"Leave me alone, Valentin!" I snapped, grabbing my bag and throwing it over my shoulder. "I'm sorry about your dad, ok? That sucks. But I am not him! Stop blaming me for everything that goes wrong, ok? You keep saying to not make things my fault, but I'm not going to do that by blaming something else, ok? So focus on yourself before you go around telling me what to do. It doesn't sound like you dad leaving was your fault, either. It just sounds like he's an asshole."

I stormed off, though in a small train there was nowhere to go. I slammed the door release button and hopped out onto the platform; my eyes so thick with tears I couldn't see any farther than my hands.

Aix Marks the Spot

The train pulled away, and I realized this was not at all my station. It didn't matter. I threw myself down on the bench and cried.

twenty-eight

THE ONLY NUMBER I HAD SAVED IN MY PHONE (WHO happened to own a car) was Jean-Pascal. Frustrated, missing being able to drive because of this stupid country, I begged him to pick me up.

"I am at... *Je suis... Le Thor?*" I said, looking at the tiny station sign.

"*Le Four?*" he said, "four-what?"

"Le Tor?" I repeated.

"*Ah! Je viens tout de suite. Pas de panique.*"

Don't panic. Yeah, right. Easy for him to say. He hadn't just alienated the only friend he had in this country, right after he went through some serious crap with his father. Which was also, once again, my fault for making a scene. What a jerk move, Jamie.

But I was right about one thing: Valentin couldn't

go around telling me how to fix my life if he wasn't dealing with his own. He couldn't tell me I wasn't allowed to feel guilty if he was running around ignoring his own problems.

Jean-Pascal took a while to reach me. Apparently, I was further from home than I had previously estimated. And he had brought the old red buggy, too, just to make things even more awkward.

"Are you all right?" he asked, as he leaned over to open my door for me. He put all his effort into pronouncing the four words. Well, three, but he made them four by careful consideration.

"Yes. No. I don't know," I replied, taking the passenger seat. As I sat down, I felt myself deflate, my body heavy and weak. "I'm sorry to have to call you…"

"Slow, please," he said, "I do not understand."

I took a deep breath.

"Thank you," I said, "I am sorry to ask for help."

"It is ok to ask," he replied. The car puttered forward, leaving the tiny station and slipping none too gracefully onto the road. "All people need. Not all ask."

We drove a couple of minutes through the empty roads, the sun crouching low on the horizon, casting its long, golden shadows on us like a net. I sunk into my seat.

"We are so worried about you," said Jean-Pascal,

causing me to sink even deeper.

"Oh," I replied. "Didn't Mamie tell you? She kicked me out."

"She is sorry she made you… run away."

"Run away?" I laughed. Not a good laugh, but the anxious, ripping-out-your-own-guts kind of laugh. "No. She called my mother a whore and told me she never wanted to see me again."

"She did not mean it."

"It didn't sound like she didn't mean it."

We continued driving in silence for a while, then Jean-Pascal, possibly in an effort to lighten the mood, turned on the radio. The first song was an oddly upbeat polka; the next, a remix of that pirate song I think came from Peter Pan. After that, I'm pretty sure they just outright played ten minutes from pirates of the Caribbean. I reached over and turned off the radio – even that sucked in this stupid country.

I wished I had the words to ask Jean-Pascal for all the help that I needed. I wish I could ask him how to reach this woman. How to piece back together a broken heart. How to keep going knowing I was the source of so many awful things.

Valentin was wrong: it was impossible to move on from them, not until you made them right. Blaming others for my problems wasn't going to solve them.

But one thing he was right about was that the hunt was now over. The desk was far out of our reach. Our last lead was dead. The last clue was long gone.

And there were no words to ask for help on this one.

"I am sorry," Jean-Pascal said, as we turned off the main road and started to make our way to Lourmarin, "that you are sad here."

Sad was one word for it. You had always called Provence home, even if you had only lived there for a short time. But I was a girl without a home, exiled from her mother country and rejected from her adoptive one. My heart had begun to beat for Provence but my blood was too American. I would never belong here, or in the world I had left what now felt like ages ago.

"It's not your fault," I said, "you have been so generous."

"People see Provence like dream," he said, "but dreams are for sleep. Real world not a dream."

"Yeah, I get that."

"Real world better. Real world real."

Insightful, this Jean-Pascal.

He pulled up in front of Mamie's gate, hitting a small beeper in his car. Just who was this man, to my grandmother? She had never said, and he had never admitted.

"Jean-Pascal," I said, nervously. But when the

question arose in my throat, another one rushed past it and reach my mouth first, "why do you drive this old car? Your new one is much nicer."

"*Pfff,*" he said, throwing himself in an elaborate, shoulder raising shrug, "you can always drive nice car. Why not drive special car?"

"Thanks, JP." As the car pulled up the gravel car port, I could tell he wasn't going to park. He turned around the fountain and stopped, ready to go.

"You do me favor," he said, poking his head back out the window, "you read one book for me. *La fin du printemps.* Your Mamie's best."

"I will, promise."

As I shut the door and made my way towards the house, I realized just how futile that promise was.

The kitchen was empty when I came in. The keys were on the table, an unasked question to lock up behind me when I came in.

I walked up through the living room, checking the oddly placed front door. It was definitely locked. No drunk Mamie on the couch this time. Good.

I owed the woman nothing. She called my mother a whore and told me I was a pawn: she had lost all of my respect in one fell swoop. I didn't bother to check if she was in her office. I knew there was nowhere else she would ever be.

Aix Marks the Spot

My room felt smaller now. I fell down on my bed, defeated, tossing my bag on the floor. The four letters were stacked neatly inside, but I no longer cared. The fifth letter was gone. The treasure, whatever it was, lost to time.

In that moment, the only person I wanted to talk to was you.

The sun was starting to set outside, painting the sky a wild shade of orange. The grass and trees knelt in pink before it. To capture the color would be a feat accomplished only by masters. I would never create a work as beautiful as it. I saw why the greats came to love this place: I would love it too, if it could ever love me back.

As if a place could love.

My phone buzzed. A text, from Valentin. I slipped it away with a flick of my thumb. And there, sitting in my inbox, was a message from Jazz.

"Haven't heard from you," she said. *"Call me when you get this, if you can?"*

I checked my phone data: there wasn't much there, and I wasn't about to waste it on Jazz. Not after how she had abandoned me the other night, when I needed her most.

She started calling me immediately, as if she had been waiting for that little silver *'seen'* to appear under her message. I would make this quick.

"I have nothing to say to you," I snapped, before she even had time to greet me, "I really don't. I have to go."

"What the hell, Jamie?" she stammered, "what happened?"

She seemed genuinely surprised: less bubbly than when I left, fully grounded and fierce. My finger hovered over the red decline button.

"What happened?" I said, "What happened is I've been living through hell! My Mamie kicked me out, and I needed you, and you weren't there!"

"Oh my god, Jamie, are you ok?" she asked.

"No, I am not ok!"

"Do you have a place to stay?"

"I slept at a friend's house. But now he hates me, so I'm back at Mamie's, though I don't think she can even tell. And I'm going to hang up now."

"Oh come on," she scoffed, "Jamie, I'm trying to help here!"

"Help? How are you helping? You're living the summer that we planned, you're still driving around, free, happy, while I'm trapped here and I can't... I can't..."

I burst into tears then. God, I was doing so much crying today. My life was in pieces, and there was no way I could put it back together again.

"Jamie," said Jazz, so stern she would have made the looney toons stand to attention, "You think I'm happy here, living my summer without you? I miss you so much! You don't even know! Every freaking day I'm worried about you. The only reason I'm still taking those classes is because you said it was fine by you!"

"Oh…" My heart – shattered as it was – was returning to its usually beat in my chest. The racing was slowing, basked in the soft, gentle tone of Jazz's voice. She radiated calm, even though the phone.

"*Oh* is right. I can't believe you thought I had abandoned you."

"You stopped talking to me." I muttered.

"I stopped talking because you stopped listening," she said, "I told you that you needed to move on and enjoy your trip. That your mother is fine. That it's not your fault. But here you are, still moping in France. In Provence! You realize I've dreamed of going there, right?"

"Not like this… not with your mom… my mom…"

"If you want to blame anyone, blame me," she said, "I'm the one who took your keys that night. I knew you would want to drive, and it was a terrible, terrible idea for you to be behind the wheel. I didn't expect any of that to happen. And I don't beat myself up about it, no: if you had been driving, I am convinced you would be dead right now. And I can't imagine a world without you in it. You got me?"

"You took my keys?"

"And I don't regret it. So if you want to blame me, go ahead. If you never want to talk to me again, go ahead. I'd rather you be in this world and giving me the cold shoulder than live in a world where you're six feet under."

"Oh my god, Jazz," I stammered, "I've been… I don't think there's a word in any language to full describe how much of a big fat idiot I've been."

We talked for as long as we could. I told her everything about my time in Provence, the good, the bad, and the ugly, everything. She told me about the art intensive I had missed, and how much she had learned and grown in such a short time. I told her about Valentin, and how confusing and weird and maddening it had been trying to figure out what we were. She told me about her current unrequited crush on the art TA who had been managing the still life portion of their course, and the funny new word her dog had learned to say.

The weight that now lifted off my shoulders didn't come from knowing she had taken the keys. I knew I couldn't be like Valentin and blame her for that night.

Instead, I realized that I could trust this girl with my life. I had known it before, but this was more proof than I could ever have imagined.

I was not alone.

"I have been a terrible friend," I told her, as we realized we would have to go.

"You've had a lot going on," she replied, "It's ok. Just recover. And call your parents, ok? They're so worried about you, your mom's resorted to texting *me*. And trust me, she does not know how to use emojis."

You had been worried about me? All this time I'm panicking about your recovery, and you're the one worried about me? I opened up the family group chat, scrolling through our conversations since I got here. My end had all been either one worded, or complete lies about everything being great.

I had to call you. I needed to talk.

I found the landline sitting next to the microwave in the kitchen and dialed up the house. It took a few tries to get the country code right, and I would probably owe Mamie a ton for making an international call, but she wasn't around to stop me.

You picked up on the first ring.

"Jamie-baby!" you sang, "how are you? How is the land of lavender and sun?"

I burst into tears. Everything I had been holding

back since the train came barreling out of me, and as it rolled it brought with it the pain from long before. The pain of what I put you through. The horror of knowing I would be the reason you would never walk again.

"I'm so sorry, I'm so sorry," I sobbed, cradling the phone to my cheek. "I'm so sorry for everything."

"Darling!" you sounded more baffled than anything else, "oh, honey, what happened?"

"Blue Jay?" Dad's voice cut in, "are you hurt?"

"No, I'm just… so sorry… for everything." I repeated. I couldn't think, no other words could go through my foggy mind. A chorus of sorries filled the receiver.

"Calm down, catch your breath," said mom, "start at the beginning."

"But you were there," I hiccuped, "I should never have called you that night, I should never have asked for…"

"Sweetie, no." Dad snapped so loudly I though there had been a break in the line, "Jamie, if you hadn't called us, you would have been at the wheel that night. You could have been the one to…"

And now he was sobbing, all attempts to hold himself together failing. I missed him, his strong arms, the way his hugs could squeeze all worry out of me.

"Jamie, if you had been at the wheel, you would never have made it home," you said. "We always want to help you. It is not your fault that this accident happened. Do you hear me? It was not your fault. And if you thought that for a second, then I'm the one who should say sorry."

"But you sent me away," I blubbered, "you wanted me out of your lives…"

"What?" Dad interjected, "we wanted you safe. We wanted to give you space to heal. We never wanted you gone!"

"I thought it was time you meet your Mamie," you said, "she's an amazing woman. What with mother's house… We thought you would be happier there."

"We thought you dreamed of Provence, like we did."

"Not without you," I said, "not without you."

And together, we sobbed across an ocean.

twenty-nine

I FELL ASLEEP WITH THE PHONE PRESSED AGAINST my ear, off but reassuring all the same. When I awoke, it had fallen between two pillows, and my wild, tired-self thought it was lost forever.

I found it, clutching it close. I had missed a few messages during the night, including a few from Jazz, probably wondering how it had gone with my parents. I wasn't ready to answer her just yet: I would have to write her a full-blown letter.

I opened up Amazon: Mamie's book, what was it again, *La Fin du Printemps*? The end of spring. I found it easily, with the orange bestseller tag boldly next to it. The cover was simple, a black and white picture of a child's feet, the hem of a white dress hanging down before it.

Aix Marks the Spot

Scrolling down, I came upon Mamie's author portrait, and my breath caught in my throat. She was stunning: her hair had been shorter when it was taken, a perfect shade of silver that would have been an insult to call grey. She rested her chin on her hand, looking out at the reader, as if to say, 'I know you, don't I?'

Looking into those flat, two dimensional eyes, I connected more with my grandmother than the entire two weeks I had been here.

I bought the book on kindle, in English: then went downstairs to grab a French copy that I had spied sitting on a shelf in the living room. Now armed with the two editions, I threw myself on my bed and began to read.

I didn't know what quite to expect from the book: I hadn't even read the blurb before purchasing it. Jean-Pascal was the one who wanted me to read it, after all. It opened on a stormy night, where three women, a mother, a daughter, and the grandmother sat around a fire. The granddaughter was only three, and her whole world was this little wooden ball, carved with intricate faces of animals. The grandmother had made it from the wood of the olive trees in her garden.

The grandmother was telling her daughter about her farm. She told her about a great freeze, that came down from the mountain and killed all the olive trees in the region, including hers. That hundreds of farmers gave up, leaving their now dead olive orchards, took up a new crop or moved into the city to start a new trade.

The forest grew up around the dead orchards, but olives are resilient. Over the years, little olive trees grew under the thick branches of pine, pushing past the carpet of needles and juniper to become not beautiful trees, but spindly olive bushes. Ugliest things you could imagine.

The grandmother swept her arm towards the olive grove outside their window. She told her daughter how before her own father died, the two of them went into a thick pine forest and lifted the olive bulbs from the earth. How they split the knotted root at every stem. How every planted bulb became a new tree, and those were the trees in their grove now.

The mother praised the grandmother for a good tale, but she did not seem to believe a word of it. She sat on the floor and played with the daughter. At the end of the night, she said goodbye, and took the toddler home. The little girl forgot the ball.

The grandmother tended her olive trees, growing the twigs big and strong for her daughter and granddaughter, but they never came home.

Townspeople came. They brought news of the granddaughter, now thriving. First, she was five. Then she was ten. Then she was a gorgeous young girl, brilliant at school. Or a beautiful bride, with a respectable husband.

The grandmother wrote letters, which she gave to the townspeople to deliver, just to be sure they were reaching her young girl. But the girl never replied.

Her mother did.

Each letter brought news of the granddaughter, but none were in her own words. The grandmother had only barely heard her toddler babble, and now she would never see her granddaughter speak.

Her grove was now a flourishing, beautiful place. Her farm was large and each tree produced the most gorgeous olives. She had grown her production so much that she had now built a press, to make olive oil, and later a little shop, to stock and sell.

But she was old. She wrote to her granddaughter, to ask if she would take the reins of the farm she had spent years building. Generations supported her until this very moment. She was ready for her lineage to take the reins.

No answer.

Finally, she drove across the country, to Paris, to find her once little girl. However, she was a farm woman, and was not made for a place as loud or as bright as the capital. She struggled to find her daughter's home, but people recognized her from the oil she made, and helped her find her way.

She finally reached the building where her granddaughter lived. Climbed the four flights of stairs - no elevator - to the apartment. Knocked on the door.

When the door opened, she saw herself.

And that's where it ended.

Trust me, I didn't understand it much, either.

I reread it quite a few times, French version in my left hand and English in my right. Just to be sure I didn't miss anything in the translation. Sure, I paraphrased a lot of it above: it was long enough to span three hundred pages and had apparently been deemed so good that not only had it won some award but had also been used during the French Literature Baccalaureate as the extract to study. Apparently, those were important things.

The latter had asked students to write a dissertation on the statement: "The grandmother's opening the door upon herself at the very end of the book represents building a future for oneself, while ignoring the needs of others." If I were to make it an SAT question, I would go much easier - The grandmother's opening the door upon herself at the very end of the book represents:

A) The granddaughter never existed;

B) The author's fear of dying alone;

C) The author really has a thing against mirrors;

Aix Marks the Spot

D) Some really deep personal turmoil which could have been resolved if the grandmother went to talk to the daughter and ask her why she just randomly started coming over when she told her the awesomest way to start an olive grove from nothing? Metal, grandma, metal.

I put the books down and landed on my bed again. I couldn't believe how long I had spent reading it, rereading it, analyzing it, as if would hold all the secrets my Mamie had been hiding from me. The anger and resentment you all had been keeping from me, as it kept this family apart. The internet tore the book apart in every possible way, examining it under different lights, but they never reached the root of the problem.

A mother and daughter don't just stop talking to their grandma from one day to the next without good reason.

Maybe that reason was because the grandmother called the mother a whore. Or told her son never to trust her. Or told them both to get rid of the child and…

It was just a story. Just a story. It wasn't our lives at all, only one side of it, altered to become fictional, changed by editors and who knows who else. It was an award-winning novel, and real life was never a novel.

It was all told from the grandmother's point of view, after all.

Sarah Anderson

I turned on my hotspot for the first time since arriving in France and picked up my computer. Friends were asking how I was, where I was at. How much had I even told them about the accident, before I was pushed on a plane and sent away?

No. Not sent away. I needed to stop blaming myself; For things I could not control and blaming others for the things I should have. You didn't kick me out. I should be enjoying my time here.

I spotted it, then, just as I started packing my life back together. The only message with an unreadable name. Valentin.

Why was he trying to reach me through Facebook?

The message he sent was brief and took me a minute to realize what was happening. Just a copy paste of an email, since I had never given him my address.

Dear Valentin,

This is so exciting! It's like being in a spy movie! Thank you for reaching out to us and inviting us to take part. If they ever make a movie about this moment, please let us know!

My husband and I were thrilled to receive your email. He loves this desk: I'm proud to say I bought it for him, for his last birthday, having fallen in love with it when we toured France together. We wanted to bring a small piece of it home and knowing the history of this particular piece made it all the more fascinating. And now, adding this modern history to it makes us love it even more: a love story, hearts crossing boundaries and countries to be together… it makes the desk all the more real!

My husband and I spent a few hours trying to find it. The letter was well hidden and must have gotten lodged deeper into the woodwork as it was shipped here. But we found it in the end, and it took both of us a lot of restraint not to read it.

We scanned the letter and have mailed you the original. Let us know what the treasure is when you find it.

Sincerely,
Dana and Louis Brown

He had done it. Despite everything we'd said, he'd still fought his way to find the clue. With shaking fingers, I clicked the letter.

thirty

Mon Amour,

My darling, look at how far you've come! This is the last clue I have to give you. At your next stop awaits your greatest prize - at least in my opinion. If you haven't broken up with me at this point, well I'm pretty sure you're going to like what you find there.

Your next clue is: Across from Provence.

Ok, I'm going to tell you where. Exactly where. Since it's your last clue, I'm going to make you work for it. So I'm sending you to the top of the St Victoire. You'll find the clue hidden under the cross.

I lost count of how many times we hiked the

mountain. That one time we climbed through that thick soupy fog might have been my favorite: it was almost impossible to tell how far we'd come, and how far we had yet to go. And at the very top, the cross looked like it was just any old phone pole. It was astounding.

But think back to the first time we hiked it together. The first time we realized we needed a respite from our work and needed the sunlight to survive. We packed our sandwiches, grabbed our water, and went.

It was nothing like Cezanne made us think it would be. All his gorgeous paintings almost made me think it would be a gently sloping stroll. Nope. It might have been March but the sun was scorching without any tree cover, and it was steep - so steep! I was out of breath five minutes into the walk.

When we finally reached the top, we had to stop by the monastery first. It was amazing how many people were up there at this hour, and how small the place actually was. I had always thought it would be, you know, an actual monastery. Like something out of a fantasy novel. But there was barely room for any one person to stay there.

Sarah Anderson

You pointed to where the rock was cut clear through, a shelf of stone in its place: the paraglider's launching point. We dared each other to stand there, at the edge. You were far braver than I was: you walked out to the metal edge, one hand poised gracefully on the rock, and looked right down at the sheer drop. Just watching you made me dizzy.

I went next. I had you stand by me, to hold me in case the worst happened. I held the wall and looked down. Oh, how the wind blew through my hair! I thought I would be pushed clear off! And I realized in that moment that I was facing my worst fears, and I was surviving. That I was standing there in the midst of one of the most terrifying drops I had ever beheld, and I was alive. I felt alive, truly alive, more alive than I had ever been before.

Since when did feeling so small make anyone feel so strong?

When I finally managed to pull myself from the view, you pointed at the words carved into the metal of the edge. CHOOSE YOUR FREEDUM. We laughed at them, while all the while I stood there, thinking about how today, we had chosen to be free. Chosen to do what would

Aix Marks the Spot

make us happy, even if it was hard.

You reminded me we had to go higher to reach the cross. The last bit was the steepest, and my heart was pounding so hard through my chest that I thought I was going to throw up. The walk went quickly. The ground leveled out and we were finally here: the cross was there before us, and it was so small. I mean sure, it's a big cross. Like what, twenty meters tall? But you'd think it being so visible that it was twice as high. I mean, I guess it's not the Eiffel tower, but . . .

Anyway. Slightly disappointed, and with my heart still beating from the drop off point earlier, we sat on the side facing our beloved Aix and tore into our sandwiches, saying nothing, just admiring the view. I put the sandwich down for a second, to drink my water, and this random dog runs up, grabs it, and runs off. I mean, come on! What were the odds?

You laugh, and without even asking, rip your sandwich in half and hand it to me. We pop open the paprika pringles and silently revel in the wonders of Provence.

Find where we were sitting. The clue will be down there. But do me a favor and remember to

sit when you get there. Sit, rest, and take in
the view. This is Provence. This is home.

So much Love,
Your Pomme Noisette.

I was shaking now. Before I knew what I was doing, my fingers were already pulling up Valentin's number and dialing him. He picked up on the first ring.

"Jamie," he exclaimed, my name on his lips like the first breath of a drowning man, "*Mon dieu*. Are you all right? Are you…"

"I'm sorry," I sputtered, "about all the things I said. Don't interrupt me, I'm not quite sure where this going, but if I stop speaking I'll lose the thread entirely. But I'm so sorry about your dad. And I'm sorry I somehow made it about me. When it's not all about me, I see that now. You were right, my parents didn't kick me out. I've been spending this whole time here trying to understand why they didn't want me that I didn't see what they were trying to give me. I read Mamie's book, you know, the creepy one with the second grandmother at the ending, and I don't understand a thing, but I think that's the problem in my family. We don't talk. I mean, we talk, but we don't understand each other. We say words and half the time they're in the right language but they are never the right ones and never taken the right way. I'm so sorry, I should have listened to you when you were trying to talk to me and I should have…"

I took a deep breath, realizing I was out of air. I practically coughed on the receiver. But just as I asked, Valentin waited for me to finish. Even if I had been right in guessing I would lose my own train of thought.

"I don't know how you found the last letter," I said, tears welling up in my eyes, "but I can never thank you enough. Thank you, Valentin, thank you."

He waited a second, hesitant. I wished I could see him in person, connect with him and tell him all the things I truly wanted to say. And I could, right now: there was nothing holding me back, not any more. But it was not the right time, and I knew it.

"I like it when you talk," he said, slowly, "I like the way your voice sounds. I like the way my language slips into your words. And I really like it when you say what you mean."

"You do?" I stammered, "it's not… I don't know, rude? Out of place?"

"No. When I met you, I was afraid everything you said was to make me get along with you. I didn't know if I liked you, or the idea of you."

"And now, you know?"

"I know that I like you," he replied, and my shattered heart started to flutter, "Isn't that the problem with so many stories? Everything would end sooner if people just talked to each other. If they all just said what they meant. Romeo and Juliet might have had a happy ending if everyone had just… talked."

"Talked. And listened."

"When you told me in the train that I never did anything, I knew you were right, though I didn't want to admit it. And I knew I had to prove you wrong. I contacted every antique dealer in Isle-sur-la-Sorgue: most did not reply. Those who did were usually a little… as you say… snippy. But one sent me to the vendor's sister, who had the record of sales. I emailed them, and they replied."

"You… you wrote to all those people."

"I did. And before you ask, I did not do it for anything, as you so angrily accused me of doing. I did it for you, because you are my friend."

"Valentin… I can never thank you enough."

"You will never have to. Do you need help for the clue?"

"No, I solved this one," I said, wiping the tears from my face, "and I think I need to do this one on my own."

"I understand," he replied. Did I imagine the drop in the tone of his voice? Maybe I did. But this was between me and my parents now. I had to finish this alone.

"But Valentin? You will be the first to know what the treasure is. We will celebrate the end of this hunt together. I could not have done it without you."

"It was my pleasure," he replied, "and if you need anything, call me. The hike is not difficult, but it is long all alone. I will be with you every step of the way."

"I know it," I said. And as we hung up, I felt three words on my lips, words I had only ever reserved for my parents and friends until today. Words that, in any language, were more than the sounds they were made up of.

I don't know if he heard it, but *I, Love,* and *You* slipped out before I could reel them in.

thirty-one

DEMAIN, DÈS L'AUBE, J'IRAIT.

I slouched across two seats of the early morning bus, the sun so low on the horizon I wondered if anyone had reminded it to get up yet. I clutched Dad's tattered and annotated copy of Victor Hugo's poetry, trying as hard I could to wrap my head around the nuances of the words. Fat chance. I understood them, but they did not come alive for me the way they did for Valentin. Still, there was something beautiful in reading a poem about dawn when you were riding across the twilit countryside the poet himself had been talking about.

Well, he had apparently been talking about Normandie, but hey, I was in the right country for once.

Oh. And it was about love after death. Oops. Still beautiful, though.

Aix Marks the Spot

The sun was up by the time the bus reached the station in Aix, and I made my way down the terminal to catch the ride to the mountain. I felt pride swelling in my gut as I took the avenue, knowing I was doing this alone, and that I didn't need any help to navigate this strange foreign world anymore. And while I had only been in Aix once before, on the day my heart shattered, I found a piece of it here, and stuffed it right back in my chest where it belonged. There was something about this city that accepted who I was, flaws and all.

The bus, per usual, drove past the stop later than scheduled. But unlike before, this did not make me angry: it came at its own time, scooped me up and took me along on my way all the same. At this hour, there was just me in the bus, sitting all the way in the back, and a couple of hikers with their large packs taking up their own seats. I looked at my tiny backpack, suddenly realizing that I had probably not brought enough at all.

The bus rolled us out of town, where the city ended abruptly, suddenly replaced with fields of vines and forests of thick, dry pines. We flashed past the stops faster than I could read them, taking the winding turns faster than I ever would have had the confidence to drive on my own.

At this rate, I was going to miss my stop. I gathered my courage with both hands and scooted up the rows of the bus.

"Excusez-moi," I stammered, *"Parlez-vous Anglais?"*

"Yeah mate," the guy with the gorgeous blonde hair replied, "kiwis, not frenchies."

"Not all of us," said the brown-haired boy, "Texas, hi."

"You alright?" Asked the girl.

"Oh, thank god," I laughed, "I couldn't figure out how to say the next bit in French! Are you going to the St Victoire?"

"Yup, you too?" asked the girl.

"Yeah, if I don't miss the stop. I have no idea where to get off."

"Barrage de Bimont!" the driver bellowed from the front seat, "The *Barrage* of *Bimont!* American?"

"Yes!" I turned to the man, who was now wearing a Stetson, of all things. I was quite sure he wasn't wearing it when I climbed onboard, or I would have noticed.

"I have got you!" he said, his voice booming like a DJ's. *"Australien?"*

"Nahn, Nouvelle Zealande!" said the two kiwis. New Zealand, I think.

"Do you like country?"

"This country? Yeah! *C'est tres beau!*"

"Non, country! *La musique!*"

All of a sudden, the PA speaker flipped on and out came the most country song I had ever heard. Sung in southern twang by what really sounded like a cowboy, whose girlfriend left him and whose dog died (not the doggy!). It was the kind of music I heard at ho-down themed parties back home.

"I love country!" the driver exclaimed, "I love America! One day, I will go!"

"Really?" I couldn't help but climb up to the front of the bus, ignoring the sign that told us not to speak to the driver. I mean, it was in French, I could pretend not to understand it. It seemed the backpackers were coming too, leaving their bags in their seats and moving up close so that the man didn't have to yell, though he still did. "That's awesome! Where?"

"South Dakota! I want to drive big bus there. Where you from?"

"Philadelphia?"

"Ah! Rocky!"

"That is so cool," said the Texan. "I've always wanted to go! I've been to Cali but never the east coast."

"East coast: Washington, New York!" The driver said with a big grin. "East coast France: Marseille, Nice, Monaco!"

"Oh yeah, we're going to Nice next," said the girl, "we're going to see as much of Europe as we can. Living out of our backpacks and everything."

She pointed at her bag, and I practically sighed in relief. It wasn't like I was going to need all that for my hike in the end. But they were crazy if they were going to hike a mountain, in this heat, with all their belongings on their backs.

The driver pulled up to a fork in the road, and stopped, opening the door as he pointed frantically up the hill.

"You walk up, up," he explained, "and then up more. When you reach cross, is top."

"Thanks so much!" I said, as the kiwis grabbed their bags, "I hope you get to South Dakota one day."

"It is the dream! Bye bye! Nice walk!"

We watched the bus drive away, basked in the song of the cicadas. The kiwis hitched up their backpacks, preparing for the ascent.

"Hey, what's your name, kid?" asked the guy with the curly hair.

"It's Jamie," I replied, "and you are?"

"I'm Matt, and this is Hazel and Dutch," he replied, pointing to his friends. "You hiking alone? Want to join us?"

"Maybe for a bit," I said, "but I'm actually here on

a mission."

"Yeah? What kind of mission?"

We made our way up the roadside, finding the trail quickly and starting our march. It wasn't steep at all: maybe Valentin had just been trying to intimidate me into asking for him to come along.

"I'm trying to find the treasure my dad hid for my mom before I was born," I replied. It felt surreal to unload the story: like a jinx had been lifted off of it, freeing me to speak my mind. "He actually set up this entire treasure hunt across his favorite cities in Provence."

Dutch wanted all the details of the hunt so far. He wanted to know everything: why dad had made the hunt in the first place, why mom had never even made it to the first clue, all that. And I found myself answering him, unabashedly.

Then we reached the top of the hill, and we were definitely not in Kansas anymore.

We had somehow been transported to the top of a gorge, great cliffs slicing a thin but immensely deep ravine through the limestone. Up ahead was a great dam, the lake behind it a deep sapphire blue, while the St Victoire mountain rose up from the depths.

And there, at the very top, the cross of Provence. My goal literally in sight.

"Everybody ready?" Asked Hazel, "it's going to be a tough one."

The talking stopped once we had crossed the dam, and the steep ascent began. I didn't even realize that Dutch had stopped asking questions until I was too out of breath to even try answering them. The incline felt vertical, and with the sun beating down on my back, every step was torture. For the kiwis and their bags of personal belongings, it must have been a hundred times worse.

And then some runner would flash past us, either on their way up or their way down, tossing a quick *bonjour* at us which we replied in breathless unison.

Every time I thought the trail evened out a little, it got steep again, repeating flat areas and steep until we broke through the line of pines. Now there was no hiding from the sun, no matter what we tried: the trek was just going to keep getting worse.

Why was I doing this again? I had nothing to prove to myself, to you. Mamie didn't know or care that I was here today. Valentin was the only one who wanted to join, and I had pushed him away out of what, personal pride?

It was probably the heat just getting me, well, heated. I took a swig of now hot water and pushed on.

I will not describe to you the pain of hiking in the

hot summer sun. I will not detail the three-hour trek to the summit - not even the summit, I learned later, the cross was not the actual summit - or how much sweat was dripping off me after just the first hour. I will tell you how nerve wracking it was to walk up a trail so close to sheer cliffs, watching the ground drop farther and farther away from you until you wondered how you could be stuck so high.

"The priory," said Hazel, "I can see it!"

From that point on, the trip felt like minutes. We casually strolled into the shaded alcove of the priory, along with the other hikers who were resting in the cool breeze. The priory itself was smaller than I expected, just a few squat buildings around a stone floor, caught safely between the cliffs of the St Victoire.

"Ready to go to the top?" Asked Dutch, hoisting his bag higher on his back. The shirt there was drenched in sweat.

"Actually, this is the part I need to do myself," I said. The trio nodded.

"We'll meet you back here for the way down, if you want," said Hazel.

"That would be great, though don't let me hold you up."

"Nah, don't worry about it."

They made their way to the path to the summit, but

I had a detour to do first. The most terrifying part of the lot.

Instead of following them up the path to the cross, I turned right, to where a massive pit seemed to dig into the mountain itself. This wasn't in dad's letter: a sign there bragged about a recent archeological dig, with eight-hundred-year-old chapels. It was hard to believe anyone climbing this mountain so long ago, let alone building a chapel on top of it. Dad hadn't mentioned that at all in his letter.

But where I wanted to go was behind the pit, around it. To where a slice through the cliff showed a beautiful blue sky. To where a short rock wall was everything between me and a few thousand-foot drop to the earth below.

Dad had made it sound like you stood right on the edge. Maybe you did, but you would have been much braver than me. I was happy enough for the solid rock wall to keep me from the fall. I stood as close as I dared, staring out at the horizon, taking in the breathtaking view. The miles and miles of rolling hills and pines, the very view that brought you and dad closer together all those years ago. Were you pregnant with me, the last time you climbed? Was I here with you, when you stood out, facing the view?

I felt like I stood there for hours. It could well have

been. The long summer days meant the sun seemed to move quickly across the sky. But there was no point in denying the inevitable. It could well be that the last clue was not where it was meant to be, and that I had climbed this whole way, done all this nonsense for nothing.

But I owed it to you to finish this.

I owed it to me.

I turned, walking away from the cliff, and made my way along the last stretch of the hike to the cross. And there I was; on top of a mountain I had seen all my life in paintings. Standing before a cross that had been carried to the top of the mountain on the back of donkeys, a beacon inviting all to find safety and peace in this turbulent world.

It was a little smaller than I expected it to be. Especially when I had just spent weeks seeing it from everywhere I went. And yet, it was perfect. Hikers sat on a bench, admiring the spectacular view. It was breathtaking from here, without the cliffs to make you feel small: up here, at the peak, I felt like a giant. I breathed in the hot dry air and let myself feel my victory. I had made it. I was at the top. I had done it, all on my own. I had slain the dragon.

And then, for the first time since the accident, I truly wanted to draw.

Sarah Anderson

I sat on the bench, between a French couple who were eating baguettes stuffed with tuna and eggs, and a man in a tight running outfit dripping with sweat. My pencil flew over the pad, picking up the details I hadn't noticed before: the steam from a far off nuclear plant, a farm making fluffy clouds; the edge of the sea, in the distance, Cassis if you squinted hard enough; the lake held back by the dam, the blue something so deep I wanted to dive from here.

"We're going to the guest center," said Matt.

His voice made me jump: I hadn't realized he was anywhere near me. The trio smiled in the most relaxed way I had ever seen: I would have thought they were stoned, if I wasn't smiling the exact same way right now. Just conquering this mountain was enough to give anyone a high.

"Feel free to leave without me," I said, and I was content with that, "if I see you when I come down, I'll join you. If not, don't worry about me: I can manage by myself."

"Let me know if you find the treasure," said Dutch, "message me on Facebook!"

I laughed. I was comfortable if the story had no ending. I found another piece of my heart on top of this mountain, and I was full to the brim with joy.

Joy. I hadn't felt this in months.

I ate my sandwich, a half stale baguette with butter and ham I had thrown together before leaving Mamie's house that morning. And then, when I was finally ready, I went to the foot of the cross, and I hunted for the treasure.

But it wasn't the stone dad had written about, was it? Of course, now that I was ok with myself, the universe had withdrawn its helping hand. The entire podium was made of some re-enforced concrete, smooth and white and not at all the rocky stock I had expected.

Oh, crap. Maybe I had climbed up here for nothing after all.

It was quicker to walk down the mountain than up it, that was for sure. I flew down the mountain, taking the steep hill steps at a time. I didn't know why I was rushing: the clue had remained hidden for seventeen years, until someone had moved it: it could wait a few minutes more.

Though I couldn't.

I broke my race at the priory, leaning against a tree to breathe. The visitor's center was miraculously open, so I dashed inside, glad for the respite from the sun's scorching rays.

My eyes darted across the tiny room. So much for a visitor's center: it only had tables and benches, empty hooks on the walls.

So back outside I went, instead slipping into the small chapel. Tiny colorful stained-glass windows let the light trickle in on ancient stone, four people spread out in the room praying or simply sitting in silence. Astonishingly, on one of the walls, a tiny glass shadowbox displayed a hat and two shirts for purchase.

Ok, so not here either.

I found myself outside again, turning on the spot, lost. For a tiny priory, this place was a maze.

"Pardon, parlez-vous Anglais?" I asked, reaching for a man in one of the shirts I had just seen inside, "Do you speak English?"

"A little bit," he said, "can I help you?"

"Do you work here?"

"I am *bénévole*. How you say, Volunteer?" He replied.

"When did they renovate the cross?"

"The cross? About… 2004?"

Crap.

"When they did, did they find anything… strange?" I urged, "like, a letter? A hidden letter?"

"A hidden letter?" he scratched his head. *"Non."*

"Are you sure? Please, it means a lot to me. I'm looking for a very special letter."

"I think… come with me."

He led me to the exit of the priory, as if we were

going to climb to the cross again, but instead turned a key in the wall and opened an old-fashioned iron gate. Inside, the ancient hallway was recently refurbished, with bright LEDs and panels on the wall. A dark door waited at the end of the tunnel.

Ok, so he was either going to open a portal to another realm or murder me. I didn't see anything in between.

But I was wrong, again. A small glass box waited under one of the banners, containing what looked like knick-knacks found during the refurbishment. An old coin. A fancy knife. A letter.

A letter.

"Oh," my jaw dropped.

"Is yours?"

I pulled the other letters from my bag, nodding.

"I sure hope so."

He took a key off his belt and unlocked the small glass box, reverently. He extracted the letter: this time it was in an envelope, the word *Amour* printed on the front in a wide and elegant hand. Not something I would see dad writing, but beautiful.

I opened it, recognizing at once that beautiful typewriter script. And I fell into the words my father had left for you, seventeen years ago, the treasure at the end of the hunt.

thirty-two

Mon Amour.

You did it, darling, you found all my clues! Now you're here, standing at the top of the world, a cross above you and, if I timed it right, with me standing right behind you.

Surprise!

I want you to keep reading, though. I think if I was to try and tell you all this, I would start sobbing and would not be able to stop. I have so much to tell you and it's hard to put them into words. Writing this letter gave me time to think them over, so I think it will the best way to tell you everything I feel.

When we kissed in the cave in Cassis, my

heart didn't stop. I didn't feel electricity or heart or anything the romance novels said. Instead, I felt calm. For the first time in my life, I was truly calm. Kissing you felt like coming home.

I think we both knew from that moment that this was special. I had dated others before, and so had you, but that was somehow different, light years behind us. It sounds cheesy, but finding you was like finding another part of myself that I didn't know I was missing, and now I cannot ever live without.

When we got stuck in Les Baux and waited for hours to get a ride back, I wasn't scared. Being lost with you wasn't a harrowing experience. I knew it was going to work out, and it did. All the while you held my hand, running your thumb over the skin for hours until it was almost raw, but I didn't want you to ever let go.

I remember thinking about that rude man from the car, who was so insulted by the fact I was speaking English, and how I wasn't offended by that, but by the fact he thought I was an American. Isn't that odd? I so desperately wanted to fit into this country, that failing to do so broke my heart. I wanted to tell him I

Sarah Anderson

was hopelessly in love with France I even fell for a Frenchman, and that this land nursed me back to life when I thought there was nothing of me left to restore.

Ok, he was a total jerk, though. I know he had no idea we knew more about French culture and symbolism than he ever would. Maybe I'm exaggerating, but that hurt, dammit.

You were there to comfort me, guide me. I came to France lost and broken and you helped me find the pieces of me in every little place we visited. You helped build me back together by showing me new sides of myself I had never known.

I found another piece in Arles, when we fought at the theatre. Sure, that's one of my worst memories of our time together so far. But that day I found my voice again, and used it to say no. No. Such a beautiful, powerful word. I found it hidden between the marble blocks and the grandstands filled with ghosts. I gave it to you. You listened.

I had missed having my voice heard.

I found more pieces of me everywhere we went. Under the eaves of the conservatory, I found my laugh. Under this cross on St

Aix Marks the Spot

Victoire, I found my strength.

All I know is that I feel whole again. When you met me, you only saw a part of me, missing chunks of who I am. So I understand if now you don't want the full me. You don't want the girl who was hurt and ran away from her problems rather than face them head on.

This letter brings you bad news. We both knew our relationship had an expiration date. We both knew when term ended my visa would expire and I would have to go back home. And I am. I am going back home. The tickets are booked and my dissertation has been handed in.

But I am coming back.

I'm not going to stay long over there. Just long enough to face Josh and make him apologize for shattering me. To use the voice I found again and that beautiful 'No'. I don't know what I'm going to do, but he's going to face retribution.

You're probably wondering what this letter is, now. Is it a break up letter? Oh, hell no. Quite the opposite. Mon Amour, there's nothing that could ever make me want to leave you. Which is why my gift to you is stapled to the next page. I'm going to give you a second to

Sarah Anderson

look. I'll wait.

Surprise! I got you tickets! I left the dates blank so that you can come and go whenever you want. I don't want you to feel obligated to come with me when I face Josh. I'm strong enough to handle that on my own, though having you there will make me happy to no end. But you showed me your world, and I want to show you mine – before I pack up and join you here.

I have accepted a job at the university. It's small, but it was enough on paper for me to apply for a work visa. The fact I got my masters here certainly helped my application. So when I get back, fully and entirely me, I'll be ready. Ready for what? I don't know.

Ready for us, maybe. If that's what you want too.

Your mother hates me, I know. She thinks I'm using you. I'm just another American girl coming to France to find my destiny. To settle down with a good French boy and, I don't know, tend a vineyard or something? What is it that those girls in movies end up doing? Or maybe she thinks I'm stealing you back to America with me, in which case she probably wouldn't be too happy with the tickets I just got you.

Aix Marks the Spot

Which is why I bought her tickets, too.

I know, it's probably not the smartest move. I mean, it seems a little counter-intuitive to invite a woman who thinks globalization is diluting the cultural heritage of her country to come to America. But I figure, it's the gesture that counts. France was willing to accept me at my worst, and I have done everything I can to embrace that culture, to build it up.

When that man yelled at us in the car - and all those other strangers who yelled at us in the street for our language choice - I felt like an outsider finally found out. I wanted to shed my American nature like a skin and just be French. But that's not humanly possible. Part of me will always be American, and I want her to meet that part. She might not accept it, but it's not going away.

I want her to understand that I don't want to make you an American. And you don't want to make me French. Together we're two different cultures building each other up. I know that scares her, and she sees that as eroding her heritage, but it's that heritage that drew me here in the first place. I don't want to hurt

```
it. It's the last thing I want to do.
  I'm rambling now, aren't I? I guess what I'm
trying to say is that I'm ready to build a
future with you. My gift to you, the treasure
at the end of this hunt, is an invitation.
An invitation to see where I'm from, and an
invitation to see where we can go.
  What do you say?


  Love you, Always,
  Ta chérie
```

You wrote the letters.

I would have dropped this one, I had been shaking so much, but my fingers were clutching it so hard it would have been impossible to pry from my dead body. This entire hunt hadn't been for you, but *from* you. Dad hadn't set this up to show you the country he loved, but you had created this to show him how much you loved his country.

How much you loved Provence.

"*Alors?*" asked the volunteer, "Is good?"

"Yes," I said, wiping my tears on my sweaty wrist, "yes, it is. Everything is going to be fine now."

thirty-three

VALENTIN WAS WAITING AT THE BUS STOP WHEN I arrived, sitting on his old red bicycle. It looked about as ancient as the priory I had just come from: half of the paint was covered in mud, the handlebars grey from years of sun damage and dust.

"Salut," I said, unable to resist smiling as I saw him there. "What are you doing here?"

"You crazy American," he chided, "biking all the way here."

"Well, what would you have done?"

"Probably stayed home."

"Then you wouldn't have found this," I replied.

It would have been much more dramatic if I had just whipped the letter out of my bag right then, but after twenty years, I was terrified of ripping it. Instead, I tapped on my backpack. It was enough for Valentin's eyes to bulge.

"I cannot believe you found it," he stammered.

"You see? This is what happens when you actually climb your mountains."

"Oh, I believe you, you know."

Before I knew what I was doing, I had wrapped my hands around his neck, and pressed my lips against his. He melted into me, his hand slipping through my hair to cup my face to his, and I found myself slipping into the comfortable smile that came when you were with someone who made your broken heart beat.

But the broken heart wasn't broken anymore. Just like you, the pieces that had shattered were together again, filled bit by bit by the country around me.

I felt whole again. Whole again, and happy. Whole plus whatever it was that I was feeling for this silly French boy, this cute face that was kissing mine.

When we finally pulled away, it was only because we were out of breath. That, and the sun was still hot at this time of day. I freed the bike from the rack and mounted it, following Valentin on the road back to the home of my Mamie.

"So, what was the treasure?" he asked, " Was it a poem?"

"You and your poems," I chided, "it was better. The

letters were from Mom, this whole time."

So I told him about the tickets you had bought for dad and Mamie to come to see your home, and the job you were taking to stay in Provence. I told him how much it must have hurt, knowing neither dad nor Mamie had seen this gesture before you ran from here.

"I read Mamie's book, *La fin du printemps?*" I added, "but it doesn't make sense. She makes it sound like my mother stole me away from one day to the next. But when she went on her rant, it sounded more like she was the one to kick dad out."

"Maybe she regrets?"

"If she ever did, then why didn't she try to talk to dad before now?" I shook my head. "It makes no sense."

"This sounds like a movie," Valentin added, "where everyone has their side of the story, but no one talks to each other so they never know the whole picture."

We pedaled up the gravel driveway, ditching the bikes near the empty fountain. I took deep breaths, trying to steady myself, but the closer I got to the house, to more difficult it was to keep my head on right.

"Pas de panique," said Valentin, "It's going to go fine."

I nodded. He was right: things could not get any worse between me and Mamie. Whatever I would risk today would make it either all go away, or I would never have to see her again.

"I'll text you," I said to him.

"If you need me, you can find me," he replied, leaning over to exchange a last kiss for the night. It was enough to make my chest all fluttery again, and for a second I was flying instead of anxious about my grandmother. Then it was over and he was pedaling away, and I had to face this dragon alone.

I opened the kitchen door. Mamie sat at the table polishing off a meal of meatballs and a glass of red wine. She looked up as I entered, inclining her head slightly.

"*Bonsoir, Jammy.*" Good evening, all prim and proper. If this were England, I would imagine I was in Downton Abbey.

"*Bonsoir, Mamie.*"

"*Tu rentres tard,*" she said. You're getting home late. I found myself blushing red.

"Mamie," I said, "We have to talk."

"*A propos de ton copain?*"

"*Non*, not about Valentin," I replied, "*A propos de toi*. And me. And dad. And mom."

I pulled my bag onto my lap and pulled out the letters, stacking them from beginning to end, and handed them to her. She pushed her plate to the side and picked them up.

"*Qu'est-ce que c'est?*"

Aix Marks the Spot

"Read them," I urged. "I read your book. Your end of spring. Now you read these. Then, we talk."

"I do not read English."

"Yes, you do."

I would have sat there at the table, watching her read, but there was something about the letters that just needed to be absorbed alone. I didn't tell her you wrote them: that would be for her to find out on her own, just like I had.

I waited in the living room, turning on the old lights for the first time since I had been there. The room looked smaller now, and in even more disarray. There was a chaotic emptiness about it, like it was underfilled, yet nothing was in its place.

When Mamie eventually emerged, she said nothing. She walked straight to me, wrapping her arms around me, tight, and sobbed into my neck. I joined her, our tears mingling, mourning the years we had never had together.

"I am sorry," she said, articulating every syllable, "I am sorry, I didn't know."

I wanted to be mad at her. I wanted to yell and scream and kick and fight. I wanted her to feel the pain that came from this distance, the pain of believing you were the reason your world was so broken.

But she already knew that pain. She had inflicted it

upon herself.

"Valentin said that we are like a movie," I suggested, sitting down with her on the couch. She reached for a drawer, extracting a massive box of tissues. The two of us partook of a good cry like one would share a bottle of wine. "That none of this would have happened, if we had just… talked."

"It is not easy," she replied, "as we do not have the same language."

"Then we learn. We learn how to speak to each other. We learn how to communicate so we can understand. It doesn't matter the language. You and dad spent my entire lifetime not talking, and you both speak French. It's not a question of language. It's a question of will."

"All these years, I could not call. I knew I could not fix what I had broken, but your father did not call either."

"Then have the courage to take the first step. Someone has to, or this will go on for the rest of your lives."

She nodded, slowly, her gaze distant. I could not forgive this woman what she had done, but I could listen.

"You need to stop clinging to the past," I urged her, "It's what's keeping you from living your present. It's what's locking you in your tower. It's what's keeping you from telling Jean-Pascal how you feel. Or your son that you're sorry."

"I am so... ashamed. I thought your mother wanted to steal my culture. I didn't realize she wanted to learn from it."

"Will you talk to her now?" I asked. No, begged. The urge to shout at her was hard to suppress. "I can phone her, right now."

"No."

My newly healed heart went cold. But her hand reached for mine, squeezing it gently.

"After seventeen years, I must do better. Be better. Are the tickets..." she paused, pursing her lips. "I need to make a phone call."

thirty - four

THE TICKETS YOU HAD LEFT FOR DAD HAD, OF course, expired. But that wasn't a problem for bestselling author Colette Martin, which meant Mamie and I were soaring over the Atlantic before the next day was out.

And eight hours in a tin can with her? Much more fun than the flight over, alone. Without the wall between us, Mamie was one of the most brilliant people I had ever spoken to. When I asked about the only book of hers I had ever read, she refused to comment on the ending.

"The ending belongs to the reader," she said, "but if I open your mother's door and see me standing there, I will still die of shock."

I didn't quite want her to die, especially not after I had just met her. The real her, this time: not the woman who isolated herself from me, from us, out of fear of herself, or making this worse, but the woman who rolled French and English words into one, making a sentences I could somehow understand though only half the words were ones that I knew.

The only setback to our little plan was customs, though I helped her fill out the ESTA quickly. Spontaneous visas to the USA did not come cheap, but she didn't grumble.

"I haven't driven a car in decades," said Mamie, scanning the sea of rentals outside the airport doors.

"You rent, I drive?" I suggested.

"You drive? My girl, you are so young!"

"America," I replied.

"America." She agreed, nodding slowly, "Will we break the law?"

We didn't, at the end. Good old Uber would be our savior. She sat up front with the nice driver as we left the airport and headed to my other grandmother's suburb, chatting amicably in broken English about this being her first time to the US.

Things got quiet when the woman dropped us off. We stood outside the flat home, staring at the single row of sunflowers before the window, the great green lawn opening its arms wide. It was unnerving how big the cars were, now that I was used to the French ones; or how much more humid it was than the air in France. How quiet it sounded without the Cicadas. Mamie took it all in in one large gasp.

We didn't need to come any closer. The door flew open and Dad was outside like lightning, hugging his mother so tight I couldn't see her through his arms, or even hear her breathing through his tears. Or maybe they were her sobs I heard, as they sputtered in French, hugging and kissing and crying on my grandmother's driveway.

And then, in the doorway, I saw you.

You were standing. Not easily, not on your own just yet. You had a walker, a massive step up from your chair that I left you with. And you were watching the reunion with tears in your own eyes, as if afraid to step forward, afraid that this moment wasn't real.

Trust me. I didn't believe it either.

When Mamie pulled away from Dad, it was to you she went first, her head bowed, her hands outstretched. And you pushed that walker forward, hesitantly at first, then gaining speed as she walked up, your mouth forming words of confusion, first in one language, then another.

"I am so sorry," said Mamie, her speech perfectly rehearsed. We had spent the entire flight over on it, and she was determined to pronounce every word right. "I am so sorry I thought-"

You didn't give her time to finish. You inclined your head forward, kissing her first on one cheek, then the other. Your hands were straining on the edge of your walker, trembling and twitching as your lips formed a bright, wide smile.

"Come inside," you said to her, "we have a lot to talk about."

I was the last one to say my hellos. I turned to dad, and we hugged, saying nothing, our words saved for where they were needed most. As I pulled away, I reached into my bag, pulling out the letters pressed so gently inside my sketchpad.

"These are for you," I said.

So, as Mamie and you built new bridges with words, Dad walked down old paths you had created together, a new culture growing out of once dry soil.

epilogue

"YOU'RE BREAKING UP AGAIN," I WAS SAYING, shaking my laptop as if that was going to help. Valentin's frozen features are confused on the screen, his face caught in the middle of an expression that could either be sadness or a laughter.

I'm sitting at the dining room table, the house suddenly full over capacity. Grandma is getting Mamie properly introduced to the kitchen appliances, the latter confused as to the lack of the electric kettle. However will she have her morning coffee?

Grandma is taking a while to warm up to Mamie, and I can't blame her. Things are far from perfect yet. Talking has resumed, apologies traded, but it doesn't take back the hurt everyone has been causing each other for almost two decades. But they are trying, all

Aix Marks the Spot

of them. All of us.

"Breaking up? Does that mean we were dating?"

"What? I don't want to break up with you! Hold on!"

I put the laptop down and grab my phone, texting him to hang on for a sec. I look up, and there's dad, climbing under the living room desk in search of the internet box.

"Dad! Don't mess with the Wi-Fi! The password is in Grandpa's office!" I yell.

"Did you just pronounce it *whiffy*?" he says, stopping in his tracks.

"No?"

"You did," says Valentin, suddenly unfrozen. "Ha! I knew I could turn you French!"

He looks adorable on that screen, my little boyfriend in a box. If he even is my boyfriend. We haven't had that conversation yet, though I have a feeling we're about to. My heart is pounding with excitement. But first things first.

"How are you? Not too bored without me?"

"A lot of Pétanque to pass the day!"

"Seriously?"

"*Non.*"

"Is that the *copain*?" you ask, scooting up on the couch, where you have been watching dad toil ridiculously under the desk.

"Maybe?" I reply.

"Is he cute?"

"Very."

"Then I approve."

"So we are not breaking up?" asked Valentin, "this sounds like the opposite."

"No," I reply. "I think we are doing the opposite of breaking up."

I dip my toes into the comfortable effortless of loving him. I think I'm going to like it here.

"So?" he asks, "you were saying? About being back in America?"

I smile. There's a lot to say: I had apparently gotten quite used to a lot of things in France I never thought I would. Like the morning coffee or the long meals, or the bread so fresh it never made it home from the bakery intact. Gosh, I missed the bread. And the cheese!

"It's taking some getting used to," I reply, "I've had mac and cheese again."

"That orange excuse for *fromage*?"

"Yeah. And guess what? I loved it."

"I take back what I say: we are breaking up."

"I agree with that!" you say from the couch.

"Mom! Quit eavesdropping!"

"Sorry, sorry."

"Yeah, the house really is too small for all of us," I replied, "but we're all trying really hard to make it work, at least for now. I might stay a few nights at Jazz's, but… I fully intend to finish my summer in Provence."

"You're coming back?" His eyes light up like fireflies at night.

"Only if you ask politely," I insist.

"Please, please come back," he begs, an overdramatic pantomime. "However will I live without you?"

I laugh. It's true, I do miss him too. We had only just started to actually know each other before I flew back, and I'm looking forward to knowing him more when I return.

"You know, I still have to visit Aix," I say, grinning. "I only saw it so briefly. But there's more. Now that Dad and Mom and Mamie are talking, well… my parents haven't been to France in ages. And since they teach French lit, well…"

"What are you saying?" His grin is so wide, I could drown in it. I can't wait to make it grow even wider.

"Well, the baccalaureate is done in two years, right?" I say. "I'm going to be in Junior year in the fall, so Mom and Dad think it might be the perfect time to move. If things go right, Mamie's house might be full again."

"Really?"

"Really."

"You know, there are schools in America that offer scholarships to international students," he said, and my heart skipped a beat.

"And you know that French schools cost less than one semester's worth of textbooks," I replied.

"What are you saying?"

"What are *you* saying?"

"I don't know what I'm saying," I said, "All I know is, long distance sucks."

I look over at my parents, sitting comfortably together on the low couch. You're leaning on dad, your eyes closed, smiling even as you drift off to sleep. He's reading your letters and holding back tears. There's a lot of tissues on his side of the room.

I look at you, and an image forms in front of you: your current selves, and your selves from seventeen years ago, two eras superimposed in one, sitting together on a beach towel in Cassis. It's like looking through a window back in time: you, with your hair long and loose, wearing a maxi dress because you hadn't predicted you would be hiking that day; dad in his ridiculous aviators, which he had bought from a north African man on the beach and he thought made him look cool. Blink, and you're gone, the real you taking their place. My mother, the woman who lost her legs and was finding them again, who would never let go of the things she loved, no matter what. Dad, the man who had lost his mother and motherland in one fell swoop, rerooting himself after the storm.

I turn my attention back to Valentin, taking in his smile, and that stray curl still sitting on his forehead. I imagine him twenty years from now, that same hair sprinkled with light grey, gentle wrinkles on his skin. I take in his face, as it is, now, smiling and eagerly waiting for me to say something, anything.

My words come out flimsy and tough, but they do the trick, and the smile, impossibly, widens.

"Et si on parlait de nous?" I ask.

Now, let's talk about us.

Acknowledgements

When I first sat down to write about my childhood in Provence, the plan was to write a non-fiction. But the words didn't come: the stories were there, they were just disjointed paragraphs, short episodes from my life and others. It took a very strange dream and a sharp reset to turn my life around, and for Provence to make me write the book I did.

Everything that happened in Aix Marks the Spot happened for real: either to me, or to a friend. Every conversation overheard on the bus or confusing interaction in town, all of it is real. Only the treasure hunt that ties it all together was invented, for cohesion's sake.

Writing this book has been the strangest and most wonderful experience of my life. Never before or since did words spill out of me in this way, and I have so many people to thank for setting me up and putting me on the path that made this story come out.

First and foremost, to my parents, Tim and Apryl. If you had not chosen Aix as our home, we certainly wouldn't be here today. I know that it's not always been easy, for any of us. Living outside of one's culture comes with a whole slew of challenges. But you choosing Aix gave me a culture to call home. I had the childhood most people could only dream of. It gave me friends that I will keep forever, opportunities that exist no place else, and a fantastic life.

In that same vein, all my wonderful friends who shared their stories with me, not knowing a decade ago that they would somehow end up in this book. Thank you Alix, Valentine, Victor, Nicolas, Laura, Lea, Lucy, Joanna. You were there for me through thick and thin and probably remember half the events in these pages. Thank you for sharing your stories, and your lives, with me.

I can't go anywhere without thanking my partner, Hugo, my own personal Provence romance. Thank you for being supportive and silly through the good times and the bad. I never thought people could live such a romance in real life. In this book, I took reality and turned it to fiction, but every day you take fiction and make it real.

To Cora, for her unbridled enthusiasm for this book from day one. For pushing me to get the whole story out, for helping me put a glossy coat of polish on it. This book would not exist if not for you. I'm so excited for us to travel Jaime's trail together one day. I can't wait to show you these places I love.

Thank you to my critique partners, Madeline, Denise, Emily, Lisa, and Heidi. It's such a privilege to have you women in my life! Aix Marks the Spot would be dull and lusterless without your keen eyes for detail.

For the woman who grounded me and helped me hear what Provence had to say: thank you, Odette. You unlocked something within me that had been hiding for years.

And to all my readers who shared Jaime's journey and connected in some small way to the story I had to tell: thank you for coming along. I hope that you enjoyed this book as much as I loved writing it. Please come visit Provence one day and see for yourselves how magical it can be.

About the Author

Sarah Anderson can't ever tell you where she's from. Not because she doesn't want to, but because it inevitably leads to a confusing conversation about where she was born (England) where she grew up (France) and where her family is from (USA) and it tends to make things very complicated.

She's lived her entire life in the South of France, except for a brief stint where she moved to Washington DC, or the eighty years she spent as a queen of Narnia before coming back home five minutes after she had left. Currently, she is working on her PhD in Astrophysics and Planetary sciences in Besançon, France.

When she's not writing - or trying to do science - she's either reading, designing, crafting, or attempting to speak with various woodland creatures in an attempt to get them to do household chores for her. She could also be gaming, or pretending she's not watching anything on Netflix.

Connect with her on social media:

WWW.SEANDERSONAUTHOR.COM

facebook.com/seandersonauthor

instagram.com/readcommendations

twitter.com/sea_author